The Prudential
Regulation
of Banks

The Walras-Pareto Lectures, at the École des Hautes Études Commerciales, Université de Lausanne

1. Mathias Dewatripont and Jean Tirole, *The Prudential Regulation of Banks* (1994)

The Prudential
Regulation
of Banks

Mathias Dewatripont and
Jean Tirole

The MIT Press
Cambridge, Massachusetts
London, England

Originally published in 1993 by Editions Payot Lausanne, Switzerland, under the title *La Réglementation prudentielle des Banques*.

Copyright © Editions Payot Lausanne, 1993.

English-language edition © 1994 Massachusetts Institute of Technology

This book was set in Palatino by Windfall Software using ZzTEX, and was printed and bound in the United States of America.

Library of Congress Cataloging-in-Publication Data

Dewatripont, M. (Mathias)
  The Prudential regulation of banks / Mathias Dewatripont and Jean
  Tirole.
     p.   cm. — (The Walras-Pareto lectures ; 1)
  Includes bibliographical references and index.
  ISBN 0-262-04146-4
  1. Banks and banking—State supervision. 2. Banks and banking—
United States—State supervision. 3. Financial services industry—
State supervision. 4. Financial services industry—United States—
State supervision. 5. Banking law. 6. Banking law—United States.
I. Tirole, Jean. II. Title. III. Series.
HG1725.D49   1994
332.1'0973—dc20   94-30751
                                                              CIP

Contents

Series Foreword

At the end of the nineteenth century, economics was taught at the University of Lausanne by two great scholars. It was at Lausanne that Léon Walras, who occupied the university's first chair of economics in 1870, developed his general equilibrium theory and Vilfredo Pareto, who succeeded Walras from 1893 to 1909, made important contributions to the analysis of "optimality" or "efficiency," and microeconomics generally. These theories brought international fame to their authors at the time and continue to provide the basis for numerous research projects in economics today.

In 1990 the University of Lausanne celebrated the centennial of its transformation from "academy" to university. On this occasion the École des Hautes Études Commerciales, HEC (Faculty of Economics and Business Administration), at the suggestion of its Département d'Économétrie et d'Économie Politique (DEEP), decided to institute a series of annual lectures to be called the Walras-Pareto Lectures. This series is therefore dedicated to the memory of the renowned founders of what is commonly known in the history of economic theory as the "School of Lausanne."

The Walras-Pareto Lectures provide internationally recognized scholars with an opportunity to present their work on particular topics in economics at Lausanne. As is usual with such a lecture series, plans were made from the start to have each work published. Editions Payot Lausanne and the MIT Press enthusiastically espoused the project, accepting to publish the lectures series in French and in English. Mathias Dewatripont and Jean Tirole are authors of the series' first publication in English. Their work augurs a long and fruitful future for the Walras-Pareto Lecture series.

Alberto Holly

Preface

This book requires little prior knowledge of finance and banking.[1] Technical explanations as well as institutional background information are often supplied in footnotes (which partly explains the large number of footnotes in this book). Likewise, knowledge of contract theory is not required, although some familiarity with it facilitates the reading of the normative analysis in part III.

The book is a research monograph, but it can also be used in the classroom. There are three potential audiences:

• *Graduate students and researchers* should be able to read the whole book. They may be particularly interested in part I on institutions, in parts III and IV on normative and positive analyses, and in the concluding remarks of part V.

• *Practitioners* in financial intermediaries and supervisory agencies might only glance at part I but read more carefully section 2.2 on the foundations of regulation of financial intermediaries and sections 3.4 and 3.5 on the analogies between the regulation of financial intermediaries and corporate governance. Chapter 5 on existing

---

1. The reader may use as background textbooks on corporate finance (e.g., Brealey-Myers 1988), banking (e.g., Garber-Weisbrod 1992 and Mishkin 1992a), and prudential regulation (e.g., Hall 1993).

banking theory provides useful background discussion, and chapters 6 and 14 give an outline of the argument and policy conclusions. Those readers already familiar with formal analysis should turn to parts III and IV for a more comprehensive treatment.

• *Undergraduate students* should be able to handle parts I, II, and the concluding part V.

An early version of this book was used as the basis for a lecture series given in December 1992 at the University of Lausanne by the second author. We would like to thank the École des Hautes Études Commerciales at the University of Lausanne for the privilege of giving these lectures, and Jean-Pierre Danthine and Alberto Holly for their cordiality and for stimulating discussion.

For advice, encouragement and criticism, we are grateful to many colleagues and students. We extend our special thanks to Patrick Bolton, Claudio Borio, John Boyd, Jacques Crémer, Jean-Marc Delporte, Jean Dermine, Patrick Depovere, Antonio Estache, Gary Gorton, Martin Hellwig, Bertrand Leton, Jean-Jacques Laffont, Colin Mayer, Marco Pagano, Peter Praet, Patrick Rey, Jean-Charles Rochet, Ailsa Roëll, Dirk Schoenmaker, Xavier Vives, Herman Verwilst and Larry White. Pierrette Vaissade typed the manuscript with extraordinary care in LaTeX. Jacques Crémer helped us with the figures. We are grateful to Dana Andrus, of The MIT Press, who edited the manuscript with skill and grace. We are also indebted to the Belgian government's Pôle d'Attraction Interuniversitaire program for a research grant (contract no. 26). The generous financial support of the partners of the Institut d'Économie Industrielle is also gratefully acknowledged.

A (slightly shorter) version of this book appeared in French under the title *La Réglementation prudentielle des Banques*, published by Editions Payot Lausanne (1993).

The Prudential
Regulation
of Banks

1   Introduction

Financial intermediaries—banks, mutual funds, insurance companies, finance companies, securities firms, or pension funds—are major players in modern economies. They provide a link between creditors and borrowers, influence the functioning of securities markets, and affect the quantity of money, the investment, and the growth of countries.

At the microeconomic level, financial intermediaries transform debt issued by firms and other borrowers into demand deposits, savings deposits, and other assets demanded by households. Bank loans constitute the bulk of the external financing of firms (Mayer 1990). For example, loans, mostly of bank origin, represented 61.9% of external financing in the United States during 1970 to 1985 when in contrast, stocks and bonds only contributed for 2.1% and 29.8% of this financing, respectively.[1] Half of the stocks and almost all

---

1. The remainder (6.2%) came from government loans, foreigners, and other firms. Also, the main source of finance of firms is internal (retained earnings). According to Mayer (1988), gross internal financing (respectively, net, after having subtracted from gross financing firms' investments in financial assets) represented 74% (respectively, 107%) of average gross firm financing in the United Kingdom between 1970 and 1985. This proportion was lower in other countries. As percentages of net financing, the proportions were for the United Kingdom, the United States, France, Germany, and Japan as follows: for internal finance 107, 90, 62, 73, 65; for loans 5, 26, 37, 12, 42; for bonds -2, 12, 1, -2.1; and for stocks -4, -3, 5, 1, 4. The remainder concerned interfirm credits. Narayanan (1991) surveys other studies on financing in Germany and Japan.

bonds and short-term bills are sold to insurance companies, mutual funds, finance companies, and pension funds. Direct finance thus represents a small share of external finance of U.S. firms. The same is true in Germany, France, the United Kingdom, and Japan. Among their other activities, financial intermediaries issue mortgages, consumption loans, and insurance policies, and they act as underwriters and hold stocks and other financial instruments of corporations and the public sector.

Beyond its principal role in the economy, financial intermediation has also attracted the attention of microeconomists because it is heavily regulated. The existence and the type of regulation is a topic of intense debate. The importance of state intervention has significant political economy consequences. Books devoted to the recent U.S. savings and loans disaster devote much space to the policy errors of the various regulatory agencies and of the politicians involved in the control of these agencies.

More generally, renewed interest in academe for banking regulation (or deregulation) was generated by the large-scale banking problems experienced by many countries. For most of the post–World War II era bank regulation proceeded smoothly: Few failures occurred, and the topic was not of widespread interest to academics and to the public. Due to a number of factors, to be discussed later, bank failures became common in the 1980s. The impact of the recent banking crises on the taxpayers will often be tough. It is, for example, estimated that the U.S. government will spend hundreds of billions of dollars during the next several decades cleaning up the S&Ls' and commercial banks' wreckage.[2] Nordic countries have spent $16 billion propping up their banks from 1989 through 1992,

---

2. Litan (1994, 519). In 1990 the Treasury department estimated the total cost of savings and loans' closures and assisted sales to between $90 and $130 billion. The Congressional Budget Office and the General Accounting Office have since projected higher costs.

and many banks still looked shaky in early 1993.[3] Japan is now searching remedies for its banking crisis. Consensus estimates of the bad loans of banks ranged from \$160 billion to \$240 billion in October 1993.[4] A number of Latin American countries (e.g., Chile, Argentina, Brazil, and Mexico) supply yet another illustration of the extent of banking crises. They experienced in the 1980s large-scale bank failures that led to (at least temporary) nationalization of many of their largest banks.[5]

Finally, microeconomists are interested in financial intermediation because of its impact on financial markets. The behavior of financial intermediaries, which in turn depends on the nature of regulation, largely determines the liquidity of these markets. This fact is, however, ignored by existing theories of financial markets. For example, traditional theories of asset pricing under uncertainty (except those based on arbitrage among assets) start from the assumption that consumers buy stocks or bonds directly. More specifically, theories that explain clientele effects and interest rate differentials by transaction costs[6] or the informational role of the stock market[7] assume that households have liquidity needs but do not consider how financial intermediaries transform these needs. A more complete understanding of financial markets should thus explicitly integrate financial intermediation.

Financial intermediation is also of interest to macroeconomists. In the short run, banks play a constituent role in the determination of the quantity of money and of aggregate business investment.

---

3. *The Economist*, January 9, 1993. A number of Nordic banks have since recovered somewhat (see *The Economist*, September 4, 1993). For detailed accounts of the Norwegian crisis and its resolution, see Steigum (1992) and Hope (1993).

4. *The Economist*, October 23, 1993. See also *The Economist*, February 26, 1994, for a discussion of planned bank-relief schemes.

5. See, for example, Brock (1992).

6. See, for example, Amihud-Mendelson (1986), Heaton-Lucas (1992), and Vayanos-Vila (1992). These authors derive the general equilibrium of a life-cycle model where consumers buy earlier and sell later assets with higher transaction costs.

7. See Holmström-Tirole (1993).

For example, banking depressions often lead to credit crunches. According to economic historians, the nature of intermediation seems to condition long-term growth as well.[8] For instance, it has been usual (until recently) to attribute part of the success of the German and Japanese economies to the close links between banks and firms in these countries.

There is a large literature[9] demonstrating a significant correlation between financial development and growth. While this empirical literature does not establish a causal link, it certainly suggests a fruitful area of investigation for macroeconomists. On the theoretical front, the financial development conjecture[10] states that real growth feeds back on the financial sector by allowing intermediaries to specialize and become more efficient; yet real growth raises the cost of labor and thus penalizes financial intermediation. There is further an interdependency between the net worths of the financial and real sectors. Insufficient banking capital constrains the supply of bank loans to firms. Conversely, insufficient capital in the real sector has an ambiguous effect on the demand for bank loans by firms: On the one hand, fewer firms have sufficient net worth to issue debt securities on the market; this raises the demand for intermediation. On the other hand, fewer firms qualify for bank credit, which decreases the number of bank loans.[11]

Despite its importance financial intermediation has generated few theoretical developments. Moreover existing theory is somewhat disconnected from regulatory concerns. Our objective in this

---

8. For an historical perspective on the importance of bank credit in Germany and Italy at the end of the nineteenth century, see Gerschenkron (1962) and the comments in Hellwig (1991).

9. Goldsmith (1969), Mc Kinnon (1973), and Shaw (1973) are early contributions to this literature. See King and Levine's (1993) evidence on 80 countries from 1960 to 1989 for state-of-the-art evidence.

10. Gurley and Shaw (1960). See Sussman-Zeira (1993) for a modeling of this conjecture, and Pagano (1993) for a survey of the empirical and theoretical literatures.

11. See Holmström-Tirole (1994) for a model in which the real and financial sectors are both constrained by the level of their assets.

book is to provide a first step in the analysis of the foundations of prudential regulation of intermediaries.[12] Our main motivation is the regulation of "banks"[13] (commercial banks and S&Ls),[14] but many of the implications of the analysis are also valid for other financial intermediaries. Indeed we will stress the commonage of issues and regulations of banks, insurance companies, pension funds, and securities funds. Real macroeconomic effects of intermediation (credit crunch, growth) will not be studied here. We will abstract from the problems of money creation as well.

Our theory is based on the following set of ideas: (1) The main concern of prudential regulation is the *solvency* of banks, namely the relation between equity, debt, and asset riskiness. (2) Since most equity is *external* (i.e., not owned by management), the solvency of banks is mainly related to the determination of the debt–equity ratio or the *capital structure* of banks. (3) The capital structure is *relevant* for bank performance only if it affects the behavior of outside claimholders. The importance of the capital structure thus comes from its allocation of control rights or external intervention rights in the internal management of the bank. (4) The *income streams* of the various claims (equity, debt, etc.) represent *incentive schemes* for their owners that guide them in their intervention behavior. (5) External intervention, and thus the allocation of control rights, affect *managerial incentives*. Ideally managers should understand that bad

---

12. Our approach was first described in Dewatripont-Tirole (1993a), where we also suggested the research lines we have pursued in the present work.

13. Here we concentrate on *private* banks and thus leave out part of the European banking sector. Note, however, that European Community competition policy limits the difference between state and private banks, and that privatization plans are expected in several countries.

14. In 1990 they represented in the U.S. $4,933 billion of assets as compared to 1,409 for life-insurance companies, 528 for other insurance companies, 1,169 for private pension funds, 806 for public pension funds, and 1,682 for mutual funds and finance companies (Federal Reserve Flow of Funds, cited by Mishkin 1992a, 47). For an account of the evolution of the allocation of financial assets among financial intermediaries from 1900 through 1990, see table 1 in Kopcke (1992).

performance will trigger outside intervention, while good performance will be followed by accommodating external behavior. The credibility of outside intervention results, in particular, from the transfer of control from shareholders to creditors when the solvency of the bank falls below a predetermined ratio. (6) The specificity of banking firms is that their debt is mainly held by *small depositors* or *other financial institutions*. Small depositors have neither the incentive nor the competence to collect information or to intervene into bank management. This is true with or without deposit insurance. The free-riding problem is such that small depositors' information is at best newspaper information or credit ratings. Moreover small depositors' reactions are limited to deposit withdrawals instead of real intervention in bank management. (We will discuss later the other bank depositors.) (7) Depositors need to be *represented* by a public or a private agent to ensure external intervention following poor bank performance.

Point 1, which states that the main concern of regulation is bank solvency, is treated extensively in chapters 2 through 4 which provide institutional background information. Chapter 2 explains banks balance sheets and income statements. It then develops a case for banking regulation as performing a monitoring service in screening, auditing, covenant writing, and intervention activities that depositors are unable or unwilling to do for themselves. From this perspective the goal of regulation is to provide active representation for depositors. Potential concerns about this "representation hypothesis" are addressed. Its realism is confirmed by an analysis of the factors that have led other financial intermediaries to be regulated or unregulated. Chapter 3 describes the main regulatory features of the Basle accords (1988) and of the Federal Deposit Insurance Corporation Improvement Act (1991). In both instances, the allocation of control rights on the bank and its freedom of action were related to its degree of solvency. We also discuss further supervisory issues: liquidity and early detection of the potential insolvency of banks, failure resolution methods, and double gearing. Then chapter 3 buttresses the case for the representation hypothesis in a comparison of the prudential regulation of banks, first with that of other financial intermediaries such as insurance companies and pension funds, and second with the covenants imposed by large debtholders on nonfinancial companies. Chapter 4 illustrates the dangers of regulatory failure through a summary account of the S&L crisis of the 1980s.

Chapter 5 surveys banking theory. While the literature has usefully highlighted some critical aspects of banking, it has not allowed for an evaluation of traditional banking regulation. In particular it has concentrated on *entrepreneurial* banks to the exclusion of *outside* equity.

Points 2 through 5 represent, in our view, the key elements of a theory of capital structure. Why should bank behavior depend on the debt–equity ratio? In the absence of external intervention in bank management, managerial behavior would solely depend on the management's own incentives, and the relative value of debt and equity would have no impact on total bank value. The possibility of outside intervention allows us to elude irrelevance results à la Modigliani-Miller (1958) and to provide a role for bank solvency.

While we offer some suggestions for why, empirically, small depositors mainly hold bank debt, the specificity of banks (point 6) is taken as a given in this book. Recall that small depositor protection is one of the primary concerns of current prudential regulation of banks and the central motivation of the prudential regulation of other intermediaries. Another motivation for the prudential regulation of banks is their essential role in the payment system and their tight interconnection in the interbank market. The failure of a single bank can have a domino effect. We abstract from this issue of systemic risk, although it is not unrelated to the solvency focus of this book. Depositor protection is a much more general concern that

applies, mutatis mutandis, to a number of other financial intermediaries. Our theory is relevant for a much broader set of institutions
than just banks.

Chapter 6 gives an outline of our argument. Readers mainly interested in policy conclusions may choose to read it as a substitute
for chapters 7 to 13 and then move to chapter 14; others may want
to skip chapter 6, or glance through it for a preview of the critical
points in the subsequent discussion.

Chapters 7 through 10 take a normative perspective of *optimal*
regulation. Chapters 11 through 13 then evaluate current regulation
and reform proposals.

The "minimalist" model of chapter 7 allows us to address the role
of a bank's capital structure. This model shows that a decrease in
bank solvency should imply increased external intervention in the
management of a bank.

Chapter 8 describes the *ideal* implementation of the optimal outside intervention policy. Its instruments are transfers of control,
recapitalization, and deposit and risk limitations. In particular, increased intervention is obtained through a transfer of control from
shareholders to creditors, through a limitation of dividends, or
through recapitalization.

Chapter 9 analyzes three important prudential issues: relative
solvency ratios, securitization, and market value accounting. The
key insight behind these three issues is the well-known idea that
managerial incentive schemes should depend on the most precise
performance measures. This simple idea has strong implications
for the definition of solvency measures. The first debate of prudential policy considered in chapter 9 concerns the adjustment of
solvency ratios to the macroeconomic environment. The "relative
ratio theory" supports a decrease of minimum solvency ratios in
recessions. In contrast, the Basle accords do not introduce such a
feature. We show that neither position is fully justified. On the one
hand, the Basle accords may unduly put the banking sector at risk

in recessions. On the other hand, the S&L crisis shows how the fall in solvency ratios leads to excessive risk taking. Our theory suggests an intermediate road between these two approaches.

The second theme in chapter 9 concerns securitization. Securitization of an asset insulates the bank from future shocks due to the asset, which can further have adverse incentive effects. The natural question is which assets should be securitized (beyond the matter of their intrinsic liquidity).

In the last part of the chapter we compare traditional historical cost accounting and market value accounting. Our discussion is similar to our earlier comparison of relative and absolute solvency ratios. In contrast with market value accounting, traditional accounting reduces the volatility of solvency indicators and isolates the bank from inappropriate control shifts. However, it ignores the impact of changes in actual solvency on claimholder behavior. Once again, our theory suggests an intermediate solution between these two accounting methods.

The important role of bank solvency in triggering outside intervention suggests that bank managers have an interest in manipulating solvency indicators in their portfolio management. Chapter 10 first returns to the costs and benefits of asset sales. Next it shows how "gains trading"—the sale of undervalued assets while overvalued assets are kept on the bank's balance sheet—is a typical managerial reaction to an optimal external intervention policy based on solvency measures.

Chapter 11 uses our theoretical framework to assess the impact of the Basle accords. We focus on three aspects. First, we analyze the extent to which the Basle mechanism—fixed solvency ratios with transfer of control following poor performance *in the absence of recapitalization by shareholders*—approximates the optimal external intervention policy derived in chapter 7. Second, since the regulation does not prevent an undercapitalized bank from selling assets in order to avoid a transfer of control away from shareholders, we study this choice between recapitalization and securitization. Finally, the minimal solvency ratio introduces a link between asset riskiness and bank solvency. We analyze the incentive properties associated with this link.

After our study of the Basle accords in chapter 11, we proceed to analyze alternative modes of regulation, private as well as public, in chapters 12 and 13. The ideal implementation of chapter 8 is very unrealistic in the presence of small depositors. Chapter 12 studies discretionary public regulation. The regulator must represent small depositors, whose interests are then internalized through the public deposit insurance. Internalizing the welfare of shareholders, subordinated debtholders, and employees instead induces excess passivity (further aggravated in the case of capture by the banking industry). Chapter 12 studies political economy problems resulting from career concerns by politicians and bureaucrats.

Chapter 13 analyzes various modes of private regulation. It shows that stand-alone private deposit insurance or credit ratings are insufficient, and possibly perverse, instruments. In particular, they provide no external intervention mechanism in case of bank trouble. Allocating control rights to uninsured subordinated debtholders instead allows for external intervention after a mediocre performance, but not after a terrible performance. Moreover an extensive use of subordinated debt raises the issue of the identity of its potential holders.

Finally, chapter 14 summarizes the main insights of the book for the prudential regulation of banks and discusses avenues for future research.

I   Institutions

2

The Nature of Banking and the Rationale for Regulation

2.1 What Is a Bank?

This section briefly compares banking activities with the activities of other firms in order to evaluate later the regulation of financial intermediaries.

2.1.1 Balance Sheet and Income Statement

A bank is a *financial intermediary* that participates in the payment system and finances entities in financial deficit (typically the public sector, nonfinancial firms, and some households) using the funds of entities in financial surplus (typically households). At the microeconomic level banks finance each other through interbank operations. Among financial intermediaries the specificity of banks is to issue *money, broadly defined*: demand deposits, savings deposits, and short-term deposits. A typical balance sheet of a bank is presented in table 2.1 (a typical income statement is provided in table 2.2).

Besides the traditional nonfinancial assets of any firm (equipments and premises), the asset side of the balance sheet includes a portfolio of financial assets: very short-term assets (cash, interbank loans, money market loans); loans and fixed-income securities

Table 2.1
Balance sheet

Assets	Liabilities
Cash	
Interbank loans	Interbank deposits
Credit to the public sector	Retail and other wholesale deposits
Credit to households	(demand, savings,
Credit to firms	and time deposits)
Equity holdings	Subordinated debt
Equipment and premises	Equity (stock issues plus retained earnings)

of variable length to the public sector, to companies (commercial loans, investment loans, real estate loans), and to households (installment loans and real estate loans); and equity of other companies in countries where *"universal banking"* is allowed (which it is not in the United States because of the Glass-Steagall Act).

The liability side of the balance sheet, which, by construction, is equal to the asset side, includes interbank deposits and then funds collected among households and companies, namely demand and savings deposits and short- or long-term deposits. Interbank deposits and large corporate deposits are called *wholesale deposits* while the others are called *retail deposits*. All of these liabilities are senior to subordinated debt, which in turn is senior to equity.[1]

Besides priority rules in the event of bank failure, it is useful to characterize deposits with respect to deposit-insurance protection. Deposit insurance typically covers small depositors (house-

---

1. It is useful here to provide orders of magnitude. For an average U.S. commercial bank in 1990, the liability side was 18% in demand deposits, 51% in savings and time deposits, 24% in other debt, and 7% in equity. The asset side was 7% in cash, 19% in public sector loans, 67% in private sector loans (including 19% in corporate loans, 24% in real estate loans, and 11% in installment loans) and 7% in equipment and premises (Federal Reserve Bulletin, cited by Mishkin 1992a).

Table 2.2
Income statement

Debit	Credit
Interest and commissions paid	Interest and commissions earned
Operating expenses	Income from equity holdings
Depreciation	
Loan (and equity) loss provisions	
Taxes	
After-tax profit	

holds and, up to a given amount, nonfinancial firms); it excludes interbank deposits. Interbank deposits are thus nonsubordinated but uninsured deposits; they are less favored than retail deposits, although they are senior to subordinated debt and equity.

Interbank operations are of two types: they include (1) very short-term loans between banks lacking cash and banks having a temporary excess of cash (e.g., through the overnight market), and (2) bank financing of commercial operations between nonfinancial companies.[2] Because of these operations banks hold credit lines with many banking correspondents, who are the bankers of companies with which the client firms of the initial banks have commercial relations.

The fact that interbank deposits are uninsured may leave the door open to potential runs that could lead to waves of failures given the importance of interbank lending. This systemic risk however leads the banking sector to rationally expect an implicit insurance mechanism that favors big banks through, for example, the central bank.

---

2. Consider a company A selling goods of value X to company B. B promises to pay A within three months. A can obtain X from its bank A' immediately and let A' recover B's debt, but A' will typically prefer to deal with B's bank B' to dealing with B directly. Consequently the three-month credit granted by A to B becomes an interbank credit between A' and B' (which then de facto grants a loan to B).

The working of this mechanism was in evidence in the 1984 Continental Illinois crisis in the United States.[3] This "too big to fail" principle in effect negates the noninsurance of big interbank deposits.

The balance sheet of the bank concerns only a share of banking activities. The assets and liabilities listed are only those granted *at present* and in a *noncontingent way*. The bank also has "off-balance" activities that do not correspond to this definition:[4]

1. *Financial service operations not linked to the granting of actual loans.* For example, the placement of securities issued by companies or the public sector in the market at large. The bank earns a fee for such services.[5]

2. *Future* or *contingent loans.* For example, documentary credits,[6] the granting of backup facilities for some financial operations, asset sales with recourse,[7] or the granting of credit lines (loan commitments). There has recently been a substantial growth in standby letters of credit, with which banks guarantee loans made by third

---

3. This was also the case recently in Scandinavia where *all* deposits were protected by the government in order to prevent generalized banking insolvency.

4. To give an order of magnitude, the "notional" exposure on off-balance sheet activities were about 85% of balance sheet assets for U.S. banks in 1986 (Ronen et al. 1990, ch 1). Any off-balance sheet item is converted into an "on-balance-sheet" loan or "credit equivalent." For example for a standby letter of credit guaranteeing a loan issued by a third party, the "notional" credit or credit equivalent is the total amount of the loan.

5. Another example is the case of a commercial loan sale without recourse that continues to be serviced by the originating bank. The no-recourse provision means that the originating bank is no longer responsible for a default on the loan; the bank then just receives a fee for servicing the loan. There is of course the issue of whether a loan sale without recourse will still be subject to an implicit guarantee by the originating bank; then the bank would keep the risk and be subject to a capital requirement on the loan. On this, see Gorton-Pennacchi's chapter "Are Loan Sales Really Off-Balance Sheet?" in Ronen et al. (1990).

6. Documentary credits imply a payment to their beneficiary only upon receiving the valid documents. Up to that moment, they stay off balance.

7. When a bank sells assets (securitizes) with recourse, it commits to paying any shortfall and therefore keeps the risk while disposing of the asset.

parties instead of issuing loans themselves. The vast majority of commercial paper issuers secure their loans with credit lines or standby letters of credit from banks. With a standby letter of credit the bank's contingent liability is the same as if it had issued the loan itself and the only difference is that the loan is taken off the balance sheet to become off-balance. (Credit lines on the other hand do not generally transfer the full credit risk to the bank.)

3. *Interest rate and foreign exchange contracts.* Namely contracts where either no principal is ever reimbursed and the exchange is in interest or foreign exchange flows (interest rate swaps or foreign exchange swaps[8]) or where one party promises to buy or sell currencies in the future at a prespecified rate (foreign exchange futures). These operations can include contingencies (options, etc.). Some of these operations directly correspond to on-balance activities: foreign exchange futures to offset foreign currency operations and the corresponding exchange rate risk, or interest rate swaps designed to reduce the interest rate risk on the balance sheet.

The balance sheet is thus only a partial picture of banking activity. It is moreover a static picture that gets modified by a reallocation of the asset and liability portfolios of the bank (this operation leaves unchanged the equity position of the bank) and by retained earnings (or by the issuance or repurchase of stock). After-tax income is the residual of the income statement of the bank, whose debit equals its credit by construction. The income statement includes both on- and off-balance operations. The after-tax income is affected first by the *interest rate margin* (interest earned minus interest due) and then by the income from equity holdings. *Commissions*

---

8. Consider an operation with a "notional principal"of $10 million, with an annual interest rate swap for five years of a fixed 10% rate against the one-year market rate (i_t) during this period. Each year t during this period, one party pays $1 million and the other pays i_t times $10 million, without payment of the "notional principal" at the end of the relationship.

can accrue from both on- and off-balance operations. Net interest income, commissions, and dividends represent the revenue of the bank. Operating expenses (personnel, premises, and equipment) as well as provisions for loan and equity losses and depreciation must be deducted from this revenue. Depreciation includes traditional losses of value of buildings and equipment. Changes in the accounting value of the loan (and equity) portfolio of the bank represent a crucial aspect of its income statement. Finally, the levy of income taxes defines an after-tax profit to be split between dividends and retained earnings. These retained earnings are added to the equity position of the bank as shown on the balance sheet.

2.1.2 Banking Specialization

Table 2.1 presented a simplified taxonomy of banking activities. In reality the quantitative structure of the balance sheet depends on the type and the degree of specialization of the bank. After the banking crises of the early 1930s[9] many countries imposed strict specialization of banking activity. For example, the United States and many European countries—but not France, Germany, the Netherlands, or Switzerland—ruled out *mixed* or *universal banks*,[10]

---

9. See, for example, Friedman and Schwartz (1963) for a description of the crisis in the United States.

10. Through the Glass-Steagall Act (1933) in the United States. Its Japanese version (article 165 of the Securities and Exchange Law) has recently been altered to allow banks to own subsidiaries, with segmented equity, allowed to hold nonfinancial equity. Britain allows for a restricted form of universal banking using separate subsidiaries, and with less equity and insurance activity than Germany, for example. See Hall (1993, ch. 9) for an extensive comparison of the U.S. and Japanese approaches to the separation of banking and securities business.

Economies of scope plead against laws such as the Glass-Steagall Act. Namely the information collected when lending to a borrower can also be used to underwrite securities for this borrower. There were two main concerns behind the passing of the Glass-Steagall Act. The first was that a bank allowed to underwrite securities may face conflicts of interest. It may underwrite poor securities for a borrower to pay the bank's poor loans with this borrower. While a bank concerned with its rep-

that is, depository institutions holding equity portfolios on their asset side, aside from loans or fixed interest securities. These countries distinguish *depository institutions*, which may not hold equity, and *holding companies*, which hold equity but do not issue deposits. Many countries moreover divided depository institutions into *commercial banks* and *savings banks*. Savings banks are specialized in collecting household savings and in granting residential mortgage loans, without being able to issue demand deposits or to grant commercial or investment loans to companies. Commercial banks instead issue demand deposits and are supposed to make short-term loans to firms.

The goal of this segmentation was to reduce the risk faced by depositors, or by the deposit insurance funds that had been created to prevent the bank runs that had led to so many failures in the 1930s. This period has also prompted complementary measures supposed to provide banking stability, such as regulatory barriers to entry[11] or ceilings on deposit interest rates.[12]

The 1970s and 1980s instead witnessed a general trend toward *despecialization* and *deregulation*. In the United States, deregulation was induced, in particular, by the phenomenon of *disintermediation*

---

utation will refrain from such behavior, less trustworthy banks may attempt to fool naive investors. Krozner and Rajan (1993) argue that despite some notorious cases, commercial banks engaged little in such conflicts of interest before 1933. They compare the performance of securities underwritten by commercial banks and those underwritten by independent investment banks (and therefore not facing a conflict of interest). They find no evidence that investors were fooled by commercial banks. However, with deposit insurance this conflict of interest might be more problematic. Depositors would not have to fear it, so only the deposit insurance fund would suffer. The second concern about the underwriting function of commercial banks was that it might increase their risk (to the extent that the underwriter buys the securities from the company and resells them to the public; the risk for the underwriter is obviously much smaller if he only promises his "best effort" to sell securities at some prespecified price).

11. The 1927 McFadden-Pepper Act in the United States had already considerably reduced the possibility for banks to engage in out-of-state activities.

12. Regulation Q imposed such ceilings in the United States.

due to deposit rate ceilings, which prevented banks from adequately rewarding depositors in periods of rising interest rates. Banks faced the competition of "money market mutual funds," which are investment funds holding very liquid short-term assets and allowing their investors to write checks against their assets in the fund. Deregulation gradually allowed banks to reconquer their competitive position against money market mutual funds.

Despecialization of financial intermediaries was motivated by a desire to allow them to better *diversify* in periods of instability of interest rates, inflation rates, and exchange rates. The example of the U.S. Savings and Loan Associations detailed in chapter 4 is significant in this respect. Regulation focused their activity until the end of the 1970s on long-term fixed-nominal-rate mortgages, while their liabilities were savings deposits that had to adjust upward with the market under the competitive threat of money market mutual funds. This problem became particularly acute in the early 1980s with the anti-inflationary policy of the Federal Reserve Board under the direction of Paul Volcker, which sharply increased nominal interest rates, especially short-term rates. Combined with the sharp recession that culminated in 1982, this formidable shrinkage of the interest rate margin of banks led the whole sector to suffer heavy losses. Deregulation was then put forward as a way to allow banks to offer new financial contracts (e.g., with variable rates) and to sectorally diversify. We will see in chapter 4 that these developments were a mixed blessing. Let us simply stress here the fact that these evolutions of the last twenty years implied a reduction in the differences among the various categories of banks, and that recent international regulations (presented in chapter 3) do not discriminate among them.

2.1.3   Bank Heterogeneity

Despite the fine segmentation of financial intermediaries, it would be incorrect to presume that intermediaries are homogeneous within each segment. A particularly telling comparison is that between small and large banks in the United States. Boyd and Gertler (1993) summarize the evidence as follows:

1. Large banks tend to choose a different asset composition from small banks. They grant more business loans and are proportionately more involved in commercial real estate and in loans to less developed countries (which have suffered large losses in the 1980s), and less in consumer loans and residential real estate, which are safer on average (this does not of course exclude bad lending policies by small banks).

2. Large banks are much more involved in off-balance sheets activities and in derivatives trading.

3. Large banks use more managed liabilities (interbank deposits, and large time deposits), which represent 40% of large banks' liabilities and 54% of money center banks' liabilities.[13] In contrast, small banks' managed liabilities account for less than 10% of their liabilities. Large banks also borrow more from abroad (they obtain more than half of their purchased funds from abroad).

4. Large banks have lower interest margins between their assets and their liabilities.

An interesting question is whether differences in behavior are linked with the widespread perception that large banks will not be allowed to fail by the central bank.[14]

---

13. Money center banks are large banks in key financial centers (mainly in New York).

14. It is worth noting in this respect that around 70% of uninsured deposits in U.S. banks are in banks larger than $1 billion. Relatedly the banks' market for certificates of deposits is tiered in that larger banks pay lower rates. Yet a similar observation is the fact that large banks purchase mainly in the (uncollateralized) federal funds market, while smaller banks use more the collateralized market for repurchase agreements (repos) as a source of funds; see Allen et al. (1989). Another piece of evidence in the same direction is that the stock price of large banks went up after Continental Illinois was bailed out, signaling perhaps that the cheap access of large banks to uninsured deposits would continue (O'Hara-Shaw 1990).

2.1.4   Deposits and Debt Position of Banks

The crucial role of debt and of its control rights in the corporate governance of nonfinancial firms has been highlighted in academic debates. Table 2.3 shows that debt, namely deposits, is quantitatively more important for banks relative to other sectors of the U.S. economy. This table should be interpreted with caution, since bank portfolios are more liquid and more diversified than those of nonfinancial firms. However, the table does indicate a potential fragility of the banking sector. In case of insolvency, control would typically be transferred to creditors or their representative, the deposit insurance fund. The debate on the optimal exercise of this control is intense, and it is reflected in the successive waves of banking regulation. The importance of debt finance explains why this debate is often framed in terms of excessive risk taking by shareholders and bank managers.[15]

The incentive effects of capital structure are particularly relevant for banks, for which debt represents the main source of finance. Where nonfinancial firms finance only a limited fraction of their activity from external sources (whether debt or equity), privileging instead the internal finance of investment (see Mayer 1988), banks face profits much too small in comparison to their assets to allow for large-scale internal finance of new credits.

In table 2.4 we compare leverage in banks with that in other financial intermediaries.[16] How should we account for the discrepancies in net worth among financial intermediaries and between

---

One should, however, investigate why large banks are large in the first place and whether uninsured deposits would not flock to them because of better management or better diversification and lower intrinsic riskiness. One could also argue that, thanks to brokered deposits, small banks also have had access to the wholesale market, although most of their liabilities are insured.

15. A hazard analyzed in academic circles since Jensen-Meckling (1976) or Stiglitz-Weiss (1981), for example.

16. For other data from 1971 through 1984, see Boyd-Graham (1984).

Table 2.3
Measures of corporate net worth by industry in the United States, 1985

Industry	Ratio of net worth to total assets	Ratio of debt to equity
All industries	0.32	2.11
Agriculture, forestry, and fishing	0.32	2.12
Mining	0.45	1.21
Construction	0.28	2.52
Manufacturing	0.45	1.20
Transportation and public utilities	0.40	1.50
Wholesale and retail trade	0.29	2.49
Services	0.31	2.25
Finance, insurance, and real estate	0.26	2.90
Commercial banks	0.08	11.00
Savings banks[a]	0.04	28.00

Source: U.S. Internal Revenue Service, White (1991, 15, 40).
a. Mutual savings banks plus savings and loan associations.

financial intermediaries and nonfinancial companies? One possible, and rather simplistic, explanation is that low net worth requirements of regulated intermediaries result from regulatory laxity. But we could look at the differences in activities. Activities calling for low-intensity monitoring generally require lower capital than those with more monitoring.[17] Although the monitoring role

---

17. In Holmström-Tirole (1994), intermediaries monitor risky borrowers and collect savings from investors (the public). Unlike in part IV of this book, the public is well informed and coordinated so that the representation problem does not arise. Investors require intermediaries to maintain a minimum solvency ratio (so the solvency requirement arises from market forces, while in this book it is imposed by a representative who tries to replicate market forces). The equilibrium solvency ratio is shown to be higher, the larger the scope for borrower mismanagement, the higher the intermediary's monitoring cost, and the larger the net worth of the banking sector. In particular, high-intensity monitoring activities should be backed with substantial amounts of capital. In contrast, intermediaries whose assets require little monitoring should be subject to looser solvency requirements.

Table 2.4
Median equity-to-total assets ratios (%)

Year	50 largest banks	Large national bank holding companies	Securities brokers and dealers	Life insurance
1980	4.63	5.60	19.51	19.71
1989	5.00	6.27	19.69	12.37

Year	Property and casualty insurance	Short-term business credit companies	Personal credit companies
1980	23.12	19.53	14.85
1989	22.29	13.76	13.30

of banks is important, many assets held by banks require less monitoring than those held by nonfinancial firms. Nonfinancial firms oversee fairly complex and risky R&D and manufacturing projects, and therefore they can be regarded as high-intensity monitoring "intermediaries." Banks, on the other hand, have, on their balance sheet, a category of safe claims (government securities, high-quality corporate debt, etc.). Loans to small business may be riskier, but their short maturity and the intensive use of collateral reduce the need for monitoring. (Moreover, banks tend to be more diversified than nonfinancial firms). In effect, while both nonfinancial firms and banks engage in substantial monitoring, there is still a quantitative difference in their monitoring intensity. A related issue to investigate might be whether nonbank intermediaries have higher solvency ratios than banks because of more lenient capital regulation, or whether the composition of their assets or the nature of their liabilities (e.g., the need for high-intensity monitoring of industrial risk for some insurers) vindicates such discrepancies.

2.1.5 Why Have Banks Failed Recently?

For a long time after World War II in many countries competition inside and outside the banking sector was restricted, and banking activities were fairly standard. It was a cozy world;[18] very few banks failed. In contrast, in the last twenty-five years there has been a sharp increase in competition, new and risky activities have been on the rise, and many economies have experienced macroeconomic shocks. Concurrently banks have been facing serious troubles.[19] Let us look at some of the factors involved:

1. *Macroeconomic shocks.* While there have been macroeconomic shocks in earlier periods, those of the 1980s had particularly adverse effects on banks. The sharp increase in interest rates, as we already noted, substantially penalized institutions that transform short-term borrowing into long-term lending. The economic slowdown also had a strong negative impact on banks, as more corporate borrowers encountered financial straits and the real estate markets tumbled in the late 1980s.

2. *Riskier activities.* A number of observers[20] feel that the nature of banking has become riskier lately. They, for instance, point to some aspects of deregulation that, in some countries, have enhanced banks' ability to hold securities. Banks have become more involved in commercial real estate as well, and they have securitized higher-quality assets such as consumer and residential real-estate loans.

---

18. As *The Economist* (April 10, 1993) notes, according to an old jibe, banking was as easy as 3:6:3 (money in at 3%, lend at 6%, on the golf course by 3 o'clock). A useful overview of the reasons behind recent instability in banking is to be found in the 62nd Bank for International Settlements Report, March 1992.
19. Hope (1993) attributes the collapse of the Norwegian banking sector to four factors: financial deregulation, external shocks (oil plunge in 1985-86 in Norway), monetary policy (expansionary in Norway), and bad banking practices. This classification clearly extends to many countries.
20. For example, Borio-Filosa (1994) and Litan (1994).

Other observers, however, argue that the diversification into new activities can reduce bank risk.

Some observers[21] are worried about the future consequences of the enormous growth in over-the-counter derivative instruments such as swaps and options. There are at least two important concerns here. The first is that the large and rapidly fluctuating exposures in derivatives make it hard for regulators to control risk. We here have in mind interest rate and exchange rate exposures: Swings in interest rates and currency rates might quickly jeopardize a bank's solvency and yet not leave regulators time to intervene. In principle, derivative instruments should be, and often are, used to *reduce* exposure to interest and exchange rate fluctuations. They have become an important element of the banks' internal risk management. The regulators' concern is not that derivative instruments will *on average* be used in the wrong direction (to increase risk instead of reducing it) but that the minority of troubled banks might use such instruments in the wrong direction in order to increase risk. It then becomes important to have reliable early warning systems (see subsection 3.3.3) that detect bank trouble and allow the regulators to limit or control trades in derivatives; regulators also try to develop systematic measures of banks' sensitivities to interest and exchange rate risks (see subsection 3.1.4).

The second regulatory worry relative to derivatives concerns the replacement-cost credit exposures. There is in principle no credit risk in a swap. For example, if I owe you x and you owe me DMy tomorrow and I default today, you will not receive x but you will not transfer me DMy either.[22] The main risk for you if I default is that you will have to replace the swap contract in possibly adverse

21. See, for example, Corrigan (1991) and *The Economist* (March 13, 1993; April 10, 1993). Many regulatory bodies have recently conducted studies about the risks associated with derivatives.
22. In contrast, the buyer (but not the seller) of an option faces credit risk because the seller might default before the option can be exercised.

market conditions. The worry about replacement costs concerns mainly the largest banks. For instance, in 1992, in the United States, 90% of the replacement cost exposure was with seven banks.[23] For these banks the ratio of replacement-cost credit exposures to total assets ranged from 12% (Bank of America) to 33.4% (Bankers Trust), which are substantial numbers compared with their net worth.

3. *More intense competition.* Competition has increased on two fronts. First, there has been more *competition among banks.* Cartel-type agreements are less tolerated than before. Restrictions on lines of business and geographical locations have been relaxed. Domestic and offshore markets have been integrated. Ceilings on deposit rates have mostly been lifted. All this has had an impact on bank profitability.

Second, the dominance of banks over *other financial intermediaries* has been seriously challenged, as shown in table 2.5 for the United States. We can attribute this partly to advances in computer technology and the development of new financial markets and instruments.[24] On the borrowing side, banks must increasingly compete with mutual funds, pension funds, and insurance companies for savings. On the lending side, highly rated firms have issued substantial amounts of commercial paper, while lesser-rated companies have also bypassed banks by issuing junk bonds.[25]

We should, however, be careful not to overemphasize the decline of banks. Banks have remained relatively strong in what is, after all, their core business: investments in illiquid assets. In particular, they still are the main providers of business liquidity. Moreover, while the bank balanced sheets have shrunk relative to those

---

23. Bankers Trust, Chemical Bank, J.P. Morgan, Chase, Bank of America, First Chicago, and Citicorp. See *The Economist* (April 10, 1993, p. 36, survey on international banking) for more detail.

24. Merton (1993), in particular, strongly emphasizes the move from intermediation to markets.

25. Commercial paper is unsecured debt issued by companies and maturing within nine months. Junk bonds are high-default-risk bonds.

Table 2.5
Share of financial assets held by major intermediaries in the United States

Intermediary	1946	1980	1989
Commercial banks	57.3	36.8	30.9
Savings and loans	4.3	15.2	11.8
Mutual savings banks	8.0	4.3	2.8
Credit unions	.2	1.7	2.1
Life insurance	20.3	11.5	12.1
Private pension	1.5	11.7	12.0
State and local government pension	1.2	4.9	7.0
Other insurance	3.0	4.3	4.7
Finance companies	2.1	5.0	5.0
Mutual funds	.6	3.4	9.4
Other	1.5	1.2	2.3

Source: Board of Governors of the Federal Reserve System, flow of funds accounts, cited in Litan (1994).

of other intermediaries, banks have substantially expanded their off-balance-sheet activities.[26] For instance, consider a bank whose corporate borrower replaces his loan by commercial paper. If this paper is backed by the bank's standby letter of credit, as is common practice, one cannot really argue here that the bank has lost market share. While the notional amount of the loan has shifted from the bank to others, the bank retains the risk, which is the central (and profitable) feature of the loan.

4. *Mismanagement.* Observers often point at mismanagement and fraud as one of the culprits for the banking crisis. There certainly has been substantial mismanagement and fraud.[27] To be sure, mis-

---

26. See, for example, Boyd-Gertler (1993) for evidence.
27. Fraud is a concern in countries with a substantial number of small banks, like the United States; mismanagement is much more likely than fraud for large banks. While the conventional wisdom is that fraud played a minor role in U.S. banking troubles (see, e.g., White 1991), Akerlof and Romer (1994) argue that fraud (e.g., structuring high-risk investments so as to obtain sizable short-term profits and

management and fraud opportunities have always existed. They simply have become more attractive to managers and shareholders in the riskier and less profitable world of the 1980s.

2.2   Why Regulate Banks?

2.2.1   Changing the Focus

There is no consensus in academe on why banks should be regulated, how they should be regulated, and whether they should be regulated at all. In our view, too much emphasis is being put on specific features of banks (transformation function, participation in the payment system, high leverage) or on various dimensions of regulation (specific requirements, deposit insurance, liquidity provision). We ought to go back to what motivates banking regulation in the first place and then proceed to logically derive its desired bundle of rules and see how these rules are affected by the specificities of banks (or other financial intermediaries).

The (alleged or real) specificities of banks may not account for the forms of regulation we observe. First, for example, the *transformation function* is performed by many nonfinancial companies. A company that invests in a ten-year R&D project or a thirty-year plant and issues lower maturity claims engages in no less transformation than a bank (there is no a priori reason for why runs should be more prevalent in the banking sector), yet there is no talk about regulating industrial firms as a rule. Second, participation in the *payments system* certainly is not a prerequisite for regulation. Otherwise, why would insurance companies or pension funds, which do not participate in this system, be regulated? Further, as Goodhart (1987)

---

long-term losses and accordingly distributing large dividends in the short run) accounts for a substantial fraction of S&L losses ($50 billion out of an estimate of $170 billion of government loss).

notes, why are five-year time accounts or individual retirement accounts (IRAs) in banks protected? Understand us well: We feel that
the protection of the payments system is important. Banks are central to this payment system and provide liquidity services to many
of the financial and nonfinancial firms. This certainly accounts for
the liquidity support offered by the central bank to member banks,
as well as for the fact that the preservation of the banking system
is often referred to as one of the two main motivations for regulation.[28] Our point is simply that the concern for depositor protection
figures prominently in the design of the regulatory system.[29]

Third, we do not view the bank's high *leverage* as a ground for
regulation. The fact that finance companies are more leveraged than
industrial firms does not make them likely candidates for regulation. The level of leverage is related to the risk on the balance sheet.
Besides, it is endogenous, and in the absence of regulation banks
could reduce their leverage in order to obtain better credit conditions.

Observers sometimes point to *deposit insurance* as an important
motivation for regulation. To some extent this puts the cart before
the horse. Deposit insurance, if desired by investors, could be provided by the private sector like most forms of insurance. Indeed
many economists have argued in favor of substantially reducing the
current coverage by the government. There is an argument, though,
according to which government deposit insurance motivates regulation rather than only being part of an optimal regulatory pack-

---

28. For example, the two main official functions of the German banking supervisory system are the protection of deposit owners and the orderly functioning of
the banking system (see Rudolph 1993). Similar motivations are given for U.S. and
French regulations.

29. We will only pay lip service to the payment system aspect of banking in our
analysis, in that the stability of the banking system will arise as a *by-product* of
government deposit insurance. We leave the analysis of the payment system for
future work. In the present work we focus on those features of banking that apply
more generally to nonpayment claims and to other intermediaries.

age: No financial system with reasonably high levels of leverage can guarantee the claims of investors if large adverse macroeconomic shocks occur. Assuming such an extensive insurance coverage is desirable, the government can use its coercive power to force other categories (noninvestors, future generations) to provide the required insurance to investors through taxes (current, or deferred through the use of public debt). These categories bear a nonnegligible risk, and they want to keep some control over its magnitude through their representative, the government. We have some sympathy with this argument but contend that the need for regulation and its "collocation" with the deposit insurance provider does not rely on the existence of large macroeconomic shocks that can wipe out the financial sector as a whole and against which depositors must be protected. Further, the concerns addressed by the large-macroeconomic-shock view if anything reinforce the perspective taken by this book.

Our approach to banking regulation is quite basic. It goes back to the view of many bankers and central bankers that regulation is motivated in particular by the need to protect the small depositors.[30] Banks, like most financial and nonfinancial companies, are subject to substantial moral hazard and adverse selection.[31] Investors therefore must perform a variety of monitoring functions: screening, auditing, covenant writing, intervention. Such functions are complex, expensive, and time-consuming. Furthermore their exercise is a "natural monopoly," in that their duplication by several parties is technically wasteful. Bank debt is primarily held by small depositors. Such depositors are most often unsophisticated, in that

---

30. The protection of depositors has motivated many banking laws. It is, for example, mentioned in article 52 of the French banking law (see Burgard 1988, 48); similarly the U.S. Federal Deposit Insurance Corporation's foremost responsibility is to protect insured depositors (Bovenzi-Muldoon 1990).

31. See, for example, Cole et al. (1993) for econometric evidence on the moral hazard problem in banking; Kane (1989) provides more anecdotal evidence.

they are unable to understand the intricacies of balance and off-balance sheet activities. More fundamentally the thousands or hundreds of thousands of customers of a bank have little individual incentive to perform the various monitoring functions. This free-riding gives rise to a need for private or public representatives of depositors. We call this the *representation hypothesis*.

The crux of our approach will therefore be to ask: *What type of control would depositors like to exert if they were sophisticated and fully coordinated? To answer this question, we must go back to the general question of optimal governance structure, which transcends banks.*

2.2.2 Addressing Potential Concerns about the Representation Hypothesis

By our representation hypothesis we, in a sense, deny banking specificity because we solely focus on control structures and small depositor representation. More precisely, we consider the specificities of banking as having quantitative, and not qualitative impacts. We see this import of corporate governance ideas as a way to enrich the banking regulation debate and not to diminish it. Let us here clarify a few points related to our argument:

1. *Why protect depositors, and not dispersed bondholders or shareholders?* A proportion of nonfinancial companies' shares and bonds are held by small, dispersed investors. These investors (who are often more sophisticated than bank depositors) face the same free-riding problem as bank depositors. Yet their claims are only slightly regulated (e.g., via disclosure requirements) and uninsured.

The reason why they are left unregulated differs for bonds and shares. Most of the bonds are issued by large or well-capitalized firms (Diamond 1991) and are relatively safe. The rating of a high-grade bond seriously limits the investor's risk. Exceptions are of course the low-quality, "junk" bonds that were much in fashion in the 1980s. They were purchased mostly by financial institutions rather than individual investors. Unlike public debt, the risky debt of nonfinancial companies requires intense monitoring. It is far less dispersed, so the representation problem does not arise.

Stocks are definitely risky. The representation mechanism that we uphold for banks exists, albeit in different form, for shares of non-financial firms. This representation is performed by private parties. In the Anglo-Saxon world (mainly the United States and the United Kingdom), dispersed shareholders are represented by large share-holders, a board of directors, potential raiders, and organizers of proxy fights. In the non-Anglo-Saxon world (e.g., France, Germany, Italy, and Japan), the control of firms is undertaken by large share-holders, and mainly by banks (Goodhart 1993; Sheard 1989).[32] Further we will argue in this book that while control by shareholders matters, control by creditors matters even more. Indeed the raison-d'être of debt is to create a tough investor who will exert discipline on management in hard times. For this reason the need for representation is even more acute for debt than for equity.

2. *Why do small investors invest primarily in financial intermediaries?* If small depositors were to deposit their money with nonfinancial firms and if banks' debt consisted only of large deposits, the focus of our study would be on the regulation of nonfinancial firms instead of banks. In fact individuals invest most of their money through financial institutions. For example, Diaz-Giménez et al. (1992) estimate that the total liabilities owed to U.S. households by financial corporations and nonfinancial corporations were in 1986 equal to 129% and 7% of GNP, respectively. This striking asymmetry is not surprising in view of the need for a "pyramid of delegated monitoring." In extremely simplified form, this pyramid

---

32. In Germany in 1974–75, the banks held 62% of the votes at stockholder meetings (by holding shares as custodians), 18% of the seats on the boards of directors, and only 9% of corporate stocks (Kregel 1992, 249).

would involve nonfinancial firms selecting and monitoring industrial and commercial projects and financial intermediaries selecting and monitoring the firms; it naturally arises in general equilibrium models of the financial and real sectors.[33]

One may wonder why, aside from any regulatory reason, households invest in debt liabilities rather than in the financial intermediaries' stocks (of course they do not always do so, e.g., claims in mutual funds are equity claims). An answer is that households are risk averse. They often want to limit the risk on assets they will need to liquidate when they become unemployed or sick, or decide to buy a house or send their children to college. Alternatively, some may want to hold a safe claim in order not to "lose their shirt" against insiders/speculators who are better informed about the value of a risky claim when they need to sell it for liquidity purposes (Gorton-Pennacchi 1990). Last, low-risk claims may smooth the payment system by reducing the cost of evaluating the real value of claims held by an agent.[34]

3. *How extensive should the regulation of the financial sector be?* We do not advocate a pervasive regulation of the financial sector. Households actually face a *menu* of unregulated (or rather lightly regulated) and regulated financial services, and this is presumably desirable. Households should have the choice to use unregulated financial institutions as long as they are made aware of the risk they face and minimal disclosure and antifraud devices are put in place. In a way, though, the government is the ultimate regulator, even in a world of low regulatory requirements. On the one hand, un-

---

33. See Holmström-Tirole (1994).

34. For views on what types of liabilities should be used for payment purposes, see White (1984) and Goodhart (1987). Another reason why some households prefer debt liabilities is that under some tax codes, there is a lower tax rate on debt (even when one accounts for personal taxes). See, for example, Miller's (1976) discussion of the pre-1986 Tax Reform Act incentives in the United States, and Brealey-Myers's (1988, ch.18) updated discussion of the issue.

sophisticated or time pressed investors must be protected against misleading promises such as deposit insurance provided by risky or poorly capitalized insurers. On the other hand, as we noted earlier, the government would be the ultimate insurer in case of a large aggregate shock. A second point related to the extent of regulation is that the need for regulation depends much on the nature of the claim and the nature of the intermediary (more on this in the next subsection). A third point is that we are in a first step interested in optimal regulation, be it public or private. Public regulation may be viewed as a situation in which the government supplies representation services to small investors (besides being the insurer of last resort). These services might also be provided by the private sector. For this reason the analysis of the costs and benefits of public and private regulations will be delayed until chapters 12 and 13.

2.2.3   Further Evidence in Favor of the Representation Hypothesis

We have two types of indirect evidence in favor of the representation hypothesis, that the prudential regulation of banks is primarily motivated by the need to represent small depositors and to bring about an appropriate corporate governance for banks. Later in sections 3.4 and 3.5 we will show that the regulation of other financial intermediaries (insurance companies, securities firms or pension funds) and the control exerted by large creditors on nonfinancial corporate borrowers are qualitatively similar to the prudential regulation of banks. This similarity with other financial intermediaries can be explained by the common desire to protect their small, uninformed and free-riding customers. This analogy between the debt covenants and control rights of creditors of a nonfinancial corporation and the methods of prudential regulation, which we review later in sections 3.1 and 3.2, reinforces the view that the regulator is first and foremost a representative of small depositors.

In this section, we come up with slightly different evidence, namely that the pattern of regulation of financial intermediaries is governed by the riskiness of claims, the dispersion of their holders, and the lack of private representatives. A summary of our argument is presented in figure 2.1.

Before detailing our argument, let us explain a few points relative to this figure. First, our description of financial intermediation is not meant to be exhaustive; it furthermore simplifies reality in order to highlight the argument. Second, we include some claims on nonfinancial corporations, since such corporations are also intermediaries in that they allocate their funds in an internal capital market. Third, "no regulation" in the figure often stands for "light regulation," that is, regulation that imposes disclosure requirements and prevents fraud, as opposed to prudential regulation. For instance, in the United States the Securities and Exchange Commission (SEC) "regulates" mutual funds. To qualify as a money market mutual fund, the fund must invest in short-term, high-quality instruments (Treasury bills, commercial paper, bank certificates of deposits, repurchase agreements).[35] A 1991 SEC rule stipulates, among other things, that a money market mutual fund must invest less than 5% in securities with less than the highest credit rating, and less than 5% in the securities of a single issuer, and that the fund's average portfolio maturity must be lower than 90 days.[36] The SEC makes sure that money market mutual funds comply with such rules, enforces disclosures and reporting requirements, and rebukes fraud. But it does not impose any capital adequacy requirement or other forms of prudential regulation (indeed shares in mutual funds are equity claims).[37] Another example of "light regulation" consists in preventing investment managers acting on behalf of private or institutional investors from engaging in fraudulent practices such

35. A repurchase agreement (or repo) is the purchase of a Treasury security with an agreement that the seller will repurchase it at a prespecified price.
36. See, for example, Gorton-Pennacchi (1993b) for a broader discussion.
37. These claims are 100% equity claims in that mutual funds are not leveraged.

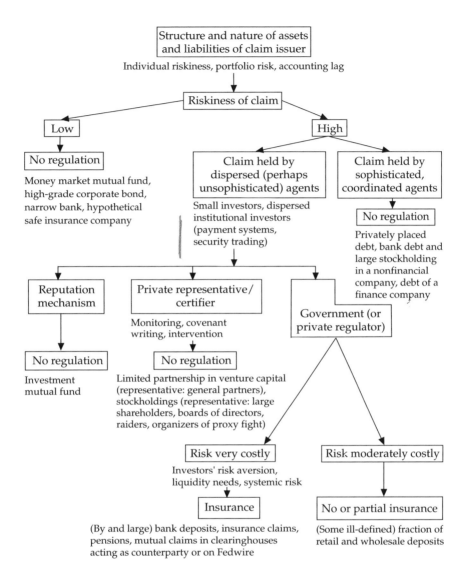

Figure 2.1
Pattern of regulation of financial intermediaries. (1) *Privately placed bonds* are bonds sold to institutions, mainly life insurance companies. Since they generally involve riskier borrowers, they call for substantial monitoring by the institution as well as more extensive covenants and slightly shorter maturities than public bonds. They are thus very similar to bank debt (except that, technically, privately placed bonds are securities, and they have longer maturities). (2) *Finance companies* borrow in large amounts (bonds and commercial paper, often backed by banks) and issue consumer loans, purchase companies' accounts receivables (factoring), or lease equipment. They are almost unregulated. (3) *Fedwire* is a continuous time settlement system in which the Federal Reserve acts as a counterpart to every trade.

as churning (trading excessively to generate commissions), back-pricing to take advantage of price movements, or investing in connected companies.[38]

Let us start with *fairly safe claims*. Having little stake, the holders of such claims are logically removed from the exercise of control over the issuer. They participate little in corporate governance, and they do not in fact raise the issue of representation. Money market mutual funds are a good example. As we noted, they are very safe equity claims due to the choice of assets. Furthermore they are open-end funds in that the shares can be redeemed at any time at a price that reflects the value of the fund.[39] So the control over management quality can fairly easily be exerted through "exit," that is, by selling the shares, rather than through "voice," that is, through covenants and intervention, to use Hirschman's (1970) terminology. A variant on the money market mutual fund is the idea of a "narrow bank," which many economists, including Friedman and Tobin[40] have advocated as a way out of prudential regulation. The idea of a narrow bank is that "insured deposits" are matched by the same type of safe, marketable assets that are held by money market mutual funds. That is, the insured deposits are very safe in the first place. The money market mutual fund's equity corresponds to the insured deposits of the narrow bank. The two concepts differ in that

---

38. In the United States, individual investors are protected by the Investment Company Act of 1940, which calls for full disclosure, marking to market, and prohibition against self-dealing (the pursuit of one's self interest with one's customer's money) by investment companies managers.

39. Managers of mutual funds are paid a management fee usually tied to the asset value of the fund.

40. See, for example, Tobin (1985). Goodhart (1987) argues that the concept of narrow banking reverses the evolution of banking. He notes that the forerunner of the Swedish Riksbank was organized in the seventeenth century "on the basis of two supposedly separate departments, the loan department financing loans on the basis of longer-term deposits and capital, and the issue department supplying credit notes on the receipt of gold and specie" (p. 79). But such an arrrangement removes profits along with the bank's risk. Banks found out that they could yield higher profits by lending long some of their reserves.

the narrow bank also holds risky assets and issues risky debt and equity. But the narrow bank's safe liabilities (the insured deposits) are insulated from the riskiness of the second group of assets. Last, the "hypothetical safe insurance company" or "narrow insurance company" would be a life or property and casualty insurance company whose payouts to policyholders (the counterparts of deposits) can be well foreseen due to the law of large numbers and whose assets are those of money market mutual funds (in practice insurance companies' policies are risky for reasons to be described shortly.)

Unfortunately, most claims are risky. Claimholders must often protect themselves against mismanagement through monitoring, covenant writing, and intervention. Regulation may then be provided by a large or group of large claimholders. The archetypical example is that of the risky debt of a small nonfinancial firm held by a bank. Relatedly there may be dispersed claimholders, but they are represented by a large claimholder/certifier such as a lead investment bank, a general partner in a venture capital enterprise, or other parties. No specific public regulation is then called for, as long as the representation function is performed (e.g., the claimholder/certifier does not secretly withdraw from the project, collude with management or other groups of claimholders, or face conflicts of interest.)

As in the case of risky mutual funds, dispersed claimholders rather than exerting "voice" through their representatives can "exit." The condition for this control mechanism to function is that the value of the claims be continuously measured so that the claims can be redeemed or sold very quickly. In particular, assets must be highly marketable (like stocks).[41]

---

41. The continuous time market pricing of the mutual funds is one of the features that differentiate mutual funds from some other investment management businesses such as pension funds. The investment management business relates to the management of an investment portfolio on behalf of a client or an institution. The portfolio manager advises or exerts discretion on the choice of assets and receives a fee for this service. Besides the swings in market value of the assets, the causes

Now we come to the group of financial claims for which the representation is performed by the government. It is worth stressing the similarities with bank deposits for a couple of the most important such claims:[42]

1. *Pension funds.* Private pension funds are set up by companies. On the liability side is the present value of expected benefits for past and future service. On the asset side is the current value of the assets of the pension fund as well as contributions for future service. The pension fund's surplus or (more often) unfunded liability is defined as a residual, as is the case for banks' equity.

Both assets and liabilities of pension funds are risky. Besides the obvious uncertainty about contributions and benefits from future services, the fund faces standard uncertainty about the value of its assets even though its portfolio is supposed to be "diversified." But there is also substantial risk on the liability side. Benefits for past service increase if few employees quit before their benefit is vested (employees are usually entitled to proportionally higher benefits when they stay five or ten years with the company), if a union succeeds in negotiating an increase in benefits, and if employees retire early. Another type of risk relates to the uncertainty about future wages in the (dominant) "defined-benefit plans."[43] In such plans

---

of losses in investment management businesses differ from those of banks, say, because of the equity nature of claims. They are linked to settlement delays and counterparty risk, and mainly to managerial fraud (fraudulent advice or nonseparation of clients' money and assets). See Franks-Mayer (1989, ch. 7) for a description of U.S. and U.K. regulation of investment management business. Franks and Mayer argue that capital requirements (which play almost no role in the United States, but some role in the United Kingdom) imposed on management may not be the proper instruments for regulating investment management. See also Mayer (1993) for a further discussion of the matter.

42. For some background on these intermediaries, see, for example, Brealey-Myers (1988) and Mishkin (1992).

43. In contrast, one in four U.S. plans are "defined-contribution plans" in which the company promises to invest a specified sum every year on behalf of the employee.

the benefit depends on the employee's salary in the final year(s). Last, the biggest risk of all is that the pension fund is underfunded as the company tries to pay obligations out of current earnings (a behavior that resembles the public pension plans' "pay-as-you-go" system), goes bankrupt, and therefore does not make up for the shortfall.

A difference with banks is that (in defined-benefit plans) equity in the pension fund is held by a single shareholder[44]—the company—which furthermore is not fully protected by limited liability. More precisely, in case of poor investment performance or unexpectedly high benefits, the company must make up the difference (though over a fairly long horizon). Conversely, the company can pocket a surplus by reducing its contributions or closing down the fund and establishing a new one. Thus, if companies did not go bankrupt, expected benefits in a defined-benefit plan would not be very risky, and prudential regulation would not be warranted. However, companies do go bankrupt and sometimes with a substantially underfunded pension fund, since companies in trouble usually provide a minimum amount of funding and invest their assets in riskier securities compared with the average pension fund.

Employees, just like bank depositors, face a collective action problem and need to be represented. They are represented by their union (when there is one) in negotiations. Besides the classic issue of whether the union represents the interests of all employees or more specific ones, there is the even more serious issue that, due to an understandable risk aversion with respect to pension benefits, the pension fund must be insured by an insurance fund, whose capital adequacy must be verified if it is private. The logic thus

---

The employees are then in principle residual claimants for gains and losses on the asset side.

44. We abuse terminology by treating defined benefits as debt claims. Technically pension funds are pass-through vehicles fully owned by the underlying investors (including employees) and are not leveraged.

resembles that of the debate between private and public deposit insurance for banks.

2. *Insurance companies.* There are two kinds of insurance companies, life, and property and casualty. For *life insurers* payouts to policy-holders (the equivalent of bank depositors) are fairly predictable (except in the case of an unforeseen disease such as AIDS). Yet life insurers face substantial risk. First, life insurance companies manage substantial amounts of assets. One reason is that a chunk of their policies (whole life policies) involves a constant premium over the life of the policy, whereas the probability of death increases over the length of the policy. The company therefore manages a surplus, which creates a risk that the company becomes undercapitalized.[45] Another reason is that life insurance companies compete with banks for medium- and long-term savings.[46] So their risk is somewhat similar to that of a bank. (They also face the same risk of non renewal of contracts as even long-term contracts impose negligible penalties for cancellation.) The assets of life insurers otherwise are, on average, less risky than those of banks, although some life insurers have purchased large amounts of junk bonds and done substantial property lending.[47]

The liability side of *property and casualty insurance* companies can be quite risky. To the traditional big risks (earthquake, great storm damage on a city, large environmental risk covered by a commercial

---

45. In contrast, term life insurance policies (for which premiums rise over time with the death probability) are pure insurance policies and involve no savings element.

46. In the United States some life insurance companies have sold substantial amounts of guaranteed investment contracts (GICs), which are shorter-term liabilities. They face an interest rate risk by financing their assets from short-term liabilities, which is similar to that faced by banks. Kopcke (1992, 53) reports that "almost four-tenths of the assets of life insurers were held by companies for which outstanding GICs were at least three times their capital in 1990."

47. Recently in the United States there has been a "flight to quality" due in particular to the 1990 regulatory requirements that penalize private placements in risky corporations. See section 3.4.

policy) can be added major changes in the legal and regulatory environment (witness the large malpractice damages recently granted by U.S. courts.)[48] On the asset side, U.S. casualty insurers invest almost 60% of their assets in bonds, another 10% in equities and little in mortgage loans and real estate (Kopcke 1992).[49]

Overall insurance companies face substantial risks. In the United States alone, 105 life insurers (out of a total of around 2,600 firms) and 74 property-casualty insurers (out of 3,800) had gone bust from the start of 1990 until May 1993.[50] Furthermore policyholders are widely dispersed and therefore need to be represented.

3. *Securities markets institutions.* Several activities related to securities markets involve substantial risk. *Investment banks* assist corporations in the initial sale of securities in the primary market. As underwriters they guarantee a price to the corporations and then bear the risk when they sell the securities to the public. *Dealers* assist in trading securities in the secondary market. They stand ready to buy at the bid price and sell at the ask price. Despite the spread between the ask and the bid, they face large market risk on their inventories. In contrast, brokers do not hold inventories. They find matches between sellers and buyers and are paid a commission.

---

48. Casualty insurers ordinarily pay their claims within a few years of writing their contracts. That is, their liabilities are of much shorter term than those of the life insurers, although life insurance policies can usually be redeemed or borrowed against by the insuree.

49. Kopcke's (1992) table 3 gives the U.S. insurance companies' holdings of selected financial assets. For 1986–90 these were as a percentage of total assets:

	Government bonds	Corporate bonds	Corporate stock	Mortgage loans
Life companies	12.8	34.9	4.7	19.6
Casualty companies	45.3	12.6	11	1.1

50. *The Economist*, May 15, 1993, p. 86. Some authors wonder whether a small S&L-type crisis is in the making (see, e.g., Mishkin 1992, 278).

They therefore do not face risk. A specialist on the floor of an organized exchange performs both functions of broker and dealer.

Not surprisingly, dealers and specialists must satisfy capital adequacy requirements. The need for representation does not result from a lack of sophistication of the parties with money at stake. Rather, as in the interbank market, the issue is very rapid transactions among a large number of counterparts, which makes self-monitoring very costly.

Note that this role of "delegated monitor" does not have to be performed by the government. For example, a number of clearinghouses set capital requirements and collect margin payments[51] on open positions from their clearing members. They also have the authority to limit or suspend the activities of the members. Accordingly they have a full-time staff that continually monitors the financial strength and the portfolio positions of the members. Their incentive to monitor is provided by their acting as a counterpart to and guarantor of every trade (in the same sense a deposit insurance fund derives incentives to monitor from the risk it endorses.)[52]

Summing up, we see that financial institutions tend to be regulated under the following circumstances. First, the claimholders are somewhat unsophisticated or free-riding (small depositors, insurance policyholders, pensioners) and/or cannot conceivably thoroughly monitor their counterparts due to the number of such parties and to the time scale involved (interbank depositors, traders on securities markets). Second, no mechanism of private representation is (or can be?) set up that would dispense the claimholders from having to monitor, write covenants, and interfere. On this second point one might wonder whether given that the claimholder

---

51. Margin payments are high-quality collateral: cash, government securities or sometimes bank letters of credit.
52. For more on clearinghouses, see, for example, Bernanke (1990), Gorton (1985), and Parkinson et al. (1992).

must be assured that a private regulator/insurer satisfies regulatory capital requirements or is insured, there exist a natural *pyramid of financial institutions*, with those at the top being publicly regulated and sometimes serving as private regulators/insurers of those at the bottom. We indeed observe that banks supply lines of credit to or guarantee some transactions of brokerage firms, clearinghouses, finance companies, and nonfinancial companies, that pension funds start playing a major role in the corporate governance of the nonfinancial sector, and that insurance companies provide credit enhancement to (bank created) trusts issuing asset-backed securities. A careful analysis of this possibility lies outside the limited scope of this book. Let us simply conclude that the motivations behind the regulation of several major classes of financial intermediaries are quite related. In section 3.4 we will see that despite important quantitative differences, their modes of regulation are also qualitatively very similar.

3   The Institutions of Banking Regulation

Current banking regulation is the result of a process of deregulation and diversification over the last twenty years. It is also a reaction to the solvency crises experienced by banks in the 1980s, and a consequence of the tendency toward international harmonization of prudential regulation, for example, through the generalized adoption of a common measure of solvency (the Cooke ratio) included in the 1988 Basle accords.[1]

The philosophy of the current regulations and of reform proposals is to allow for healthy competition in banking while improving discipline through sufficient capitalization at any time. The challenge for such a philosophy is the difficulty to control solvency ratios through balance sheets and income statements, which may provide a distorted picture of reality because of accounting lags.

Of course another regulatory challenge concerns the response of the system to a generalized undercapitalization of the sector

---

1. The Basle accords were designed by the Basle committee. The committee's members are senior officials of the central banks and supervisory agencies of Belgium, Canada, France, Germany, Italy, Japan, Luxembourg, the Netherlands, Sweden, Switzerland, the United Kingdom, and the United States, and they meet four times a year (usually at the Bank for International Settlements in Basle).

The Basle accords concern only international banks. However, their application by the European Union covers all credit institutions. While the accords were signed only by the above countries, similar rules have been voluntarily adopted in many other countries around the world.

due to an adverse macroeconomic shock, such as a crash in the stockmarket or the real estate market, a wave of failures in an industrial sector, or a threat of default by sovereign borrowers. Experience shows that the temptation is then great not to stick to the regulatory requirements. In later sections we will come back to the credibility problem facing these solvency ratios and to the intervention of the authorities supposed to enforce them.

At this writing the coordination of regulatory activities initiated by the Basle accords has not been completed. In fact the Cooke ratio, which is supposed to ensure the stability of banks, only covers *credit risk* and thus deals solely with the *identity of banks' debtors*. It abstracts from market risks, and in particular from *interest rate risk*, which is due to the volatility of the term structure of interest rates, and to the traditional asymmetry of duration between bank assets and liabilities. More sophisticated Cooke ratios are being studied in order to control for the interest rate risk involved in banks' on- and off-balance activities (more on this later in subsection 3.1.4).

3.1   The Basle Accords

In this section we detail, as an illustration, the implementation of the Basle accords at the European Union (EU) level.[2] The main elements of banking regulation were defined by the EU on the oc-

2. See the brochure published by the EU Commission, "Completing the Internal Market: Situation upon January 1, 1992, Volume 1, A Common Market of Services," January 1992, pp. 5–30, as well as the *Official Journal of the European Union*, L322-30 of December 17, 1977, L33-16 of February 4, 1987, C 36-1 of February 8, 1988, L 124-16 of May 5, 1989, L 386-1 of December 30, 1989, L386-14 of December 30, 1989. This section mainly focuses on the 1988 Basle accords; subsection 3.1.4 considers a preliminary proposal for reform made by the Basle committee.

casion of the 1992 Single Market program, and they very closely follow the Basle accords.

3.1.1 General Dispositions

First, the regulation does not distinguish among the various categories of banks, bundling them all under the heading "credit institutions."[3] The regulation moreover *harmonizes* the banking activity throughout the EU.[4] For example, it concerns *consolidated balance sheets* of banks. The regulation confers supervisory power on the authority of the country where the banking group is incorporated. The regulation stresses the ability of banks to settle throughout the EU. Finally, it prevents discrimination in the deposit insurance system, between national and foreign banks on a given national territory, and for national banks between the national and foreign territories if the foreign country has no explicit deposit insurance system.

3.1.2 Capital

The key to current prudential regulation is the obligation to continually meet minimum capital adequacy ratios.[5] The regulation first precisely defines capital on a consolidated basis. Capital consists of two parts:

---

3. These are defined as "any company whose activity consists in receiving deposits or other funds to be reimbursed from the public and in granting credits on one's own behalf"(*Official Journal of the EU*, L322-30 of December 17, 1977).

4. For a detailed description of harmonization problems at the EU level, see Chiappori et al. (1991).

5. This discussion closely follows the EU Commission's brochure "Completing the Internal Market," pp. 19–20 and 26–27. For further details on the Basle accords, see Barbour et al. (1991), Bhala (1989), and Hall (1993). Hall's chapter 8 provides a comprehensive and useful comparison of the application of the Basle accords to the United Kingdom, United States, and Japan.

1. *Tier 1 capital, or "core" capital.* This includes stock issues[6] as well as disclosed reserves[7] without any limit. There is no goodwill (intangibles) in tier 1 capital.

2. *Tier 2 capital, or "supplementary" capital.* This includes elements like perpetual securities,[8] "undisclosed reserves,"[9] subordinated debt with maturity exceeding five years, and shares redeemable at the option of the issuer.

Tier 2 capital cannot exceed 100% of tier 1 capital as a contribution to total capital. Moreover shares redeemable at the option of the issuer and subordinated debt cannot exceed 50% of tier 1 capital. A third element of capital concerns "provisions for general

---

6. Equity capital is common stock, plus noncumulative perpetual preferred stock. (Preferred stock must be paid before any dividend distribution. Unpaid dividends do not accrue if it is noncumulative, and there is no maturity date if it is perpetual).
7. Disclosed reserves are reserves created by appropriations of retained earnings, share premiums, and other surplus.
8. For instance, perpetual cumulative preferred shares.
9. Undisclosed reserves, "whatever their legal or accounting definition, present the following features: (a) they can be freely used by the credit institution to cover losses related to normal banking activities, when these have not yet been identified; (b) their existence appears in the internal accounts; (c) their amount is set by the management of the credit institutions and verified by independent external auditors" (Official Journal of the EU, L124/18, Article 3.1). Undisclosed reserves are thus available to cover yet unidentified future losses, just as the "provisions for general banking risks," which are however subject to stricter accounting rules. For example, a bank that decides to retain an amount y to cover unidentified future losses and has a loan portfolio valued at x may either present a balance sheet where loans are valued at x and where y appears on the liability side as "provisions for general banking risks," or simply value loans at $x - y$. The undisclosed reserves then are treated as provisions for identified loan losses in the income statement of the bank. This technique corresponds to one of the many practices of company income smoothing (see Fudenberg and Tirole 1992 for a theoretical analysis of this phenomenon). Since undisclosed reserves are bundled together with identified loan losses, the reader of the accounts does not know the extent to which these losses are real or not. The treatment of undisclosed reserves is one of the areas where discrepancies arise across countries. For example, while undisclosed reserves are allowed to be counted as tier 2 capital by EU regulations, they are not part of the capital of U.S. banks.

banking risks": Temporarily, they are part of tier 1 capital; they do not count for the limits concerning tier 2 capital.

Intuitively the hierarchy "tier 1 capital/provisions for general banking risks/tier 2 capital" concerns the degree to which capital is *explicit* and *permanent*. Indeed reducing the accounting value of equity and of official reserves is a delicate and public operation, since it necessitates approval at the shareholder meeting upon a proposal of the board of directors. Provisions for general banking risks instead only require a decision of the board of directors. Both categories appear explicity in the annual accounts of the bank. In contrast, undisclosed reserves, which are part of tier 2 capital, appear only in the internal accounts of the company and thus do not constitute public information (even though the internal accounts are verified by external auditors). Subordinated debt, on the other hand, while appearing explicitly in the accounts of the bank, *must* be repaid at some point.

Beyond these distinctions the characteristic of capital is to be subordinated to deposits and other traditional bank liabilities, and not to be due in the short run: Indeed subordinated debt (which *must* be repaid at some point) must be of a duration of at least five years initially, without any early reimbursement obligation. Moreover the subordinated debt portfolio belonging to tier 2 capital must satisfy, at any moment, a minimum average maturity requirement.

Finally, the regulation enumerates elements of a bank's assets that must be deducted from capital: for example, equity holdings and subordinated debt from other credit institutions if these are in excess of 10% *of their capital*, and the same equity holdings and subordinated debt below 10% of their capital for the amount that exceeds 10% of the capital *of the bank that holds them*. This way the regulation prevents artificial infusions of capital through crossholdings, in cases where consolidation of accounts is not required (see also subsection 3.3.3).

While the Basle accords ensure a uniform definition of capital across countries, country regulators have some discretion in their monitoring of the banks' accounting practices (in particular with respect to the level of provisions for loan losses) and in their choice of tier 2 capital: A commonly cited discrepancy is that U.S. banks cannot count their latent gains on securities holdings as capital while their Japanese counterparts (following the accords) can count up to 45% of their latent gains on securities holdings as tier 2 capital (there are a number of other differences among countries; see Hall 1993, ch. 8).

3.1.3 Risk-Weighted Assets and Solvency Requirements

The regulation requires capital to be equal to at least 8% of total assets of the bank (including its off-balance activities) after applying risk-weighting coefficients to the assets. The precise regulatory rule is

$$\text{Capital} \geq 0.08 \left\{ [\sum_i \alpha_i \text{ On-balance assets of type } i] \right.$$

$$+ [\sum_{i,j} \alpha_i \beta_j \text{ Off-balance assets of type } i, j]$$

$$+ [\sum_{i,k} \hat{\alpha}_i \gamma_k \text{ Off-balance exchange or}$$

$$\left. \text{interest rate contracts of type } i, k] \right\},$$

where i represents the nature of the borrower, and j and k the nature of the operation. In particular, we have

$\alpha_1 = 0$ for cash, loans to member states of OECD, their central banks and loans backed by them, as well as loans in national currencies to other states and central banks,

$\alpha_2 = 0.2$ for loans to—or backed by—international organizations, regions, and municipalities from OECD, OECD banks, and those of other countries if their maturity does not exceed one year,

$\alpha_3 = 0.5$ for residential mortgage loans that are fully backed by the mortgaged asset,

$\alpha_4 = 1.0$ for all other loans, in particular loans to nonbanks, equity holdings, and so on.

For off-balance assets the weight of the borrower is multiplied by a weight $\beta_j \in \{0, 0.2, 0.5, 1.0\}$ that expresses *the riskiness of the operation*. For example, an unused credit line, of initial duration less than a year or revocable instantaneously without any restriction, receives weight $\beta_j = 0$. An unused credit line of initial duration in excess of a year has $\beta_j = 0.5$. And $\beta_j = 1.0$ for future contracts (committing the bank to buy in the future) or acceptances.[10]

For interest rate or foreign exchange operations (swaps, futures, options, etc.) the weight of the borrower ($\hat{\alpha}_i = \alpha_i$, except for $i = 4$ where $\hat{\alpha}_4 = 0.5$) is multiplied by a weight γ_k which is applied to the notional (implicit) principal.[11] This principal is evaluated either at its initial value for the entire duration of the operation or at its market value at each instant (which varies with interest rate and foreign exchange fluctuations), depending on whether the bank declares this operation initially as a "hedging" or as a "trading" operation. The weight γ_k increases with the duration of the operation and is higher for foreign exchange than for interest rate contracts. It is higher for principals evaluated at their historical value rather than at their market value. Weights vary from 0 to 0.025 for market values and from 0 to 0.05 (plus 0.01 to 0.03 per year beyond two years) for historical values.

The denominator of the capital adequacy ratio thus represents the *accounting value* of bank assets adjusted for their *individual risk*. The

---

10. Acceptances allow the beneficiary of this credit to obtain credit on his or on his suppliers' behalf from the bank, up to a predetermined limit; the beneficiary must reimburse the bank at a predetermined date.

11. See chapter 2, note 8, for an explanation of notional principal.

regulation does not take into account the *portfolio risk* of the bank; that is, it does not take account of the correlation among assets or between assets and liabilities. For example, it abstracts from *interest rate risk*, which can expose the bank's net worth to considerable fluctuations. Interest rate risk depends on relative durations as well as on the degree of variability of loan and deposit rates. The bank can reduce interest rate risk by balancing loan and deposit terms, by indexing loan or deposit rates, or by using several financial instruments such as interest rate swaps with institutions having offsetting insurance needs. However, under current regulation some of these operations *raise* capital requirements.[12] Similar points can be made about *exchange rate risk.* These two forms of risk will be discussed in the next subsection.

Another case in point is the regulatory treatment of *netting*. The measurement of risk weighted assets does not try to match assets and liabilities. That is, it a priori does not matter whether the bank's borrowers are also its lenders. In principle, however, the degree to which these borrowers and lenders match affects the risk faced by the bank. Suppose that bank *A* owes $100 to bank *B*, to be paid tomorrow. Suppose further that bank *B* itself is meant to reimburse $100 to bank *A* tomorrow. The international regulations attribute the same credit risk for bank *B* whether bank *B* owes $100 to bank *A* or to some other bank. Yet, if bank *A* fails to repay tomorrow, bank *B* in a netting system may cancel its payments to bank *A*, but will need to reimburse the $100 if it has borrowed it from another bank. Alternatively, bank *A* and bank *B* can sign today a "novation contract" canceling their respective claims. Novation contracts are actually the only form of netting that is recognized by the Basle

---

12. While interest rate swaps are designed to reduce the overall interest rate risk of the bank, they actually raise capital requirements by adding a new source of risk, linked to the risk of failure of the party with which the swap has been contracted. The swap agreement must then be replaced at possibly adverse market conditions.

accords. [13] Novation eliminates the capital requirements that each must incur by lending to the other, unless netting is recognized in the first place. There is thus some logic to allowing netting. Indeed netting is an important concept for the development of interest and exchange rate swaps. The possibility of not facing a risk on the gross exposure, and risking only a replacement cost, makes swaps more attractive. Accordingly the Basle committee has been reflecting on a proper allowance of netting in recent years.

We should hasten to add that both from a legal and a theoretical viewpoint, the issue of netting is not yet settled. Countries differ in their treatment of netting. There is, for example, no universal legal doctrine as to whether claims should be considered on a gross basis (separately) or on a net basis, should a bank fail in a net settlement system.[14] Matters have not been clarified on the theoretical front either. Note that in the previous example banks, by canceling their claims, are actually transforming each other's claim into a claim that is senior to other claims in the same priority group. Should this "seniorization" be considered efficient?[15]

---

13. Technically a novation contract is "a bilateral contract between two counterparts under which any obligation to deliver a given currency on a given date is automatically amalgamated with all other obligations for the same currency and value date, legally substituting one single net amount for the previous gross obligations." A novation contract then is obviously restrictive, since it requires obligations to be denominated in the same currency and due the same day, although the two counterparts can expand the scope of applicability of novation agreements by entering further contracts that match and are amalgamated with the existing ones. There is a fortiori no recognition of multilateral netting (e.g., the netting of claims such as "A owes B $100, B owes C $100, and C owes A $100") in the Basle accords.

14. In a net settlement system, payment orders sent during the day are aggregated at the end of the "day" on a multilateral basis.

15. This question would be meaningless in a complete contract world. The priority structure and the dilution possibilities within each category of debt would be fully specified. Contracts between financial intermediaries, however, are far from being complete (partly because of the very short time scale involved in writing such contracts), and the judge must guess what the parties would have wanted to specify in the contracts if they had had all opportunities to "do things right."

Another drawback of the current regulation is that it poorly accounts for the *market value* of the bank's assets (except for interest rate or foreign exchange contracts where market value *may* be taken into account). To be sure, it would be exceedingly difficult to subject *all* assets to market value accounting, yet there are assets, in particular, securities traded in thick markets, for which regulation could give more weight to market value accounting. Not doing so raises the risk of *accounting lags* in the measure of a bank's insolvency, a risk that is exacerbated by potential accounting income manipulation (gains trading) by banks.

In the absence of accounting lag, the regulation would fully protect depositors or their insurers, as long as "the national authorities take steps to remedy the situation" if the capital-to-assets ratio falls below 8%. This provision may mean a potential control shift to the authorities, who could obligate the credit institution to recapitalize.

3.1.4 Interest Rate and Other Market Risks

Regulators have long realized that the sole focus on credit risk gives a very imperfect measure of bank riskiness and that the 1988 accords need to be extended to measure banks' exposure to market risks (interest rate risk, exchange rate risk, equities risk, etc.).[16] The Basle committee produced consultative proposals on this topic in April 1993. Our goal is not to give a detailed account of this complex and unsettled topic but simply to illustrate some of the ideas and difficulties in the case of interest rate risk (see section 3.4 for the market risk attached to security trading).

The basic proposal defines a set of maturity bands[17] and identifies *net* positions within each band across all balance and off-

16. Similarly in the United States, the 1991 FDICIA requires supervisory agencies to develop interest rate risk measures.
17. There are thirteen bands in the committee's recommendation. The American proposals include six bands.

balance sheet items. To each band is assigned a duration weight. For example, this weight in the proposal may range from 0.20% for positions under three months to 12.50% for positions over twenty years. The weights serve as benchmarks and are multiplied by other weights that depend on assumptions on the volatility of interest rates (to reflect discrepancies across countries). The sum of all the weighted net positions yields an overall interest risk indicator that measures the sensitivity of the net worth of the bank to changes in interest rates.[18]

There are nevertheless several difficulties in defining a bank's interest rate risk:[19]

1. *Maturity of claims.* It is hard to specify precisely in a regulatory rule the exact duration of a number of assets and liabilities. For instance, prepayable mortgages may, as their name indicates, be paid back by borrowers before their formal maturity. Furthermore the expected duration of a prepayable mortgage is not fixed; it depends on the evolution of the interest rate after it has been issued. Still on the bank's asset side, but off-balance, the fraction of lines of credit that are effectively used by corporate borrowers depends on market conditions. On the liability side, one must make assumptions on the fraction of savings and demand deposits that will be rolled

---

18. A simple weighted-sum could yield an indicator equal to zero. Suppose that a bank has 100 in assets, 50 with overall weight 1 (short term) and 50 with overall weight 10 (long term), while all its debt liabilities (e.g., -100) have weight 5.5 (medium term). The weighted-sum indicator is then equal to zero. A more conservative approach would consist in performing only *partial netting* across duration bands and taking, for example, an average of the above indicator and of the weighted sum of the *absolute values* of asset and liability positions across duration bands. Such suggestions have been made not only for interest rate risk but also for the market risk faced by securities firms and banks (see section 3.4). One could make use of further information (e.g., on the covariance among duration bands) supplied by econometric estimations of the term structure.
19. See the Basle committee's 1993 Consultative Proposal on Interest Rate Risk for more discussion.

over; again, the stickiness of deposits is not an independent random variable, since it depends on market conditions.[20]

2. *Correlation across types of risks.* Deriving an accurate measure of interest rate risk may not suffice if one is unable to determine its correlation with other types of risk. For example, a rise in the interest rate may be correlated with an exchange rate appreciation. One would then want to measure the correlation between interest rates and exchange rates.[21] Another example is credit risk. As Hellwig (1993) argues, a reduction in interest rate risk may raise credit risk, and therefore capital charges on interest rate risk may result in more borrower default. Hellwig gives the example of indexed mortgages. Unlike fixed-rate mortgages such mortgages insulate the bank against variations in market interest rates. However, when the interest rate increases, more borrowers are unable to meet their monthly payment and default.[22]

3. *Capital requirements.* Capital requirements on risky positions ought to give banks the proper incentives to manage their risk. It may not be optimal to induce intermediaries to refrain from engaging in risk management through low capital requirements. On the other hand, and as Hellwig (1993) argues, aggregate risk (e.g., interest rate risk) is nondiversifiable, and it is a priori unclear whether intermediaries should be forced by high capital requirements to search perfect insurance against such risk.

---

20. There is yet the issue that most claims pay off over a number of periods (like bonds) or involve several transactions at any given point of time (like swaps). One technique to address this issue is to convert each coupon or principal payment (for a bond) or each leg of a transaction (for a swap) into a separate asset in order not to have to define "average" positions and to have a better view of the bank's overall riskiness.

21. In a similar manner, but at a more disaggregated level, the correlation among currency rates could be used to measure exchange rate risk.

22. The bank may then foreclose on the properties, but the real estate prices may be depressed by high interest rates.

While the ultimate goal of the Basle committee is to obtain a reasonable measure of interest rate risk, the intermediate goal, in this period of regulatory groping toward better techniques, is more modestly to define some rough estimate that will be used to identify outliers (banks with substantial interest rate risk). In this approach[23] no capital requirement is yet levied on interest rate risk, but banks with large interest rate risk are under intense supervisory scrutiny.

3.1.5 Activity Restrictions

While the key regulatory instrument in the Basle accords concerns capital adequacy ratios, there exist direct limits to excessive risk taking too. First, there are *restrictions on universal banking*. Banks are not allowed to hold nonfinancial equity for more than 60% of their capital. Derogations are possible provided they are backed at 100% by additional capital that does not figure into the computation of the Cooke ratio. Second, there is a *control of "large risks."* A "large risk" is defined as a loan that exceeds 10% of the capital of the bank that grants it. In general, banks are not allowed to have any single large risk in excess of 25% of their capital, and the sum of large risks cannot exceed 800% of their capital. Banks are required to keep regulatory authorities informed of all their large risks.

3.1.6 Deposit Insurance

The main elements of the 1988 regulation concern bank long-term value as opposed to liquidity. They focus on solvency instead of risks of liquidity crises. Other institutions of course exist to help banks face such risks, like the interbank market or the central bank, lender of last resort.

---

23. This approach has been adopted by American regulators.

However, these mechanisms do not rule out panics when a bank becomes insolvent, if depositors fear they will not be fully reimbursed in case of failure. Such panics can generate a liquidity crisis and accelerate the bank's failure. In fact the absence of bank runs in these recent years of large shocks is the outcome of depositors' trust in the *deposit insurance* system. Even in the United States where the banking sector faced massive insolvencies depositors were almost always fully reimbursed, though explicit deposit insurance was limited to $100,000.

The reason why regulatory authorities go for full insurance of course is the fear of contagious bank runs once depositors lose faith in the banking system. The anticipation of this policy is clear: In the United States interest rates on large deposits, legally only very partially insured, did not rise relative to those on smaller deposits, which enjoy much higher legal protection in relative terms.

The European situation is similar to that of the United States. The only difference is that legal protection is less available and even nonexistent in some countries (the objective of the EU commission is to coordinate explicit insurance, though at a much more modest level than in the United States. It proposed 15,000 ecus per depositor; this level was subsequently transformed into a reimbursement of at least 90% of the first 20,000 ecus (around $24,000) by the EU's finance ministers, to take effect on January 1, 1995.). Once again, it is clear that implicit insurance is much higher, and possibly unlimited, even for the legally uninsured interbank deposits.

Note finally that existing insurance systems do not provide adequate incentives to banks, since insurance premiums are based only on the total volume of assets and not on risk taking by the bank. This means that healthy institutions provide a sizable subsidy to unhealthy ones. It should be noted, though, that it is extremely difficult to devise proper risk-based premiums, especially if those are to be determined in a transparent, nondiscretionary manner. And, in fact, proposals to introduce risk-based premiums have been very timid.[24]

3.2 U.S. Regulation

The preceding discussion stressed the European experience and provided a comparison with the United States only in the case of deposit insurance. The American circumstances are relatively similar to those of Europe, especially in the matter of capital adequacy ratios. A major difference, however, is the specialization of banks: In the United States there is no universal banking. Savings banks or savings and loan associations are further distinguished from other banks. In fact the 1991 regulation reinforced this specificity in that these institutions must hold residential mortgages for at least 70% of total assets. Yet rules stressing geographic specialization are being phased out, just as the EU commission attempts at easing the entry of foreign banks into each member state. This deregulatory action extends to deposit rate ceilings. To be sure, regulators are aware of the dangers of combining deposit insurance with unrestricted deposit rates, whereby insolvent banks attempt to attract new deposits through higher rates to finance risky projects in the hope of becoming solvent again. In case of bad realizations of these risky loans, the deposit insurance fund pays the bill instead of shareholders if the bank is already insolvent. This strategy was used in the 1980s by some U.S. Savings and Loan Associations, as we will see in chapter 4.

---

24. For example, in the United States, the 1991 Federal Deposit Insurance Corporation Improvement Act requires risk-based premiums for deposit insurance. In 1992 the FDIC proposed premiums ranging from 23 cents per $100 deposits for the healthiest banks to 31 cents per $100 deposits for the weakest. There is a large theoretical literature on the pricing of government deposit guarantees. See, for example, Merton-Bodie (1992) for references.

Because of the heavy losses of depository institutions, the U.S. Treasury drafted in February 1991[25] a reform plan for deposit insurance that would improve the regulatory process and strengthen capital adequacy rules. Perhaps the most innovative proposal was the elimination of restrictions preventing the banks from underwriting or entering insurance activities and against out-of-state branching. But the insurance and securities firms' lobbies succeeded in defeating this plan.

In December 1991 the Federal Deposit Insurance Corporation Improvement Act (FDICIA) was passed. It is a more timid version of the earlier Treasury plan. Its main idea is to reduce the discretion of regulators (whose number is also cut) through *rigid and gradual intervention* rules. Bank solvency is rated from 1 to 5: (1) well capitalized, (2) adequately capitalized, (3) undercapitalized, (4) significantly undercapitalized, (5) critically undercapitalized. The highest rating allows for diversification toward riskier activities. A lower rating implies some constraints, and the lowest one inevitable liquidation or complete asset sale. Downgrading by one step prevents the bank from expanding total assets or distributing dividends without the approval of the regulator. Downgrading by two steps forces the regulator to require recapitalization, merger, or the appointment of a new management team. Moreover the Federal Reserve banks must absorb their loan losses if they lend to troubled institutions. The capital adequacy ratios are stricter than those defined by the Basle accords, suggesting to some observers a pessimistic market share outlook for the weak American bank-

---

25. "Modernizing the Financial System: Recommendations for Safer, More Competitive Banks." Many other proposals were made. See *The Economist*, August 10, 1991, pp. 67–68, for a partial presentation of these proposals, and *The Congressional Budget Office* (1990) for a much more detailed list. Mishkin (1992b) evaluates the merits of the Treasury proposal. Estimated costs of commercial bank failures for the Federal Deposit Insurance Corporation (FDIC) for the years 1992–94 is evaluated at $31 to 43 billion by Barth, Brumbaugh, and Litan (1991).

ing sector. Finally, as in the Basle accords the reforms concerning market value accounting and capital ratios based on portfolio or interest rate risks are left for future resolution.

3.3 Some Other Supervisory Issues

We now turn to some other important aspects of banking supervision. This discussion will by no means be exhaustive. We still leave aside a number of relevant issues such as the coordination of regulation and deposit insurance internationally.[26]

3.3.1 Liquidity and Early Warning Systems

The solvency ratio provides a succinct picture of a bank's assets and liabilities. But, since a single number cannot adequately summarize what has intrinsically multiple attributes, regulators keep tabs on a few other key variables. Prominent among these variables are measures of liquidity. As is the case for nonfinancial institutions, liquidity problems often signal that the bank will fail. In fact regulators often do not wait for a liquidity problem to occur before they pay attention to the short-run position of the bank. They ask banks to report various liquidity ratios. There are two related issues concerning liquidity measures.

First, *why* should regulators care about liquidity at all? After all, capital adequacy requirements are meant to ensure the bank's solvency. Now, if a bank is solvent but faces an imbalance between short-term payments and short-term income, the bank should be able to borrow (e.g., on the interbank market) against future earnings, and the liquidity problem should be solved without undue

---

26. On this topic, see for example Carosio (1990), the appendix in Goodhart's (1993b), the chapters by Laub and Kane in the book edited by England (1991), and chapter 3 in the Basle committee's report 8 (1992).

liquidation of longer-term assets. In other words, liquidity problems are always solvency problems.

As we noted earlier, any solvency measure is, however, necessarily imperfect. A bank may be solvent according to the accounts, yet potential lenders may balk at lending to it. A run on the wholesale market may then occur, forcing the bank to sell some of its long-term assets at distress prices. The liquidity problem that was triggered by the market's questions about the bank's solvency feeds back on its actual solvency by lowering the value of its assets. Alternatively, the central bank or a government agency may be drawn into lending to the bank (against low-quality collateral or by not foreclosing on a debit position in the payment system), a situation that it would like to avoid. A requirement that the bank have enough liquid assets—that is, assets that are quickly marketable at a price close to their value if they stayed with the bank while possibly reducing the average yield of the asset portfolio—lowers the risk faced by the deposit insurance fund.

Second, how does one capture the notion of liquidity? To illustrate the difficulty posed by this *measurement* issue, note that one must determine which assets are marketable and which are not. A riskless asset that pays a fixed amount thirty years from now is very liquid, since potential buyers and the seller have symmetric information about its future payoff. In contrast, a one-year credit line to a borrower whom only the bank knows well is fairly illiquid. There is therefore no necessary relationship between an asset's maturity and its liquidity. Staying on the lending side, there is further the question of what fraction of (off-balance-sheet) commitments will be drawn down. It may, for instance, be the case that many borrowers make simultaneous use of their credit lines with the bank. It may also happen that a number of long-time borrowers request new loans and that the bank feels obligated to grant them for fear of letting the competition in. Similar issues arise on the borrowing side. For example, the fraction of deposits that are rolled over or the rate of arrival of new deposits may be uncertain.

The focus of the 1988 Basle accords on solvency and consequent neglect of liquidity problems does not mean that central bankers have ignored liquidity issues. These issues were discussed in their reports on the payment systems. Also chapter VI of the 1992 *Report on International Developments in Banking Supervision* synthesizes the best liquidity management techniques used by major banks and exhorts banks to adopt such techniques if they have not yet done so.

In a number of countries supervisory authorities have traditionally required banks to report their various liquidity measures.[27] In Principle II of the 1961 Banking Act, the German regulation (besides capital adequacy requirements specified in Principle I), even applies a "maturity matching" principle for financial institutions to limit long-term lending to the level of long-term funding (Kregel 1992; Rudolph 1993). The French banks are required to report quarterly their "liquidity ratio" for the forthcoming month and the two previous months, as well as their liquidity forecasts for months 2–3, 3–5, and 6–11 following the report.[28] This liquidity ratio (which is required to exceed a certain threshold) results from a complex computation. Very roughly, it measures the ratio of (some estimate of) the short-term certain and potential income over (some estimate of) the short-term certain and potential disbursements. Weights are applied to reflect the marketability of assets in the ratio's numerator. For instance, short-term Treasury bonds receive a weight of 90% to 100%, while equity has a weight of 50%. Similar assumptions are made to account for probable disbursements in the denominator of

---

27. For more on early warning systems, see the special issue on "Commercial Bank Surveillance" of the *Economic Review* (1983).
28. Règlement nø88.01, February 22, 1988 (modified, February 23, 1990.)

the ratio. For example, included there are 20% to 30% of deposits (as a measure of nonrenewals), 70% of certificates of deposits, and 50% of (some class of) off-balance-sheet commitments.

The U.S. financial regulatory agencies have traditionally used an early warning system, called the CAMEL (capital adequacy, asset quality, management, earnings, liquidity) system to identify problems. Here liquidity, capital adequacy, and asset quality are the three key variables. The bank receives a composite grade from 1 (best) to 5 (worst). As demonstrated in table 3.1, this system seems to function relatively well even though some problem banks have succeeded in evading detection. In a sense early warning systems may be viewed as attempts at incorporating such relevant information as liquidity into the solvency measure. While these systems have traditionally been used to identify potential failures, they can also define "generalized capital requirements" which, if not met, constrain the bank to issue new shares or to refrain from distributing dividends.[29]

3.3.2   Handling Bank Failures[30]

The way a bank is handled when failure is imminent affects incentives in a number of ways. It affects the willingness of potential lenders to lend to the troubled bank, the willingness of the supervisory authority to intervene, and the willingness of the bank managers to act efficiently if they stand a chance of keeping their jobs under some forms of failure resolution. Excluding forbearance

---

29. The 1991 U.S. Treasury proposal notes that undercapitalized, unprofitable banks may still pay dividends (table 5, p. X-14). It observes that "in 1989, for example, 18 banks with equity ratios between zero and three percent, with an aggregate return on assets of -2.64 percent, paid dividends amounting to 35 basis points of assets."

30. There are several good references on the topic of this subsection, including Bovenzi-Muldoon (1990), Goodhart-Schoenmaker (1993), and the U.S. Treasury Proposal (1991, ch. 1).

Table 3.1
Examination data for 347 failing banks: January 1, 1989, through September 9, 1990

| CAMEL rating | Never | Months prior to failure that bank first achieved CAMEL rating | | | | | | | Total |
		Less than 6	6 to 12	12 to 18	18 to 24	24 to 30	30 to 36	Greater than 36	
5	11	87	79	82	37	18	14	19	347
4 or 5	3	12	26	40	45	58	42	121	347
3, 4, or 5	0	2	5	15	32	46	46	201	347

Source: U.S. Treasury Report (1991).
Note: Banks receiving assistance are not included. Included are all commercial and insured savings banks failing during the period, with CAMEL ratings assigned both through the examination process and through other means.

(which consists in lowering the capital adequacy requirement or not enforcing it), there are basically *four* ways for a regulatory agency to handle bank failure. Only one of these leads to liquidation of the bank.

Suppose that a bank cannot meet its obligations, or alternatively that while not yet defaulting, it falls below some critical level that makes the supervisory agency take control of the bank's destiny. The agency can choose among:[31]

1. *Liquidation (payoff resolution).* The bank is closed and put under receivership. Insured depositors are paid immediately the full amount of their claims (so they do not suffer a delay in reimbursement; this prevents runs by small depositors shortly before the failure.) Uninsured funds are frozen, although a conservative estimate of what they are likely to recover in bankruptcy may be paid. The deposit insurer maintains a claim in the bankruptcy proceedings. In the United States the FDIC has equal standing with uninsured depositors and other general creditors, and it receives a proportionate return on its claim from the liquidation.

---

31. U.S. terms for the four methods are in parentheses.

2. *Merger (purchase-and-assumption transaction.)* A healthy bank, which may be the highest bidder in an organized auction, acquires all (or some of) the failing bank's assets and liabilities. The deposit insurer makes a cash payment or else purchases some of the bank's bad assets at an inflated price in order to facilitate the purchase. The only immediate effect on insured depositors is that the name of their bank has changed. In principle uninsured creditors may lose money in the transaction, although most often in practice in the United States and a number of other countries *all* depositors' claims are assumed.

3. *Government loans or transfers (open-bank assistance).* The supervisory agency or the central bank provides financial assistance, purchases, or guarantees some of the bad loans made by the bank to keep it afloat.[32] An open-bank assistance may be accompanied with concessions from management (which may also well be replaced) and from uninsured creditors and shareholders who are asked to bear some of the losses. (Other banks may also be asked to contribute.) Such negotiation may, however, be made difficult by the urgency caused by the impending default.

4. *Government ownership (bridge bank).* The government may take full control of the bank by infusing capital. For example, a number of large troubled Latin-American banks were nationalized in the 1980s. A similar case is occurring in Norway, where lately several large banks have had substantial solvency problems. In Norway the main instrument of the Government Bank Insurance Fund (established in 1991) is recapitalization, whose effect is de facto nationalization of the beneficiary bank.[33]

---

32. For example, in recapitalizing Crédit Lyonnais, the French Treasury is devising a scheme that will allow the troubled bank to sell a portion of its bad loans with a Treasury guarantee on these loans.

33. See Hope (1993) for an extensive discussion of the failure-resolution method in Norway.

Table 3.2
Ten largest FDIC failure-resolution transactions through year-end 1989

Date	Bank name	Type of transaction[a]	Assets (in billions of dollars)
07–29–88	First Republic Bancorporation	BB	33.7
09–26–84	Continental Illinois	OBA	33.6
03–28–89	MCorp	BB	15.4
04–20–88	First City Bancorporation	OBA	11.2
04–28–80	First Pennsylvania	OBA	8.0
09–01–85	Bowery Savings Bank	OBA	5.3
07–20–89	Texas American Bancshares	BB	4.3
10–28–74	Franklin National Bank	P&A	3.7
03–20–82	New York Bank for Savings	OBA	3.4
11–28–81	Greenwich Savings Bank	OBA	2.5

Source: Bovenzi-Muldoon (1990).
a. BB = bridge bank, OBA = open-bank assistance, P&A = purchase and assumption.

In the United States, since 1987 the FDIC can own and operate a bank until a more permanent solution can be arranged. The bank's management is replaced, and shareholders lose their investment. A newly chartered bank, the bridge bank, is created. This enables the bank to avoid disruption and to start reorganization while potential bidders prepare for a purchase-and-assumption transaction. The bridge bank's existence is limited to two years (with a possibile third-year extension).

Table 3.2 gives some indication of the FDIC's revealed preference among these methods.[34] The 25% of bank failures in the 1970s and 1980s that resulted in liquidations concerned small banks, and none of the ten largest FDIC resolution transactions involved a payoff

---

34. Goodhart-Schoenmaker (1993) contains a cross-country survey of 104 recent failures in 24 countries.

transaction. The largest payoff transaction was for the Penn Square Bank (1982), with $250 million in insured deposits and $220 million in uninsured deposits.[35]

The FDIC's mandate is to minimize the "expected cost" of failure resolution. In particular, the FDIC must run a statutory cost test showing that the alternative measure is not more costly than a liquidation. While straightforward in principle, the exercise of this mission in practice involves a fair amount of judgment. On the one hand, it is hard to forecast the costs of a liquidation or a merger. On the other hand, the cost does not need to be limited to the FDIC's monetary outlay but can include the cost of some externalities, such as the disruption of a local economy. "Systemic risk" figures prominently among these externalities. The losses incurred by uninsured depositors or creditors may create difficulties for other banks or financial intermediaries through several channels. First, the losses borne by the wholesale lenders may jeopardize their solvency.[36] Second, and with more immediate effects, the payment system may be seriously disrupted due to the large intra-day exposures among banks. Third, the participants in the wholesale market may learn that uninsured deposits are no longer de facto insured, and runs may occur on a number of banks. For these reasons, authorities have usually preferred to bail out

---

35. The 63rd Annual Report of the Bank for International Settlements (1993, 170–81) contains an interesting comparison of the recent management of financial distress in the United States, Japan, and the Nordic countries. In terms of assets of failing commercial banks, liquidation accounts for a small fraction of assets in the United States (5.2%) and is almost unknown in the other countries. Mergers and acquisitions represent 73.8% of the assets in the United States, 31.6% in Norway, and are not used at all in Finland, Sweden, or Japan, which rely exclusively on open-bank assistance (as opposed to 21.1% for this method in the United States and 68.1% in Norway.) Government takeovers represented 24.8% of assets in the United States, 30.2% in Norway, 83.5% in Finland, and 86.3% in Sweden.

36. For instance, when Continental Illinois failed in 1984, 66 banks had uninsured deposits at that bank exceeding the value of their equity; another 113 had deposits between 50 and 100 percent of their capital (U.S. Treasury 1991).

uninsured depositors and have refrained from liquidating large banks.[37]

While new rules try to limit the ability of the FDIC to pay uninsured claims, some observers find these rules still too timid. For example, statement 76 of the Shadow Financial Regulatory Committee (1991)[38] argues that "it is still possible for the FDIC to read the statute to permit payment of uninsured depositors in full (by generously overestimating liquidation costs) or to override the limitation itself by working an emergency procedure for perceived systemic risk; the Fed could still support an insolvent institution with advances by absorbing the interest charges." Last, we should point out that there has begun a theoretical analysis of the impact of the regulatory structure; in particular, it concerns an examination of the institutional separation between supervisory and monetary agencies in their failure resolution methods (see Goodhart-Schoenmaker 1993; Repullo 1993).

3.3.3 Conglomerates and Double Gearing

One of the most elusive questions in prudential regulation is whether to allow and how to supervise a conglomerate involving a regulated financial intermediary. In this subsection we do not attempt to provide an answer to this question; we just try to formulate what we perceive to be the debate.

---

37. Exceptions to this too-big-to-fail policy for the financial sector are BCCI and Drexel-Burnham-Lambert (which was not a bank) which were allowed to fail. As noted, for example, by Goodhart-Schoenmaker (1993), these financial institutions had become by and large outsiders (other financial institutions had shied away from them), so their failure was not perceived as having large systemic implications.

38. The statements of the Shadow Financial Regulatory Committee (a group of independent experts from academia and private organizations who assess and respond to policy initiatives and suggest regulatory reforms) can be found in the *Journal of Financial Services Research*.

Background

In the United States the 1953 Bank Holding Company Act limits conglomerates that include a bank to activities that are "closely related to banking." This has been interpreted as including in particular thrifts, finance companies, insurance companies, and securities affiliates. Some[39] have proposed that the Bank Holding Company Act be modified to allow some low-risk activities for which the bank's distribution network could be an asset (insurance, mutual funds). Others want to go further and allow U.S. banks to hold equity in nonfinancial companies (as is already the case, with various limits, in France, Germany, Italy, and Japan).

Transfers within a bank holding company are fairly restricted by law.[40] Loans or extensions of credit by an FDIC insured bank to an affiliate are limited for transactions involving any one affiliate to 10% of the bank's equity and for all affiliates to 20% of the bank's equity, and must be fully collateralized with high-quality collateral. More important, the bank is not allowed to operate other forms of transfers such as purchasing low-quality assets at their book value instead of their market value.

In continental Europe the current formation of large "bancassurance" conglomerates is vividly debated. European banks and insurers have been busy building loose alliances through small cross-shareholding, merging, or else extending internal operations (e.g., a number of banks have developed their own life insurance subsidiary). They want to exploit their broad distribution networks to offer one-stop shopping services to their customers. Regulators are currently pondering over the appropriate measure of solvency for these emerging conglomerates.

---

39. For example, Robert Glauber, former undersecretary for finance at the U.S. Treasury Department at a London Business School seminar.
40. Section 23A of the Federal Reserve Act; for details, see General Accounting Office (1987).

Firewalls and Spillovers

A major concern of bank regulators is that a healthy bank might suffer from the failure of a nonbank affiliate. They have in mind two issues:

1. *Undue transfers.* Regulators are worried about the possibility that a bank affiliate may be forced to rescue a troubled nonbank affiliate, thus reducing the value of bank deposits, or, equivalently, increasing the expected loss of the deposit insurance fund. We have seen that direct transfers are seriously limited by law. But there are transactions that are more complex to monitor. The actual market value of an illiquid asset sold by the nonbank to the bank may be debatable. Complex arrangements involving third parties may also seriously obscure the nature of the transfer.

A related difficulty is posed by the partial merger of activities, which may be a raison d'être of the conglomerate. The conglomerate might allocate key personnel or bias its choice of data bases to favor one affiliate over the other, or it may engage in cross-subsidies in the common marketing of products to their customers (bundled as in the case of life insurance tied to a mortgage loan, or unbundled). Note that such arguments extend beyond the mere issue of the rescue of a nonbank affiliate. More generally the conglomerate will allocate its resources so as to optimally arbitrage among opportunity costs. It may allocate some of its risky activities to the bank affiliate if the price of its debt (deposits) is insensitive to risk taking.

These forms of arbitrage are familiar to economic theorists, since they occur in the industrial sector as well (e.g., when a regulated utility purchases equipment or other inputs from an unregulated member of the conglomerate). If they are indeed hard to monitor, they provide a case for a regulation at the conglomerate level on a consolidated basis, with perhaps an additional regulation at the affiliate level (for reasons to be developed later).

Yet regulating conglomerates on a consolidated basis, while per-haps natural for a pure banking conglomerate, presents difficulties: How does one combine prudential rules for banks and nonbanks such as insurance companies? Perhaps more important, how does one deal with the fact that some affiliates (finance companies, non-financial companies, etc.) are not subject to regulation themselves?

2. *Market perceptions.* Consider the case of a healthy bank whose nonbank subsidiary (or parent company) is failing. If the bank and its subsidiary are legally separate, the bank is not liable for the losses incurred by the subsidiary's creditors. Courts may sometimes "pierce the corporate veil" and not respect the bank's limited lia-bility if the management and financing of the two companies are too intertwined (which may actually be why the conglomerate was formed in the first place).

But, even if the legal separation between the bank and its sub-sidiary is affirmed, the bank may want to come to the rescue of the subsidiary. As is sometimes observed,[41] the bank has "its name on the door" of its subsidiary. The failure of the subsidiary may damage the bank's reputation, and its source of funds might dry up. Indeed a number of American banks have voluntarily assumed responsibility for the debts of their subsidiaries,[42] even though in principle they are not allowed to do so (the penalties for breaking the law in this matter are weak).

Cross-shareholdings and Double Gearing

A different concern of regulators is how to account for cross-shareholdings. As a motivation for the corresponding (sometimes quite obscure) debate, recall that for each extra $1 invested in a risky asset such as a share in a nonfinancial company, banks must

---

41. For example, in Pierce (1991).

42. See General Accounting Office (1987, 23–24) for examples.

add 8 cents of equity to their own capital. Yet, if the risky asset is an equity participation in another bank, the bank must add $1 in equity. What then is so different about a bank that vindicates a twelve-and-a-half fold increase in the capital requirement?

To begin with, consider two banks (or one bank and one insurance company) with the following simplified balance sheets:

Bank i	
A_i	D_i
	E_i

Bank i	
$A_i + \Delta$	D_i
	$E_i + \Delta$

Case 1: No cross-shareholdings   Case 2: Cross-shareholdings

In the absence of cross-shareholdings (case 1), bank i ($i = 1, 2$) has debt D_i, assets A_i, which for simplicity are all risky and therefore receive weight 100% in the computation of the solvency ratio, and equity $E_i = A_i - D_i$. Assume, for instance, that each bank meets exactly the capital requirement, so

$$r_i = \frac{A_i - D_i}{A_i} = 8\%, \quad i = 1, 2.$$

Suppose now that each bank takes an equity participation for $\$\Delta$ in the other bank (case 2). The solvency ratio increases to

$$r_i' = \frac{A_i - D_i + \Delta}{A_i + \Delta} = \frac{0.08 A_i + \Delta}{A_i + \Delta}.$$

Then, if Δ is equal to $x\%$ of A_i, the solvency ratio increases by almost $x\%$ for x small. This is the "double-gearing" phenomenon. The same capital, in a sense, is used twice to permit leverage and asset expansion. On the other hand, the consolidated balance sheet, and therefore the solvency ratio, are unchanged:

Bank 1 plus bank 2	
$A_1 + A_2$	$D_1 + D_2$
	$E_1 + E_2$

Note that the consolidated outcome corresponds at the individual level to a 100% equity requirement for a participation in another bank, which is indeed the rule in practice.[43]

There is little new here. The same issue arises in the measurement of the capitalization of the stock market of a country. It is well known, for instance, that despite the recent Japanese stock market fall, the total value of Japanese stocks far exceeds that of U.S. stocks. One point of departure between the two countries is that Japanese firms hold more of each others' shares than their American counterparts. But the total value of stocks in the economy exceeds the total household investment in shares; the size of the discrepancy depends on the matrix of cross-shareholdings and is larger for large cross-shareholdings. The relevant number for measuring the true value is the smaller value.[44]

This analogy can also be used to illustrate the complexity of the double-gearing problem. To obtain the real value of a stock market, one must invert the matrix of cross-shareholdings in the same way one must invert the input-output matrix of an economy to know the real consumption of each primary input by each final output. A full elimination of double accounting of net worth similarly requires looking at the cross-shareholdings, not only within the banking or regulated financial sector but also in the economy as a whole. This is trivially illustrated by the case of an unregulated "nonfinancial company" F which receives a loan Δ from bank 1 and invests this amount in shares of bank 2, which thereby can expand its assets by $\Delta' = \Delta/(0.08)$ and its debt by $d_2 = (0.92)\Delta'$:

---

43. In contrast, there are currently wide variations in the accounting of cross-shareholdings of insurance companies. On this, see CEA (1993).

44. To illustrate this, suppose that there are two firms in the economy, each with a forecasted profit of 1 and owing a fraction y of the shares of the other. The total value of the shares listed on the stock exchange is $V_1 + V_2$, where $V_i = 1 + yV_j$. So $V_1 + V_2 = 2/(1 - y)$. But the value of the households' holdings is $(1 - y)(V_1 + V_2) = 2$.

Bank 1	
$A_1 - \Delta$	D_1
Δ	E_1

Bank 2	
A_2	$D_2 + d_2$
Δ'	$E_2 + \Delta$

Bank 1 plus bank 2 plus F	
$A_1 - \Delta$	$D_1 + D_2 + d_2$
$A_2 + \Delta'$	$E_1 + E_2$

Loan $\searrow$ $\nearrow$ Equity participation

Firm F	
Δ	Δ

Case 1: Nonconsolidated accounts   Case 2: Consolidated accounts

So much for the accounting illusion. But who cares? Regulators certainly do. The asset growth that would be created by cross-shareholdings would raise the expected cost for the deposit insurance fund. *In theory* this increase in risk is irrelevant as long as the extra risk translates into an increase in the price of debt. *In practice*, however, deposit insurance premiums are little if at all sensitive to risk taking, and an incentive is created for the use of such artificial inflation of net worth to fuel the growth of risky assets.

Consolidation or/and Stand-alone Regulation?
If deposits were simply a risky claim with a payoff distributed according to an exogenous distribution, the logic of consolidation would be unassailable. But *why are there separate entities in the first place?*

To obtain a broader perspective, let us come back to the representation hypothesis, according to which the supervisory authorities represent depositors. In this view the authorities must indeed have a clear view of how risky their claim is. But they are also part of the corporate governance of the banks. They must provide adequate incentives to managers and shareholders of *individual* banks. This is actually a major justification for the existence of capital adequacy requirements, as we will later show.

Consolidating two companies into one with a single group of shareholders and a single group of debtholders affects incentives by diluting performance measures and outside interference in management. To illustrate this point, consider two banks. Each starts with 8% equity. Bank 1's equity rises to 9%, while bank 2's falls to 2%. By the theory developed in the third part of this book, the fall in bank 2's solvency should lead to corrective action by creditors (the deposit insurance fund), since incentives for corrective action are best provided by the conservative claimholders. But there is no reason to expose bank 1 to corrective action. Yet, if the two banks are subject to a single capital adequacy requirement (full consolidation), control rights shifts to the creditors of the holding, which does not meet the 8% requirement (unless bank 2 is much smaller than bank 1 and unless shareholders are willing to recapitalize the holding). Because they take control of the full entity, creditors (or the deposit insurance fund) are able to impose their conservative bias not only on bank 2 but also on bank 1, which does not deserve it.

While a good approach to the supervision of conglomerates will need to address individual incentives, it will also need to ask *why the conglomerate exists in the first place*. One simple reason may be regulatory arbitrage. For example, in the United States bank-holding companies can be used to circumvent branching restrictions. Another instance of regulatory arbitrage is the use of double gearing. However, and more interestingly, in their formation conglomerates may have efficiency motivations. The conglomerate structure may submit its affiliates to higher-intensity monitoring than would the capital market. Alternatively, the mergers or cross-shareholdings may be motivated by economies of scope, such as those brought about by the merger of two complementary distribution networks, that might be difficult to implement through a simple contract. Still another reason that is sometimes invoked for the existence of conglomerates is that activities that have different sensitivities to the business cycle or to interest rate variations can be merged to provide insurance against macroeconomic shocks; it remains to be explained, though, why the same outcome could not be accomplished through contracts (e.g., swaps) on financial markets. More work remains to be done before we have a clear understanding of the regulation of conglomerates.

3.4 The Regulation of Nonbanks

Although this book's primary focus is on banking regulation, it may be useful to describe briefly the regulation of some other financial intermediaries. One reason is that we stress the commonage of motivations for regulation (see section 2.2), and this translates into similarities in the regulatory rules. Another reason is that the conceptual framework for banking regulation is likely to shed light on various aspects of the regulation of nonbanks.

3.4.1 Pension Funds

Because of their specific governance structure the regulation of pension funds may be less related to banking regulation than that of insurance companies and securities firms. Yet there are a number of striking similarities, especially for defined benefit plans on which we focus here.

The current U.S. regulatory framework was set up in the 1974 Employee Retirement Income Security Act (ERISA). This act requires companies to make minimum contributions, to make up for any shortfall over a (long) period of time, and guarantees that pensions will be paid. By analogy with banks, the deposits to be protected are the defined benefits, the prohibition against paying large dividends corresponds to the requirement to make minimum contributions, and the need to recapitalize when solvency falls under some minimal ratio becomes an obligation to make up for unfunded liabilities. Asset-risk weights are replaced by a looser requirement of diversifying the asset portfolio and of not taking excessive risk ("being prudent"). Self-investment is also limited to 10% of total assets.[45]

The pension funds' Federal Deposit Insurance Corporation is the Pension Benefit Guarantee Corporation (PBGC). Like the FDIC until recently,[46] the PBGC charges a flat (risk-unrelated) premium for its insurance. Premiums increase in the case of underfunding, however. The PBGC makes up for most of the deficiency if the company goes bankrupt (the PBGC is ahead of all unsecured creditors to recover money). But it is seriously understaffed and audits less than 1% of the insured plans every year, and, like the FDIC, it tends to be seriously undercapitalized. Some bankruptcies have been very costly, such as that in 1987 of the LTV Steel Company, which forced the PBGC to pay out $400 million per year to LTV pensioners (while the PBGC takes in only $280 million in premiums.)[47] Indeed, recently several observers have worried about a possible S&L repeat. The Shadow Financial Regulatory Committee (in its statement 93, March 1, 1993), citing evidence collected by the Congressional Budget Office and the General Accounting Office, estimates that the PBGC is probably insolvent on a current value basis by as much as $35 billion. Reforms have been suggested that would improve

---

45. There are also substantial analogies in terms of behavior. For instance, Bodie et al. (1987) find a significant relationship between the firm's profitability and the discount rates they choose to report their pension liabilities. This is similar to the behavior of troubled banks that try to dissimulate their poor health by engaging in gains trading (see chapter 10) or not provisioning enough for loan losses. Another finding of Bodie et al. is that a pension fund with a higher proportion of unfunded liabilities invests less in bonds. This is similar to the behavior of a troubled bank gambling for resurrection. For more on the governance structure of pension funds, see their article and Bulow-Scholes (1983).

46. See Mishkin (1992).

47. For example, Mishkin (1992), *The Economist* (October 2, 1993, p. 84), and the Shadow Financial Regulatory Committee (Statement 93, March 1, 1993).

auditing and reporting, strengthen capital requirements, charge premiums related to risk, and so forth. The debate on pension funds regulation thus resembles the (more advanced) one on banking regulation.

As in banking regulation the regulator may be unwilling to intervene in case of underfunding. For example, in 1993 General Motors' pension fund was underfunded by $20 billion with no immediate solution in sight.[48] Forbearance is typical, even though the law allows the PBGC to take over underfunded pension plans (and gives it a lien equal to 30% of the firms' net worth).

Other countries have regulations roughly similar to those of the United States (see Davis 1993 for a good survey), which is nevertheless exceptional in linking premiums to the degree of underfunding. Some countries have specific asset portfolio restrictions (e.g., Japan and Switzerland). But there are big differences among countries in the *importance* of pension funds relative to pay-as-you-go social security systems. At one extreme are the very significant pension funds in the United States, the United Kingdom, and the Netherlands, and at the other extreme, a very minor function of pension funds in France, Germany, and Italy. Current demographic trends promise to increase their importance everywhere, and with them the need for adequate regulation.

3.4.2 Insurance Companies

The regulatory rules for insurance companies are much less uniform that those for banks. They are also evolving fast. So we will

---

48. In the case of General Motors, one may wonder whether the PBGC would induce bankruptcy even if it had the power to do so, given that the bankruptcy would have a widespread impact on GM's suppliers, employees, clients, lenders, and local communities. The fear of systemic risk is reminiscent of the reluctance of regulators to close large banks that are deemed "too big to fail."

take only a glance at them, which should be sufficient for our purpose.

In the United States insurance is regulated at the state level. Insurance contracts are covered by guaranty associations. The losses incurred when an insurer goes bust are in principle paid by other participating insurers, although it is generally agreed that an implicit put is written on the state and federal governments (i.e., the authorities will pick up the remaining liabilities in case of bankruptcy).[49]

The National Association of Insurance Commissioners (NAIC), which is the association through which state regulators set nationwide standards, has recently set up new risk-based capital adequacy requirements. Capital is defined as assets minus the actuarial calculation of liabilities. The rules heavily favor low-risk assets (e.g., bonds) over higher-risk ones (e.g., equity). For example, for life insurers the capital requirements on government bonds and equity are 0% and 30%, respectively (compared with 0% and 8% for banks).[50] Furthermore the 1990 new rating guidelines created six quality categories for insurance company assets, NAIC-1 through NAIC-6. Only the top two, NAIC-1 and NAIC-2 correspond to investment-grade ratings from rating agencies. The new statutes put limits on the amount of insurers' investments in NAIC-3 through NAIC-6 categories, as well as higher reserve requirements for such assets. While insurance companies have historically played an important role in financing companies that cannot obtain appropriate ratings for public bond issues, the new regulations have caused a collapse in the private placements in below NAIC-2 companies.[51] Last, the risk-based standards adopted in 1993 specify that as the ratio of

---

49. See, for example, Kopcke (1992, 45).
50. *The Economist*, May 15, 1993, pp. 86–89.
51. See Emerick-White (1992) and Carey et al. (1993).

an insurance company's (risk-adjusted) actual-to-required capital level falls progressively below one, successively stronger regulatory actions are implemented (in the same way the FDICIA calls for progressively stricter interference as a bank solvency ratio falls).

In the European Union regulation is more centralized than in the United States. There are also similarities with banking regulation[52] in that it rests on three pillars: capital requirements, asset portfolio restrictions, and intervention by the regulator (restructuring plan, mandatory closure, sale or absorption) in instances of violation of these requirements. Portfolio restrictions insist on the marketability of assets and on avoiding excessively concentrated risks (e.g., no more than 10% of assets in a single construction project, or no more than 5% of assets in financial securities of a single firm). The capital requirements (or "solvency margin") are *not* risk-weighted. Beyond this, for *life-insurance companies* the capital requirement is computed partly, as is the case for banks, from *balance sheet* information. Indeed, thanks to the law of large numbers, it is reasonably easy to compute the expected liability facing the insurance company. "Mathematical reserves" represent the net present value of the company's expected liabilities minus the net present value of premiums still to be paid by the insuree. They are equivalent to deposit liabilities of banks. Insurance regulation requires capital to exceed 4% of mathematical reserves, which must have been computed "prudently." An important issue is that these liabilities are computed net of reinsurance, but only up to 85% of gross liabilities. Specifically an expected liability of $1,000 that has been reinsured for $400 counts as $850; if it has been reinsured for $100, it counts as $900. The idea is that reinsurance lowers the risk of the insurance company *provided* the reinsurer is not insolvent. Otherwise, the

---

52. See the three directives on life insurance and the three directives on non-life insurance in the Official Journal of the European Communities (L228(16-8-73), L63(13-3-79), L172(4-7-88), L330(29-11-90), L228(11-8-92), and L360 (9-12-92))

insurance company is responsible for the full risk.[53] This explains the median course of action taken by the regulator.

One key difference between deposits and mathematical reserves is that expected liabilities multiply the *contingent* liability of the insurance company by the *probability* of accident. Typically this liability exceeds mathematical reserves (because probabilities are lower than 1 and because mathematical reserves are defined net of future premiums to be paid by the insurees) so that the difference between the two, called *capital at risk*, is positive. The insurance company faces an additional capital requirement of 0.3% of the capital at risk, net of reinsurance up to 50% of its level.

Concerning *non-life-insurance companies*, the capital requirement is not computed on the basis of balance sheet information but on the basis of *income statement* information. Capital must exceed the maximum of two amounts: a proportion (between 16% and 18%) of premiums charged for the current year (again net of reinsurance, up to a point) and a proportion (between 23% and 26%) of *yearly* settlements (actual and expected) of the last three (or seven) years (again, net of reinsurance settlements up to a point). One difference with life insurance comes from greater heterogeneity in non-life insurance, which induces the regulator to focus not only on expected future liabilities (approximated by premiums) but also to control for actual risks or settlements in the recent past. A second difference with life-insurance companies is that non-life insurees do not accumulate assets that can be identified as their own on the insurance company's balance sheet. Moreover non-life-insurance contracts are typically of much shorter duration than life-insurance contracts. These reasons have induced the regulator to focus on income statement information instead of balance sheet information.

---

53. One can draw a parallel between reinsurance and securitization. "Real" securitization, or securitization without recourse, means that the asset has been sold by the bank, which is not affected any more by riskiness in its future return. Reinsurance differs from securitization in that (1) it concerns liabilities rather than assets and (2) in case of an accident the insolvency of the reinsurer transfers the whole risk *back* to the insurer-reinsuree who loses the benefit of the reinsurance contract.

3.4.3 Securities Markets Institutions

Like for insurance companies, the regulation of securities firms is not uniform and is still in the making. There is general agreement that capital adequacy is very important for efficient trade. There is less agreement on the specifics. At any given moment in time, a securities firm has securities on the asset side ("long positions") of its balance sheet, and other securities on its liability side ("short positions"). Its aggregate portfolio risk should decrease when, ceteris paribus, the portfolio is more "balanced," that is, when the sum of all long positions minus the sum of all short positions—or its *net* position—is close to zero. Indeed in that case the securities firm should be less vulnerable to aggregate (market) shocks. However, regulators do not agree on whether the basis for regulation should be the *net* position or the *gross* position (i.e., the sum of all long positions plus the sum of all short positions). The United States and Japan use a variant of the gross position, the United Kingdom the net position and the European Union and the Basle Committee favor considering both.[54] The European Union will, from 1996, require firms to have equity equal to 2% of their gross position plus 8% of their net position. The motivation for this rule is that the

---

54. Dimson-Marsh (1994) detail the approaches currently used. All require capital to exceed some specified fraction of portfolio risk. The U.S., or "comprehensive" approach, defines two variables L and S as the sums of all long and short positions, respectively, and computes portfolio risk as $\max(L, S) + \max[\min(L, S) - \mu \max(L, S), 0]$. If, as in some countries, $\mu = 0$, only the *gross* position $(L + S)$ is considered. In the United States, however, $\mu = 0.25$.

The "building block" approach favored by the European Union and the Basle committee defines portfolio risk as a weighted average of $(L + S)$ and of $\max(L - S, S - L)$, that is, of the *gross* and the *net* position.

Finally, the U.K., or "simplified portfolio," approach starts from Sharpe's simple and celebrated CAPM model where portfolio risk is expressed in terms of market variance and of each security's beta and residual variance. The "simplified portfolio" approach adds the assumptions that (1) all securities' betas are equal to 1 and (2) all securities' residual variances are equal. This approach requires estimating only two parameters: the market variance and the individual security residual variance.

net position reflects general market risk, while the gross position takes into account the risks of the individual securities, including credit risk.[55] An empirical study by Dimson and Marsh (1994) suggests, however, that while much better at tracking *actual* portfolio risk than the U.S. approach, the European Union approach is dominated by the U.K. approach. Indeed this last approach seems closest to portfolio theory not only by focusing on net positions but also by taking into account the degree of diversification across individual securities.[56]

There are of course some differences between the regulation of banks and securities firms. For example, bank assets are often illiquid and reported at historical cost. In contrast, trading positions are usually reported at their market value. This makes the measure of the equity position of securities firms very volatile. Accordingly, and unlike banks, securities firms can include in their capital a high proportion of short-term debt if it is subordinated and subject to a lock-in clause.[57] In fact the Basle committee suggests that banks could also use such "tier 3" capital (subject to further restric-

---

55. The Basle committee's position is defined in its April 1993 consultative proposal on "The Supervisory Treatment of Market Risks" (e.g., see pp. 27–32). Its motivation for including both measures is given on pages 27–28:

> As with debt securities, it is proposed that the minimum standard for equities should be expressed in terms of the so-called "building-block approach." This means that the overall capital requirement would consist of separately calculated charges for the "specific" risk of holding a long or short position in an individual equity, and for the "general market risk" of holding a long or short position in the market as a whole. Specific risk has some parallels with, but is broader than, credit risk in the sense that it exists whether the position is long or short. General market risk is the risk of a broad market movement unrelated to any specific securities. The long and short position in the market would be calculated on a market-by-market basis, i.e., a separate calculation would have to be carried out for each national market in which the firm held equities.

56. See note 54.

57. A lock-in clause stipulates that neither interest nor principal may be paid if capital falls under some threshold.

tions) to support the market risks in their trading of equities and debt securities,[58] their normal banking business remaining subject to the standard tier 1–tier 2 requirements. Another difference (in the United States) between the two regulations is that security traders are not explicitly covered by federal insurance but rather by guaranty funds provided by all surviving members. Regardless of the current differences, the goal is to move toward a convergence in capital requirements of banks and securities firms (if only because banks and securities firms compete in the securities markets). The rules described above are meant to apply both to securities firms and to banks' trading activities.[59]

To sum up, there are substantial analogies between banking regulation and those of pension funds, insurance companies, and securities firms. We of course do not deny that there are some important differences. In particular, banks are central to the payment system and to the supply of money. Their regulation includes features such as the access to liquidity provided by the central bank that do not exist for other intermediaries.[60] Broad principles of prudential regulation are, however, identical.

3.5 Is Banking Regulation Different from Corporate Governance?

As a further piece of evidence in favor of the representation hypothesis, we would like to stress the strong analogy between banking regulation and loan agreement covenants. That is, we argue that the control of banks by their regulators is not all that different from

---

58. See pp. 9–12 of the 1993 consultative proposal on market risk.
59. Banks must keep separate "trading books" and "banking books."
60. Nonbanks do not have access to liquidity facilities, although in some cases the central bank may intervene to facilitate their access to liquidity (e.g., after the October 1987 crash the Federal Reserve pressured large New York banks to provide liquidity to securities firms and clearinghouses).

the control of nonfinancial companies by banks. Admittedly there are a number of discrepancies that can be attributed to four factors. First, the activities of banks and firms are not identical, and it is natural to observe a few differences (in the same way that the regulation of insurance companies is somewhat qualitatively different from that of banks). Second, the regulator in the case of banks is public. A feature common to most public regulations, be it of banks or of other firms, is that the regulator's discretion is limited.[61] By contrast, banks have a bit more flexibility to use subjective information to tailor their loan agreements to the fine characteristics of the borrower. An illustration of this may be the fact that net worth or liquidity requirements are often specified in loan agreements both in absolute and relative terms, while regulatory requirements are usually expressed only in terms of ratios. Third, the interests of the public regulator extend beyond his or her stake in a particular bank. In particular, the bank's failure affects other banks that have lent to it, and therefore the regulator indirectly.[62] (An analogy at the corporate level could be that of a bank who has a monopoly position on strongly interconnected firms in a region or town). This may partially explain why, in practice, the regulators are not as insistent as commercial banks on recouping their money. Fourth, unlike a bank with a borrower, the regulator can only indirectly control the amount it "lends" to the bank; for the depositors lend to the bank, and it is only through deposit insurance that the regulator becomes the de facto lender.

Despite some differences, the philosophy of prudential regulation strongly resembles that of loan agreement covenants:[63]

---

61. On the reasons for such limited discretion, see Laffont-Tirole (1993, chs. 11-16).

62. Of course the regulator may also pursue other objectives than depositor representation: financial system stability, monetary growth, and so forth. We will return to this point in chapter 12.

63. A useful description of covenants in standard loan contracts can be found in Zimmerman (1977). His statement of the philosophy of loan agreements is quite instructive for our purpose:

1. *Capital adequacy, risk weights, and activity restrictions.* Standard loan agreements demand capital adequacy. For instance, the ratio of total debt to tangible[64] net worth may be required not to exceed a given level. The difference in activities makes risk weights even more complex to define for nonfinancial companies than for banks. Rather than defining such risk weights, loan covenants restrict risk in other ways. Lenders generally require various forms of casualty insurance (as well as life insurance for a key principal in a closely held business). They include various covenants restricting asset growth (ceilings on capital expenditures and on leases). They also restrict the activities of the borrower in several ways: They may earmark the use of the proceeds of the loan to the purchase of specific investments and may forbid sales of assets, changes of business and/or of management, without the bank's consent.

2. *Liquidity and early warning systems.* Standard loan agreements specify minimum levels for a number of financial indicators. The

---

Through the loan agreement, the bank creates a clear understanding with the borrower as to what is expected of it. In doing so, the bank establishes its control of the relationship and provides for several basic functions to effect that control.

The lender attempts to ensure regular and frequent communication with the borrower by using certain covenants in the loan agreement. The communication results in an up-to-date assessment of the borrower's financial situation and its general management philosophy.

When the bank requires that the borrower maintain certain financial ratios, it is accomplishing several objectives. On the surface these covenants provide triggers or early warning signals of trouble, which will allow the bank to take rapid remedial action. The borrower is made aware of where the minimum performance cutoffs are. However, the banker is also helping the borrower set reasonable goals in terms of financial condition and growth. In some cases, a "growth formula" is created which states that until a specified set of financial conditions is met, the borrower may not be eligible for further debt.

All these controls—required ratios, ratio goals, required actions and forbidden actions—may seem arbitrary or restrictive; but applied wisely, they are not. The process lets all parties know where they stand, thus reducing the number of unknowns or uncertainties in the loan relationship.

64. Banks, like regulators, dislike counting nontangible assets, such as goodwill, that have no liquidation value.

latter, in particular, apprehend the borrower's liquidity position. Working capital is typically one of the key variables in this respect. For instance, the ratio of current assets to current liabilities is required to exceed some threshold.[65] But other constraints (on profit to assets, sales to receivables, etc.) can be imposed as well.

3. *Handling of failures.* In a standard loan agreement the bank can call the loan in early ("declare all sums of principal and interest immediately due and payable, without presentment, demand for payment, or notice or dishonor or other notices or demands"). The bank can also force default if the borrower fails to pay an installment or violates a covenant. In case of covenant violation the bank may face roughly the same choices as a banking regulator. Forbearance, liquidation,[66] or renegotiation (resulting in debt forgiveness—the analogue of an open-bank assistance—or, if the bank is allowed to hold equity, a debt-equity swap—the analogue of government ownership). There are of course a number of (country-specific) differences, and there is no point here entering the intricacies of bankruptcy laws.

4. *Cross-shareholdings and participations.* The double-gearing problem discussed in subsection 3.3.3 seems to be less relevant in the bank-borrower relationship for several reasons. First, the allowed leverage is smaller. Second, loan agreements usually prevent the borrower from purchasing assets, making loans to or guaranteeing obligation of another person, firm, or corporation, except in the or-

---

65. Current assets are assets that will normally be turned into cash within a year. Current liabilities are liabilities that will normally be repaid within a year.

66. The "too-big-to-fail" nightmare of regulators has a counterpart in bank-borrower relationships, often stated as: If you owe the bank $100,000 you are in trouble; if you owe the bank $10 billion, the bank is in trouble. It is much easier for a lender to keep a reputation for being tough in front a small borrower than in front of a large one (Goodhart 1993a). Of course in the regulatory context the "too-big-to-fail" policy is motivated primarily by the systemic risk.

dinary course of business; investments in securities are restricted to government securities.

We have compared prudential rules and loan agreement covenants. A similar comparison would apply to the covenants of privately placed debts. The institutions (mainly life insurance companies) that purchase privately placed bonds from below-investment-grade corporations impose tight covenants.[67] These covenants commonly include restricted payments (ceilings on dividends or stock repurchase that depend on earnings and previous payments), restrictions on leverage (or net worth requirements), and limitations on liens and asset sales. Affiliated transactions (which might give rise to nondividend transfers to shareholders) are usually prohibited (see again subsection 3.3.3 for a description of similar constraints in banking regulation). Last, privately placed debt agreements also specify the governance of the borrower-lender relationship in case of covenant violation. The agreement may set a "cure period" during which the borrower must comply with the covenants (this is analogous to a prudential rule giving banks a chance to recapitalize or take other corrective actions if the regulatory requirements are not met). If the borrower does not comply at the end of the cure period, the lender may require immediate repayment of the principal.

Interestingly these covenants are more numerous and more restrictive, the lower the borrower's credit quality.[68] Recall that regulated banks also have less freedom of action, the lower their net worth or their regulatory rating (indirectly through the risk weights of the Basle accords or more directly through restrictions on activities under the FDICIA rules.)

---

67. See Carey et al. (1993, 81), Smith-Warner (1979), and especially Kahan-Tuckman (1993) for evidence on privately placed debt covenants.
68. Carey et al. (1993).

One possible line of departure between prudential regulation of bank loans and privately placed debt is the greater discretion "enjoyed"[69] by private lenders compared to regulatory agencies. Kahan and Tuckman (1993) argue that some covenants in privately placed debt agreements are likely to be violated even in the absence of managerial misbehavior. Lenders (who collect much more information than, e.g., public debtholders and therefore are well informed) renegotiate the contracts, while regulatory agencies in principle are tied by less discretionary enforcement of prudential rules, even though they have some discretion as to the measurement of solvency ratios. We will come back in detail to the discretionary–nondiscretionary regulation dilemma in chapter 12.

---

69. This discretion is a double-edged sword. As has been emphasized by the literature on the "soft budget constraint"(Dewatripont-Maskin 1990), it may be ex ante optimal for a lender (a principal) to commit not to renegotiate a contract with a borrower (an agent), even though renegotiation is ex post Pareto optimal. The perspective of such renegotiation is likely to have a negative impact on the borrower's incentive to avoid getting into trouble.

4

The Example of
the U.S. Savings and
Loan Associations

In this chapter we very briefly describe the S&L crisis in the United States. The S&L crisis is the most famous and best-understood case of recent troubles in banking regulation. It has received a lot of attention in the economics literature, and we direct the reader toward books devoted to this topic for a detailed analysis.[1] We focus here only on the main features of this episode in order to highlight the challenges of banking regulation.

4.1   S&L Fragility with Respect to Interest Rate Risk

The regulation that followed the banking crisis of the early 1930s ensured banking stability, especially S&L stability, thanks to (1) deposit insurance, (2) strict geographical and functional specialization, and (3) barriers to entry and deposit rate ceilings.

Cracks appeared in the system when high short-term interest rates made it hard for credit institutions to keep attracting deposits. The problem was particularly acute for S&Ls, which typically borrowed short (liquid savings deposits) and lent long at fixed rates (mortgages). The dilemma facing the industry and the regulators was the following: Lifting regulation and raising deposit rates implied a deterioration of profitability, while not raising them implied a sharp reduction in available deposits.

---

1. See, for example, Dab (1991), Kane (1989), and White (1991).

In the 1960s deposit rate ceilings were kept in place, leading in some instances to temporary disintermediation. These became acute with the high inflation of the 1970s and the development of money market mutual funds at the end of the decade. The situation became critical with the monetarist policy of Paul Volcker and the subsequent sharp increases in interest rates. The aggregate net interest rate margin of S&Ls became negative in 1981 and 1982, and the percentage of loss-making S&Ls rose from 3% in 1979 to 30% in 1980, 70% in 1981, and 80% in 1982 before dropping back to 40% in 1983.[2]

4.2 The Initial Regulatory Response

The regulatory response to this fragility was threefold: First, in order to allow S&Ls to better diversify, their activities were deregulated: flexibility of deposit rate setting in order to allow S&Ls to counter disintermediation, permission to grant variable-rate mortgages in order to stabilize interest rate margins, widening of the credit activities in order to reduce the specialization in residential mortgages (commercial real estate, installment loans, credit card loans, corporate securities). Second, the government lent money to troubled S&Ls that were unable to raise new capital (1982 Garn–St. Germain Act). Finally, capital adequacy ratios were reduced and intervention rules for undercapitalized S&Ls were substantially weakened.[3] The dilemma faced by the regulators was that strict implementation of the regulation (i.e., the sale or liquidation

---

2. Data from the Federal Home Loan Bank Board (FHLBB), the regulatory body of the Federal Savings and Loan Insurance Corporation (FSLIC, the S&L deposit-insurance fund), cited by White (1991, 70).

3. The regulatory response to the S&Ls' problems must be contrasted with the response to the almost simultaneous problems faced by the largest commercial banks (see, e.g., Litan 1994 for a discussion). In 1982 Mexico was unable to pay interest on its debt. Other developing countries might have jumped on the bandwagon, had Mexico defaulted. The nine U.S. "money center banks" had loans outstanding to Latin American countries equal to almost twice their equity capital.

of insolvent S&Ls and the reimbursement of all depositors up to $100,000) was impossible given the low level of capitalization of the Federal Savings and Loan Insurance Corporation (FSLIC). Congress and the President were unwilling to use tax dollars to recapitalize it. The economic argument used against implementing current regulation at the time was that S&Ls were victims of an unexpected temporary macroeconomic shock. According to this argument, it was unfair to penalize them through sale or liquidation. Instead, it was better to wait for an improvement in their capital position (thanks to a gradual rise in the interest margin following the rise in mortgage rates). Moreover despecialization was supposed to prevent such problems in the future, thanks to better diversification.

Capital adequacy requirements were relaxed in two ways. First, the minimum ratio was lowered from 5% to 3% in the early 1980s. Second, accounting rules were softened in comparison to generally accepted accounting principles (GAAP). Note that these may already allow for methods that delay the acknowledgment of a deterioration in capital position. Indeed historical cost accounting (as opposed to market value accounting) leaves the door open to the sale of assets whose value has risen in comparison to their initial accounting value, while assets whose value dropped are kept by the company, which tries to minimize provisions for such losses of value. This is the practice of "gains trading," which can be used to avoid admitting insolvency. The detection of insolvency was also made harder by changes in accounting practices. Indeed regulators introduced regulatory accounting practices (RAP) in order to spread over time the losses incurred in selling underwater assets.[4]

The Federal Reserve (through currency swaps) and the U.S. government (through advance payments of commodities as well as direct lending) kept Mexico afloat, which de facto recapitalized the money center banks. Although perhaps still insufficiently capitalized, the latter did not develop into troublemakers the way thrifts and a number of other commercial banks did.

4. "Loss deferral accounting" allowed thrifts to book the loss of such assets as goodwill to be amortized over a number of years and to reinvest the proceeds in assets earning high yields.

Table 4.1
S&L solvency under different accounting practices

	RAP solvency between 3% and 5%		RAP solvency below 3%		RAP solvency above 3% and GAAP solvency below 3%	
	Number	Assets (billions)	Number	Assets (billions)	Number	Assets (billions)
1982	1,077	337	71	13	166	52
1983	1,104	377	48	13	245	67
1984	1,041	446	71	15	374	95

Source: Federal Home Loan Bank Board (cited by White 1991, 86–87).

While the goal of this policy was to reduce the inefficiency associated with gains trading by inducing banks to restructure their asset portfolio, it also contributed to a further weakening of the S&L capital adequacy requirements.[5]

These accounting changes thus worsened the accounting lag in the detection of insolvency. This lag was already a big problem, since capital ratios were computed as an average of the last five years and since new S&Ls benefited from a twenty-year transitory period.

Table 4.1 shows that these measures had a very significant impact. As far as orders of magnitude are concerned, the number of S&Ls at that time was around 3,100, and their combined assets went from $750 billion in 1982 to $1,000 billion in 1984.

It is clear from the table that this regulatory softness was very effective. Only a very small number of institutions were in contradiction with the official capital adequacy minima. And FSLIC intervention could focus on a "respectable" proportion of these (63 in 1989, 36 in 1983, and 22 in 1984). On the other hand, lots of institu-

---

5. Another feature of the regulatory changes was the incentive given to adequately capitalized S&Ls to acquire less capitalized ones by allowing them to set very optimistic "going concern values" for these acquisitions on their balance sheets.

tions were dangerously close to insolvency. But accounting changes rationalized the inability (or unwillingness) of authorities to carry out regulatory intervention.

4.3   The Dual Adjustment Process

The regulatory gamble proved correct *on average*. Most S&Ls became profitable and solvent again in the mid-1980s. A significant problem arose, however, with those S&Ls that were deeply insolvent in the early 1980s, and that abused the new freedom induced by deregulation to engage in "gambling for resurrection," knowing that further potential losses would be covered by depositors or, more probably, by the FSLIC.[6] A number of tightly held S&Ls even engaged in outright fraud. In a typical scheme a bank manager who is also the largest shareholder would grant a money-losing loan to a friend and would receive money from him or her on the side. Such looting is a particular concern in small banks. It is related to gambling for resurrection in that it is more likely to occur when the bank is poorly capitalized. The manager/large shareholder is then more willing to incur the risk of getting caught. Yet, as Akerlof and Romer (1994) argue, looting can be distinguished from gambling for resurrection on the following ground: Looting is a deliberate plunge into negative net worth while gambling for resurrection intends to give the bank a chance to get back to positive net worth.

In fact, in contrast with loss-making nonfinancial firms, which typically experience a reduction in growth following financial distress and liquidity constraints, the combination of deposit insurance and flexible deposit rates allowed troubled S&Ls to easily attract new deposits. Deposit rate deregulation even led in the 1980s to the emergence of "deposit brokers," which tried to obtain the highest

---

6. See, for example, the analyses of Dab (1991) and White (1991).

rates for their clients' savings, independently of the solvency of the S&Ls, which was a concern solely for the FSLIC.

As a consequence, S&Ls experienced significant growth in the troubled 1980s, especially those S&Ls that were finally sold or liquidated at the end of the decade (as shown by Barth et al. 1989 who consider 205 insolvent S&Ls sold or liquidated by FSLIC in 1988). Further, those S&Ls that had diversified relatively more into nontraditional riskier assets[7]—commercial real estate, land loans, corporate securities—were also the less capitalized, and had higher intangible assets as a proportion of total assets displayed on their balance sheets.

4.4 Regulatory Cleanup by the FSLIC and the Congress

After a period of extreme forbearance, the FSLIC started to react in 1985, trying to better control undercapitalized S&Ls. Its new policy included credit ceilings, as well as a gradual strengthening of capital adequacy requirements: introduction of instantaneous ratios instead of five-year averages, increase of the minimum ratio from 3% to 6%, abolition of the RAP in favor of a return to GAAP, and tripling of the FSLIC regulatory staff.

While these measures limited the problems caused by insolvent S&Ls, the undercapitalization of the FSLIC prevented real discipline. The situation thus worsened while political opposition (fostered by the insolvent S&Ls lobby) prevented the recapitalization of the FSLIC. This problem plagued its liquidation and subsidized sale activity until 1988. That year finally witnessed the FSLIC restructure 205 institutions, amounting to 7% of total S&L assets, a volume that was four to six times bigger than that of the previous five years.

This restructuring attracted a lot of media attention, given its cost for the FSLIC: $30 billion against total assets of $100 billion for these

---

7. FHLBB data, cited by White (1991, 116).

restructured S&Ls. Of course these sums were used to pay depositors, not S&Ls themselves or their shareholders, even though the media described them as a "bailout." The FSLIC action was criticized, but it is unclear that it wasted money in this badly needed restructuring process. The Congress, however, punished the FSLIC, which was partly used as a scapegoat. In effect the FDIC (the deposit insurance fund of commercial banks) absorbed the FSLIC and took over its responsibilities.

New regulation was adopted in 1989 and 1991. Additional recapitalization was granted, as well as increases in insurance premiums, which remain, however, solely a function of asset volume. Several observers thus complain that healthy institutions keep subsidizing troubled ones.

II

Theoretical Perspective

5   Existing Banking Theory

The current banking regulation which we described in chapter 3 strongly stresses bank *solvency*. It is designed to prevent moral hazard in banking. It simultaneously tries to foster competition in the sector through unrestricted deposit rates and, at least in Europe, strong despecialization of banks. Essentially, regulation aims at an optimal trade-off between *incentives for quality and competitiveness* of bank services and *the solvency and stability of the industry*.

Can economic theory provide an assessment of the current focus of regulation? Further, can it unveil specific features of banking activities that vindicate the existence of regulation in the first place? We will start our discussion by stressing three banking functions put forward by current banking theory: transaction cost reduction (including the organization of the payments system), monitoring, and liquidity creation. As we will show, beyond quantitative differences, there is no sharp contrast between banks and nonfinancial firms. We will then briefly present some contributions in the spirit of industrial organization, before studying explicit regulatory models. Finally, we stress the need for a theory of the capital structure of banks as a foundation for an evaluation of prudential regulation.

We have not tried to make our discussion exhaustive. Hellwig (1991) contains a full discussion of some of the themes described in this section. A comprehensive survey is also provided by Bhattacharya and Thakor (1993) and by Freixas and Rochet (1994) in their forthcoming book.[1] Our bias is toward theoretical issues, since the main purpose of our book is to contribute to the theoretical foundations of banking regulation.

5.1 Reduction in Transaction Costs

As stressed by Gurley and Shaw (1960), banks transform the credit portfolio demanded by borrowers into a deposit portfolio desired by lenders. This transformation has two faces. First, banks engage in *term transformation*. Firms like to finance their projects with long-term credits. Households, instead, prefer short-term deposits for liquidity reasons. Banks are able to supply this transformation (as detailed below), though nonfinancial firms could themselves issue demand deposits or short-term savings contracts. However, it would be costly for small investors to write debt contracts with firms (these are complex agreements with restrictive clauses on firm activities). Moreover small investors typically like to diversify their risks, which would multiply contracts and transactions costs. An intermediary is able to exploit returns to scale by writing and enforcing debt contracts with firms.

Second, banks reduce transaction costs through the *payment system*. For example, a firm or individual who receives a check does not have to verify the solvency of its issuer. Such verification for each transaction would be very costly. Centralizing this process at the level of financial intermediaries avoids wasteful duplication of verification costs.

---

1. This book offers an up-to-date, detailed, and rigorous overview of the new economics of banking. It also contains an extensive discussion of regulation, and will be useful to the careful student of banking theory.

This vision of banking activities,[2] although relevant, is only partial. It has in particular few implications as far as the control of banks and regulation are concerned.

5.2 Delegated Monitoring

5.2.1 Information Provision as a Natural Monopoly

A firm that looks for debt financing has typically a choice of public debt or bank debt. Public debt is inefficient in so far as it forces each lender to assess the firm's solvency.[3] This results either in a duplication in monitoring costs, or in suboptimal monitoring due to free-riding.[4] It is thus to be expected that public debt is often issued by high-reputation firms (Diamond 1991) or by firms whose healthy equity position reduces the probability of failure (Hoshi-Kashyap-Sharfstein 1991).[5] In contrast, a firm with limited equity, with no reimbursement history or reputation for solvency (e.g., because of its small size or its young age) must be closely monitored. Given the natural monopoly aspect of information provision (Leland-Pyle 1977; Campbell-Kracaw 1980; Diamond 1984; Ramakrishnan-Thakor 1984), it is logical for such a firm to apply for bank debt.[6]

---

2. Some aspects of this transaction cost theory are particular cases of the more general delegated monitoring theory, which we will study in the next section.
3. Or, at least, to continuously update rating information provided by specialized agencies.
4. Gorton and Pennacchi (1990) suggest that debt is a less information-intensive asset than equity, and thus attracts a relatively less-informed pool of buyers.
5. One exception to this argument is the junk bond market. Still it is true that bank debt constitutes the main source of external finance for small- and medium-sized firms.
6. Besides returns to scale in information provision, Campbell and Kracaw stress economies of scope due to the information obtained by the bank in its management of a firm's bank account.

Another and quite common mechanism to get around incentive problems between the bank and its borrower consists in granting a loan commitment, that is, to promise future lending at pre-specified terms. A loan commitment represents an option for the borrower, who may or may not exercise it depending on its opportunities. Loan commitments can reduce borrowing rates, and the associated moral hazard problems on the borrower's side, against a commitment fee paid up front and which the borrower will treat as sunk when making effort or project choice decisions (see Boot, Thakor, and Udell 1987, 1991; Berkovitch and Greenbaum 1990).[7] Moreover Boot, Greenbaum, and Thakor (1993) note that many loan commitment contracts give banks freedom to unilaterally terminate the contract (using "material-adverse-change" clauses). They argue that by not abusing this flexibility, banks are able to efficiently enhance their reputation for fair behavior.

The natural monopoly vision of bank debt has recently been questioned. Several authors (e.g., Fischer 1990; Sharpe 1990; Rajan 1992)[8] argue in favor of duplication. In Rajan's work, for example, a bank that is the sole creditor of a firm quickly starts dominating its potential rivals, thanks to its knowledge of the firm's solvency. These rivals could of course try to offer more attractive loans to the firm but will be worried about the "winner's curse." That is, their offers will be accepted precisely when the firm's traditional bank becomes pessimistic about its solvency (Broecker 1990; Riordan 1993). As a consequence the firm's traditional bank gradually acquires monopoly power over the firm. It can thus partly "expropriate" the firm's investments through high interest rates. As in the Williamsonian dual-sourcing theory in industrial organiza-

---

7. See also Bester's (1985, 1987) analysis of collateral as a check against adverse selection and moral hazard in noncontingent loans.

8. Similar ideas in favor of nonexclusivity of bank financing can be found in Hellwig (1991) and von Thadden (1990).

tion,[9] ex ante duplication costs may be more than offset by the protection competition offers to a firm's investment. It is interesting to note in this respect the difference between the German and Japanese financial systems (Narayanan 1991). These two countries have traditionally had underdeveloped stock and public debt markets, with banks playing a prominent role.[10] In Japan a single dominant bank takes care of most of the financing inside an entreprise group (*keiretsu*). In contrast, large German firms often rely on at least two banks (as well as on their access to the Euromarkets).

5.2.2   The Diamond Model

To model the natural monopoly character of banking, Diamond (1984) starts from an incentive problem inside nonfinancial firms. Each firm is managed by an entrepreneur and enjoys no reliable accounting system. The lender is unable to observe the entrepreneur's financial return, and thus his ability to recoup his loan depends on costly audits. The optimal (deterministic) contract between the entrepreneur and his lender (Townsend 1979; Gale-Hellwig 1985) is then a debt contract with a fixed reimbursement amount, and audit plus confiscation of the entrepreneur's return in case of failure to fully reimburse the creditor. The existence of a bank allows the entrepreneur to avoid the duplication of audit costs by all creditors. But the role of the bank is still very limited: It is merely a common auditor hired by a syndicate of lenders.

To obtain a richer theory of banking, Diamond introduces a moral hazard problem for the bank. This innovation is welcome given the prominence of moral hazard in banking discussions. Diamond then points out another form of increasing returns to scale by showing

---

9. See Farrell-Gallini (1987) and Shepard (1988).

10. Dewatripont-Maskin (1990) and von Thadden (1990) analyze models where bank finance induces firms to take a long-term perspective, a feature often associated with the German and Japanese economies.

that the moral hazard problem within the bank decreases when the size of the bank increases. In fact moral hazard completely disappears when the bank holds a fully diversified credit portfolio. To see this, assume that the bank grants credit to a continuum of firms, promises a fixed payment to each of its depositors, and accepts ex ante a significant (ex post) nonmonetary penalty (incurred by its managers) should it fail to honor such promises. Because of the fixed payments promised by the bank to its depositors, the owner-managers of the bank are residual claimants of the bank's profits provided that it pays its depositors. In case of independent project returns, profits are deterministic and allow the bank with probability one to avoid failure. There is no moral hazard problem for bank managers, since they are residual claimants. The first-best outcome is then achieved through a single active bank in the economy. This result would hold even if the bank's owner-managers had limited liability: They would still have no incentive to induce the bank to fail because they would not get any return from this event.

Banking competition in this model does not necessarily lead to the above first-best optimum. Yanelle (1988, 1989) shows the existence of multiple equilibria induced by Diamond's increasing returns through diversification, when individual depositors are not protected by deposit insurance. Indeed a bank with lots of depositors and thus lots of loans is well-diversified and enjoys a smaller probability of failure; it can attract more depositors. Consequently, as in the network externality literature, bank size can be self-fulfilling. This can lead to allocative inefficiencies; in a world where banks are differentiated, depositors can, for example, all go to an intrinsically inefficient bank. Moreover Yanelle analyzes competition on both deposits and bank credits. Returns to scale lead to the optimality of a single active bank, but once having monopolized deposits, this bank will tend to abuse its market power against entrepreneurs. Similar network externality arguments have been presented by Matutes and Vives (1992) and Winton (1991).

5.2.3   The Diamond Model and Banking Regulation

The Diamond model is a very significant step toward the theoretical understanding of the specificity of banks in the lending process. It has, however, two limitations from the point of view of banking regulation:

1. It cannot explain the existence of outside equity, either for banks or for nonfinancial firms. Only debt, together with the right to audit when there is insufficient repayment, has value. This absence of outside equity is problematic for an analysis of regulation because of the prominence of regulatory capital adequacy requirements.[11]

2. It eliminates all moral hazard or bank failure risk. This is counterfactual in light of banking history. One issue concerns the diversification hypothesis. Beyond regulatory restrictions on banking activities and organizational costs linked to bank size, credit institutions specialize by necessity as well as choice: by necessity because information costs are smaller when one's portfolio is more homogeneous; by choice because bank shareholders and managers may deliberately choose risky strategies because of limited liability (Jensen-Meckling 1976) and thus privilege positively correlated asset returns even in the presence of constant unit costs of information acquisition (Emmons 1991; Rochet 1991). Another reason why riskless portfolios are not realistic is the impossibility of diversifying systemic (macroeconomic) risk.

5.3   Liquidity Provision

While delegated monitoring models concern bank assets, liquidity provision models focus on their liabilities (Bryant 1980; Diamond-

---

11. Matutes and Vives (1992), who build on the Diamond model, thus focus on the optimal choice of deposit insurance premiums in their policy analysis.

Dybvig 1983).[12] In the famous Diamond-Dybvig model, depositors do not know in advance whether they will face liquidity needs in period 1 or 2. At date 0 they sign a contract with their bank that specifies the interest rate they obtain if they withdraw their deposits in period 1 or 2; then they learn about the timing of their liquidity needs. The bank does not know whether the depositor who withdraws in period 1 really needs cash at that period. If many depositors withdraw in period 1, the bank must liquidate some of its long-run investments, and this implies economic losses. The bank thus faces the risk not to be able to repay depositors who plan to withdraw in period 2. The fact that many depositors withdraw in period 1 thus prompts other depositors to imitate them; this is the bank run phenomenon.[13] The bank faces the following dilemma: Either it invests in short-term assets and does not fulfill its term transformation role, which is inefficient, or it faces the possibility of bank runs when it invests at least partially in illiquid long-term assets.[14]

There exist simple ways of obtaining the "right equilibrium," where only depositors who really need cash in period 1 withdraw at that date. For example, public or private deposit insurance eliminates depositors' concerns about the ability to withdraw at date 2.

---

12. There is a large literature on liquidity provision summarized, for example, in Freixas-Rochet (1994). Von Thadden (1994a, b) provides a lucid discussion of the role of the "incentive compatibility constraint" (the fact that agents not facing a liquidity need may want to take their money out of the bank and reinvest it somewhere else when reinvestment opportunities are good). He shows that even though in some cases this constraint can be made nonbinding (Diamond-Dybvig 1983), its existence quite generally generates a loss in welfare by limiting insurance across realizations of liquidity needs.

13. The Diamond-Dybvig model also admits an equilibrium without runs. Other models introduce objective systemic information, which sometimes implies a unique equilibrium, with runs (Postlewaite-Vives 1987; Jacklin-Bhattacharya 1988; Chari-Jagannathan 1988).

14. Cone (1983) and Jacklin (1987) have shown that banks are not needed if investors can directly buy nonfinancial firm securities. A security market without transaction costs does at least as well as an intermediated economy.

This is in fact an essential argument in favor of deposit insurance. Another method is to let the authorities act as lender of last resort, in favor of solvent but illiquid banks. A third method is to allow the bank or the regulator to suspend convertibility beyond a given level of withdrawals (those of people with liquidity needs in period 1). This method leads to potential moral hazard problems. For example, a troubled bank could prevent depositors from withdrawing their money.

The consensus in favor of deposit insurance is quite broad among regulators. Some economists suggest limiting deposit insurance as a way to reduce moral hazard problems and to better discipline banks. Depositors can then react to negative information about a bank's health by withdrawing their money (Calomiris et al. 1991; Emmons 1991; Rey-Stiglitz 1992). This threat can induce bank managers to behave optimally. Calomiris and Gorton (1991) also show that a "first-come, first-served" rule induces depositors to monitor banks. The idea of limiting deposit insurance for small depositors is, however, not really widespread; partial insurance for large deposits (provided it cannot be circumvented by splitting and multiplying deposits) is instead more popular. We come back to this issue of large uninsured deposits in section 13.3.

A useful application of the Diamond-Dybvig model is the general equilibrium analysis of Hellwig (1993). He uses their liquidity risk framework to focus not on bank runs but on the optimal return of deposits in the presence of macroeconomic risk. More precisely Hellwig assumes uncertainty at date 0 about the short-term interest rate between dates 1 and 2 (which reflects investment opportunities as of date 1). As in the Diamond-Dybvig model the role of financial intermediaries is to allow for insurance contracts against liquidity needs at dates 1 and 2. If the bank can observe liquidity needs, that is, verify that date 1 withdrawals are really necessary, the optimal contract shares risk between individual types. A higher short-term interest rate between periods 1 and 2 may lead to a lower interest rate for date 0 deposits withdrawn in period 1 as well as a higher interest rate for date 0 deposits left in the bank until period 2. The intuition is that better reinvestment opportunities for (short-term) assets maturing in period 1 make it less attractive to pay interest on money withdrawn at date 1. There is no reason to promise non-contingent interest rates on demand or savings deposits. Their remuneration should instead covary (negatively) with interest rate risk. Hellwig shows further that when liquidity needs are private information, the Pareto-optimal covariation may not be sufficient to induce depositors without liquidity needs in period 1 not to withdraw at this date when the short-term rate in period 1 is too high. Incentive constraints then limit feasible insurance.[15]

Liquidity transformation and deposit insurance are very relevant for regulation. In the presence of generalized explicit or implicit deposit insurance, the regulatory debate on these issues has lost some of its importance. In fact current debates mainly concern capital adequacy ratios rather than liquidity issues. The problems raised by the Diamond-Dybvig model may become relevant again in the event of credible moves to limit deposit insurance.

5.4 Competition in the Banking Industry

A classical theme in industrial organization is the absence of internalization by firms of their externalities on other firms or consumers. The general implications of this behavior are suboptimality of a firm's price, product choice, quality, investment or R&D decisions and a role for intervention by a regulatory authority. Similarities can be drawn for the banking industry. Several

---

15. Hellwig also shows that under this incentive compatibility constraint it may become optimal for society to liquidate long-term projects, even though in his model liquidation and reinvestement in a new asset is always dominated by keeping the long-term asset until its maturity.

recent contributions have applied IO (industrial organization) tools to banking.[16] For example, Chiappori et al. (1993) study interest rate competition between spatially differentiated banks that enjoy market power. They show that deposit rate ceilings (as still practiced in France) increase the number of bank branches and may induce "overbranching." As was in evidence among airlines before deregulation in the United States, limited price competition increases the profitability of attracting new customers and ensures strong quality competition. Chiappori et al. show that such regulation can lead to "bundling," where banks grant loans provided they can also manage the borrowers' deposit account. This strategy allows banks to circumvent regulation, in the same way as vertical integration or barter can circumvent input price regulation in IO.

Matutes and Padilla (1991), in another relevant application of IO methods, analyze automated teller networks. They focus on banks' incentives to make their networks compatible in the absence of regulation. A single network is efficient but may fail to emerge because of its effect on competition: Through a single network banks reduce differentiation and end up competing more severely for deposits.

It is important to adequately use IO methods for the analysis of the banking sector. The IO approach seems much better suited for the understanding of some banking strategies than for an analysis of current regulation. IO theory has been much more successful from a positive than from a normative point of view. Its current banking applications, while quite worthwhile, do not really distinguish banks from other industries. They thus inherit the usual ambiguous welfare predictions of IO.

---

16. See also Gual and Neven (1992) for an empirical analysis of the impact of deregulation on banking competition in Europe.

5.5   Regulatory Models

The models that most closely address prudential regulation issues take a simpler view of banks, abstracting from explicit delegated monitoring or liquidity provision. They all concern *entrepreneurial banks,* so deposit finance is assumed to be the only source of outside funds and outside control.

One type of model stresses the risk-taking bias implied by the inability of depositors (possibly encouraged by deposit insurance to invest in deposits) to observe the asset portfolio risk chosen by the bank (Merton 1977, 1978; Bhattacharya 1982). In such a world, capital requirements reduce risk taking and, under deposit insurance, the implicit subsidy from deposit insurance. However, by changing the equilibrium scale of operations of the bank (the banking entrepreneur may react to a decreased profitability by investing less of her own wealth in the bank), capital requirements can also affect in ambiguous ways the desired asset composition of a risk averse bank owner (Koehn-Santomero 1980; Gennotte-Pyle 1991; Rochet 1991). Consequently it may be the case that higher capital requirements may *raise* some banks' failure probabilities. Davies and McManus (1991) show that the same ambiguity concerning risk taking is present when one increases the net worth level at which banks have to be automatically closed.[17]

---

17. While these models presuppose pure debt finance, it may be possible to find situations in which it is optimal for the banking entrepreneur to enter a pure debt finance contract and in which results are not fundamentally altered. Daltung (1994) uses the Townsend-Gale-Hellwig costly state-verification model to obtain such foundations. She shows that excessive risk taking is a natural consequence of the private information obtained by banks in their delegated monitoring function, *with* or *without* deposit insurance. The presence of an insurance scheme can again *worsen* or *alleviate* excessive risk taking in her setup. Capital constraints are useful only if the deposit insurance scheme is underpriced, that is, if it subsidizes banks in expected terms. Otherwise, since a rational insurer correctly predicts the level of risk taking and prices it accordingly, it is in the entrepreneurial bank's interest to put up

A number of authors have also analyzed the link between competition and prudential concerns. They have stressed the fact that the expectation of future rents makes it more costly for a bank to fail and introduces a mitigating factor against excessive risk taking. Bhattacharya (1982) has argued that deposit rate ceilings could act as such a deterrent against risk taking. Besanko and Thakor (1993) have shown that lower entry barriers can be Pareto worsening if they induce a large increase in risk taking. Finally, Chan, Greenbaum, and Thakor (1992) have argued that the existence of sufficient rents may be a precondition for a useful role for risk-sensitive deposit insurance premiums.

Another recent branch of banking theory considers the optimal regulation of a single banking firm that has private information (about cost or quality) and takes unobservable decisions. Some of the techniques used here were developed in the context of natural monopoly regulation, such as telecommunication or electricity companies, but can also be applied to oligopolistic firms.

An important idea from this branch of banking theory is the benefit of introducing *menus of options* from which the bank chooses depending on its characteristics. Instead of imposing a rigid regulatory scheme to all banks, it is better to allow them to self-select. Such menus already exist to a certain extent. For example, some financial sectors are regulated, while others are not (or almost not). Another example concerns some reform proposals presented in chapter 3 where more capitalized banks are allowed to engage in riskier activities. A well-capitalized bank's choice between distributing dividend and facing regulatory oversight, and retaining earnings and enjoying more freedom of action, can be seen as a choice within a menu.

---

enough of its own money to credibly commit not to engage in excessive risk taking. Once again, however, there is no place for outside equity in this model.

In the model of Rochet et al. (1993) a bank may be either efficient or inefficient. The degree of efficiency is private information to the owner-manager (who owns 100% of the equity) and unobservable to the regulator. The bank's profit also depends on privately observed managerial effort. The manager is risk averse. The regulator offers the bank an incentive scheme, inducing self-selection on the basis of the fraction of risky assets chosen by the bank and of the profit-sharing scheme between the bank and the regulator. Rochet et al. show that in the optimal scheme efficient managers obtain relatively more insurance and are allowed to take relatively riskier actions (since, by assumption, effort and intrinsic efficiency are more important for risky than for nonrisky assets).[18]

A challenge for all models of optimal banking regulation surveyed here is the introduction of a role for the bank's capital structure decisions. The introduction of outside equity poses the problem of the irrelevance of the financial structure of the bank in the presence of optimal managerial incentive schemes, as in the famous Modigliani-Miller theorem (1958). In other words, capital ratios do not affect the bank's behavior, which is entirely determined by managerial incentive schemes. Two approaches can lead to the emergence of a role for the capital structure and for capital ratios. One approach allows for occasional involvement of claimholders in the management of the bank. This is the road taken in this book. Another approach consists in imposing exogenous constraints on managerial incentive schemes by linking them to some claims, like equity (e.g., as done since Jensen-Meckling 1976).[19]

---

18. This normative result illustrates the problems of a laissez-faire policy combined with deposit insurance where, ceteris paribus, less efficient banks take riskier actions because they are less fearsome of bankruptcy. Gennotte (1990) analyzes a positive such model where he derives a bimodal distribution of the banking sector similar to that of the U.S. S&L industry in the 1980s.

19. See, for example, Giammarino-Lewis-Sappington (1993).

5.6   The Need for a Complementary Approach

This brief survey of banking theory has uncovered a number of useful paradigms to describe the workings of the banking industry. Two types of models have stressed the specificity of banks: as delegated monitors for their lending activity and as liquidity providers for their depository role. We have stressed the fact that such models are of limited use for prudential regulation. Liquidity provision models are more concerned with panics, contagion, and systemic risk than with the solvency of individual banks. At first, delegated monitoring models may appear closer to the concerns of prudential regulators, but the potential for diversification through increased size makes regulation unnecessary. Limiting the extent of diversification would allow them to be used to analyze regulatory issues (deposit insurance pricing, capital requirements). There is one caveat, however: Since all of these models concentrate on *entrepreneurial banks*, they allow for only *inside equity* and not *outside equity*.

This problem is serious in that, at least for large- or medium-size banks, most equity is held by outsiders. Moreover regulation is concerned primarily with capital requirements; the source of equity finance is not a factor. Without outside equityholders analyzing the impact of recapitalization in such models is impossible. This is unfortunate, since regulation tries to alter shareholders' incentives to discipline managers through higher capital requirements. (Regulation based on balance sheet information is also ruled out by many of these models, whose starting point is the absence of accounts, so a debate between historical cost or market value accounting would be irrelevant.)

For all these reasons it is natural to try and complement existing banking theory by an approach that gives an explicit role to outside equity. One specificity of our argument in this book is to consider banks as regular firms except for the fact that their debtholders are small and dispersed and thus need to be represented. Our starting point is thus a model of the capital structure of firms in which both debt and equity are active participants. Recent models of corporate finance have used the incomplete contract paradigm to include out-side claimholders in the management of firms,[20] even though they do not simultaneously rationalize debt and outside equity. We build upon their insights to provide such a model which, together with our "representation hypothesis" forms the basis of the remainder of this book. The following chapter presents a nontechnical overview of our approach and results. Chapters 7 through 13 detail the analysis, and chapter 14 provides a summary of our policy insights as well as some remarks on directions for research.

---

20. See, for example, Aghion-Bolton (1992), Bolton-Scharfstein (1992), or Hart-Moore (1994, 1990b, 1989).

6   Outline of
                       the Argument

This chapter details our modeling approach as well as our main insights as they unfold in the following chapters. Readers mainly interested in policy conclusions can read it as a substitute for chapters 7 through 13, before moving to chapter 14, which summarizes the lessons of our approach for banking regulation.

As we explained earlier, in our view, banking regulation stems primarily from the desire to protect ordinary uninformed, free-riding depositors (the "representation hypothesis"). Our approach consists *first* in viewing a bank as an ordinary firm, and *second* in introducing the market failure stemming from the depositors' collective action problem.

Chapter 7 thus starts with a simple model of the banking firm. Since banking regulation tries to control the capital structure of financial intermediaries, we first relate our general theory of the capital structure of a firm. As we explained in section 5.6, the theoretical corporate finance literature has not yet supplied a full-fledged model of debt and equity in a managerial firm. In particular, we need to develop a model that can simultaneously rationalize (1) managerial incentive schemes, (2) multiple securities giving control rights as well as income streams to their owners, and (3) a regular pattern of such securities with emphasis on debt and (outside) equity.

Our theory starts with the standard managerial moral hazard problem within a firm, and the equally familiar idea that formal incentive schemes (bonuses, stock options), while useful, are limited by imperfect verifiability of firm performance. Consequently additional incentives are provided by the possibility of *external involvement* in management by outsiders. For example, shareholders, in particular through the board of directors, can put the firm under the control of a holding company, ask the manager to reverse a decision, to divest a division, to cancel a project, to forgo some perks, or to leave. Similarly, and perhaps more important as we will see later, debtholders (e.g., a main bank for a nonfinancial company) can force the firm to take such decisions by threatening to provoke failure by refusing to extend a credit line or to reschedule claims.

Of course managers dislike interference and prefer to be left doing whatever they want to do. Therefore managerial discipline is best provided by promising a low level of interference in case of good performance and a high level of interference in case of a mediocre one.

Such a disciplining device raises two questions: How can one accurately measure performance? How can one *commit* to an external interference policy if, as is assumed in incomplete contract theory (Grossman-Hart 1986; Hart-Moore 1990a; Aghion-Bolton 1992), such policies or the exact circumstances under which they are picked cannot be contracted upon in advance? The first question relates to the reliability of accounting systems as well as the room for short-termist actions by managers. Indeed the threat of intervention implies an incentive for managers to hide problems, possibly in the hope they will disappear, but at least to "buy time." Chapter 10 details how such problems arise in the banking context, where it has taken the form of "gains trading" (selling assets which are undervalued by the accounts while keeping those which are overvalued). There we show the existence of a trade-off between the disciplinary effect of outside interference and the resulting inefficiency due to gains trading.

More important for our argument is, however, the issue of *commitment* to a given interference policy. Our key assumption is that external intervention cannot be precisely specified, so outsiders upon whom control is conferred must be given incentives to intervene in the proper way. We thus have a "double moral hazard problem" for outsiders as well as managers. This enables us to predict a systematic pattern for securities' return streams and control rights, since outsiders' incentive schemes are provided by the return streams attached to their securities.

In reality, this systematic pattern does exist: Equityholders, with a *convex* return structure in firm performance, typically have control in *good* times, while debtholders, with their *concave* return structure, have de facto control in *bad* times. To accord with the forms of interference discussed above, and also to be able to match this observed correlation between return streams and control rights, it is natural to assume that interference leads to a *decrease in risk*. This is clearly realistic if interference means canceling some projects, divesting a division, imposing safe projects or securities, or liquidating part or all the company. In such cases claimholders with a concave return structure (debtholders) are more prone to interfere (are tougher) than those with a convex return structure (shareholders). Combining this with the general point that interference should follow a mediocre performance, we thus conclude that *control should shift from soft claimholders (equityholders) to tough ones (debtholders) in case of mediocre performance.*

Our theory thus rationalizes the existence of outside equity and debt, and of control by *partisan* or *biased* principals. Indeed the nonlinearity of their returns with respect to firm performance makes credible the carrot (relative passivity) as well as the stick (activism) that help discipline managers ex ante.

The optimal interference policy does not only consist in allocating control between equityholders and debtholders. As we show in chapter 8, the incentives of the controlling claimholders must further be adjusted within each control region through, say, net worth adjustments (recapitalization, dividend distribution).

To see this, consider a banking firm that makes short-term (one-period) and long-term (two-period) loans to industry and faces in period 1 managerial moral hazard in its management of both types of loans. The bank's first-period profit v (net of first-period deposit withdrawals) is realized; more generally, v could stand for any objective information that would be recorded in the bank's balance sheet at the end of period 1. The second-period profit η is not yet realized, although a signal about the prospects of the bank or its environment might accrue at this stage. Let the bank's period-two obligation to depositors be equal to D, and let $\bar{\eta}$ denote the historical cost (value of the principal) of the long-term assets. The balance sheet at the end of period 1 is thus

Assets	Liabilities
v	D
$\bar{\eta}$	E

where net worth or equity E is, as usual, defined as a residual. Assume that v is reinvested in a safe asset, say, a Treasury bond, at the market rate of interest of zero. According to the international agreements, the safe asset has weight 0, while the industrial loans $\bar{\eta}$ carry full weight. The Cooke ratio at the end of period 1 is then

$$r = \frac{v + \bar{\eta} - D}{\bar{\eta}}.$$

A straightforward reinterpretation of the allocation of control to shareholders in good times ($v \geq v^{\min}$ for some $v^{\min}$) and to debtholders in bad times ($v < v^{\min}$) is in terms of Cooke ratios:

Letting $r^{\min} \equiv (v^{\min} + \bar{\eta} - D)/\bar{\eta}$, shareholders keep control if and only if

$$r \geq r^{\min}.$$

We are now in a position to discuss net worth adjustment in each control region. For conciseness, let us focus on shareholder control (the conclusions are the same for debtholder control). Suppose that the bank's performance v deteriorates. Net debt $D - v$ increases, so the bank is less capitalized, in the sense of a lower Cooke ratio. Shareholders are then more tempted not to interfere to reduce risk (formally the set of signals about second-period prospects that lead to risk taking expands). This is easily understood: For example, if net debt is large, the shareholders can make money only if they "gamble for resurrection." Indeed the evidence shows that the S&Ls that took the most risk were the undercapitalized ones. We can conclude that poor performance is followed by reduced interference, yielding a clearly perverse incentive for managers. A recapitalization compensating the deterioration of the balance sheet counters this perverse evolution of the balance sheet. Conversely, in case of brilliant performance shareholders want to play conservatively in order not to jeopardize their newly acquired assets; a dividend distribution then helps reduce the level of interference. For debtholder control we can apply a similar net worth adjustment rule, together with an *uncontingent* transfer of control when r falls below $r^{\min}$. Chapter 8 builds an *equivalent* external control mechanism that specifies for each r below $r^{\min}$ a level of recapitalization $I(r)$ that shareholders must accept in order to retain control. Shareholders may be ready to do this in order to prevent debtholders from choosing conservative actions. The higher $I(r)$ is, the lower the incentive for shareholders to pay it, and thus the tougher the expected interference for managers.

Chapter 8 thus details ways to implement optimal external inter-ference. The key elements are a contingent control mechanism, net worth adjustments, and possibly a recapitalization scheme that al-lows equityholders to retain control even after poor performance if they wish so.

Chapter 9 introduces *aggregate risk*, which is beyond managerial control, in order to see how it should be treated in the optimal in-terference mechanism. International regulations state that a bank's Cooke ratio must exceed 8% at all times. Many have criticized this rule on the grounds that it is harder for a bank to reach 8% in a banking recession than in a boom. As a matter of fact, regula-tors have often been more lenient during banking recessions. For example, in the early 1980s when the S&Ls were badly hurt by interest rate shocks, the regulators lowered solvency standards sub-stantially, first by lowering the floor from 5% to 3% and then by adopting new lax accounting procedures; they could accordingly declare most S&Ls "solvent." Regulators defended their "relative ratio" policy precisely on the grounds that solvency requirements should be indexed on the cycle.

Taking an incentive approach to banking sheds light on this de-bate between *absolute and relative ratios*. Informativeness theory (Holmström 1979; Shavell 1979) implies that banks should be in-sulated from uncertainty that they do not control. For example, suppose that bank i's verifiable variable entering the Cooke ratio v_i is the sum of an idiosyncratic risk v_i^I and of an aggregate risk v^A (real estate, interest rate, loans to LDCs, etc.) common to all banks. Theory recommends that bank management not be affected by v^A. All of this is standard. What is less well understood is that this reasoning does not call for a simple relative ratio rule because the incentives of outsiders in control must be accounted for (the double moral hazard problem for insiders and outsiders is the key to most of our discussions).

To understand this, suppose that the minimum solvency ratio is equal to 8% in the absence of any aggregate shock and that a macroeconomic downturn lowers the solvency ratio of all banks by 6%. A bank that would have normally reached a ratio of 8.5% has a ratio of 2.5%. To leave control to shareholders, as is appropriate, the solvency requirement should be lowered to 2%. However, shareholders do not behave in the same way when the real solvency is 2.5% and 8.5%. Indeed, following the downturn, they may want to gamble for resurrection. To complement the relative ratio rule (which preserves the proper allocation of control), one must also recapitalize the bank by an amount (here 6%) contingent on the average profitability of banks with a similar balance sheet composition to account for the altered incentives. Of course a recapitalization may not be easy, especially in a downturn when many other banks are also trying to recapitalize. One may then consider alternative instruments such as pro-cyclical deposit insurance premiums or any other government policy that would have the effect of helping banks in a downturn and tax them in a boom.

The same informativeness reasoning may shed light on another important policy debate: Should one record a bank's assets at their *historical cost* (as has always been done) or at their *market value* (assuming that this value can be measured)? Returning to our two-period framework, assume now that the bank's second-period profit is $\eta + \epsilon$, where η is not yet realized in period 1 and ϵ is some macroeconomic shock that is revealed in period 1. For example, ϵ reflects news on the real estate market, the interest rate, or the value of loans to LDCs. Macroeconomic shocks are of particular interest because they can often be measured more objectively than idiosyncratic shocks, and therefore give the best chance to market value accounting.

The balance sheet and the solvency ratio for the two accounting methods at the end of period 1 are as follows:

Market value accounting

$v + \epsilon$	D
$\bar{\eta}$	E

$$r = \frac{v + \epsilon + \bar{\eta} - D}{\bar{\eta}}$$

Historical cost accounting

v	D
$\bar{\eta}$	E

$$r = \frac{v + \bar{\eta} - D}{\bar{\eta}}$$

It can immediately be seen that market value accounting, but not historical cost accounting, involves an excessively volatile allocation of control under a capital adequacy requirement. On the other hand, historical cost accounting does not adjust the shareholders' incentives, who again are induced to gamble for resurrection in case of an adverse shock. Historical cost accounting, like the relative ratio rule, insulates the allocation of control from exogenous noise but takes no account of the effect of this noise on shareholders' incentives. Market value accounting, like the absolute ratio rule, improperly allocates control. The policy implications, including the need for a median policy, are the same as for the treatment of macroeconomic shocks in general.

Observe that *securitization* of assets is partly a substitute for market value accounting, except that there the manager of the bank has discretion over which assets are sold, which may lead to gains trading. Chapter 9 also makes a distinction between the timings of the resolution of idiosyncratic and aggregate uncertainties. When the first precedes the second, securitization improves the informativeness of performance about managerial effort, while it is the opposite when aggregate uncertainty comes first. An example of the first case is home mortgages, where market uncertainty can dominate the value of the loan after some years; an example of the second is an R&D industrial loan whose idiosyncratic components can take ten years to be realized. Our model suggests that only the first type of loan should be securitized if managerial discipline is to be promoted.

Chapters 7 to 10 take a *normative* perspective. They outline a model of firms that rationalizes multiple outside claimholders and contingent control. As such, they are applicable to banking and nonbanking firms alike. The specificity of banks we highlight is the dispersion of its debtholders, and their lack of competence or incentives to exercise the control rights typically exercised by banks themselves for nonfinancial companies. Consequently depositors must be *represented* to allow for the usual disciplining device associated to the capital structure. Chapters 11 through 13 turn to various ways in which the depositors can be represented.

Chapter 11 focuses on the current regulatory framework, based on the Basle accords and on the Cooke ratio. This framework involves some elements of the optimal intervention mechanism described previously. In particular, it introduces a net worth requirement and the possibility of transferring control to a depositors' representative in case the bank falls short of it and shareholders refuse to recapitalize. However, the chapter stresses two shortcomings of the system:

1. In the region of unconditional equity control (net worth above the minimum solvency ratio), dividends can be distributed fully for any given improvement in performance so that the net worth ratio is independent of performance: Managers are thus not rewarded for improved performance (as they would be if successful banks were allowed *lower* net worth ratios). In contrast, when bad performance makes the net worth ratio fall below the minimum level, the recapitalization requirement to that minimum penalizes managers more the worse the performance, which serves as a discipline device.

2. More important, by not distinguishing between idiosyncratic and aggregate risks, the Cooke ratio introduces penalizing recapitalization requirements in the case of adverse macroeconomic shocks and is thus too harsh on managers in those times. This would call for temporary help for banks.

In chapter 12 we address another shortcoming of regulatory systems which, like the Basle framework, is based upon *public agencies*. A public agency that receives control after poor performance (and possibly refusal by equityholders to recapitalize the bank) is meant to represent depositors, or debtholders, and thus *to follow an interventionist course*. This is meant to be excessively tough in comparison to ex post efficiency and will of course not be welcomed by bank managers.

One can thus question the degree to which regulators may be committed to such interventionist behavior when there is banking industry, and even congressional, pressure. The S&L crisis is a telling example, since it led to regulatory forbearance and even cover up. In chapter 12 we show how a regulator in charge of ex post intervention, but also of ex ante monitoring, may be tempted to be passive instead of interventionist ex post in order to cover up failed monitoring that could harm his or her career prospects. Such political economy considerations rationalize the current attempts at limiting regulatory discretion, even though they may come up at the expense of flexibility in the disciplining of bank managers.

In the face of these limits of public regulation, chapter 13 addresses reforms that try to give more of a role to private parties. We evaluate them against the requirement that poor performance by the bank be followed by an interventionist outsider put in charge to counter the perverse incentive stemming from decapitalization. It is clear then that while potentially helpful as part of an optimal regulatory mechanism, rating agencies or a private deposit insurance scheme *alone* do not solve the problem. In fact a deteriorated rating or higher deposit insurance premium following poor performance even reinforce the perverse effect of decapitalization.

A serious drawback of pure rating or insurance premium schemes is that there is no debtholder representative. Can a large debtholder take on this role? It can, on the one hand, discipline management in bad times and, on the other, add another cushion to equity in order to reduce the potential intervention of deposit insurance. We stress, however, that these two functions are largely incompatible: As an equity cushion the large debtholder may be effective provided that its claim is *junior* to insured deposits. However, in the event of a big recession that wipes out the value of equity, the big debtholder would in fact become residual claimant and behave like (passive) equityholders. Disciplining managers in bad times requires uninsured debt to have the same priority as deposits, and to serve as a complement rather than a substitute to deposit insurance.

III Normative Analysis

7   A Simple Model

7.1   The Model

In this chapter we develop a framework that we will later use to assess current banking regulation. The simplified balance sheet of a financial intermediary is at each instant t:

Assets	Liabilities
Loans (L_t)	Deposits (D_t)
	Equity (E_t)

where equity is held by shareholders and necessarily $L_t = D_t + E_t$. The structure of the liability side is endogenous in our model.

The model aims at analyzing the effect of governance structures on managerial moral hazard. There are two periods, $t = 1, 2$. At the beginning of period 1, initial deposits D_0 and equity E_0 are used to finance loans $L_0 = D_0 + E_0$. The quality of these loans depends on the manager's effort $e \in \{\underline{e}, \bar{e}\}$, where $\underline{e} < \bar{e}$. Only the manager observes e. The high effort is socially efficient but costs K to the manager, while the low effort costs nothing. K may represent either the manager's valuation for a low-pressure job of selecting loans or the private benefit received by distributing loans to his or her "friends" rather than to the best borrowers.

Two pieces of information on the quality of loans are revealed at the end of period 1. Let

$$\pi = v + \eta \tag{1}$$

denote the yet unobservable final profit of the bank. v is the *verifiable* first-period performance. It includes the value of loans maturing at date 1 as well as net capital gains on other assets. For the moment we assume that v is reinvested in safe assets (e.g., Treasury bonds) at the market rate of interest, which we normalize at zero;[1] alternatively the income v does not accrue before date 2, but its value is realized (revealed) at date 1. In contrast, η denotes assets whose value is yet unrealized at date 1. Besides v, the market receives a second signal $u \in [\underline{u}, \bar{u}]$ concerning the realization of the random variable η. We assume for simplicity that u is a sufficient statistic for (e, u) to predict η. Let $\bar{\eta}(u)$ denote the expectation of η given the market's information at the end of period 1, and let $\bar{\eta}$ denote the corresponding historical cost (the value of the loans' principal).

There are two accounting methods. *Historical cost accounting* (or the generally accepted accounting principles, or GAAP) measures the total value of loans at date 1 at level

$$L_1 = v + \bar{\eta}. \tag{2}$$

Market value accounting makes use of market information:

$$L_1^{MVA} = v + \bar{\eta}(u). \tag{3}$$

For instance, the accounting value of a bond held by the bank is equal to its principal (adjusted by past interest payments) under historical cost accounting, but reflects the evolution of market interest rates under market value accounting. Similarly, under market value accounting, changes in interest rates affect the valuation of consumption loans and mortgages, and securitizable assets can be recorded at their market price. We will mainly focus on historical cost accounting. Market value accounting will be analyzed in chapter 9.

---

1. See section 11.3 for a study of reinvestment in risky assets.

The two signals v and u are performance measures. Both are positively correlated with managerial effort. In a special case, though, only v is affected by effort. The signal u then stands for variables, such as market interest rates, real estate prices, or macroeconomic fluctuations, on which the manager has no influence. The density of v is $\bar{f}(v)$ if $e = \bar{e}$, and $\underline{f}(v)$ if $e = \underline{e}$. Similarly the density of u is $\bar{g}(u)$ if $e = \bar{e}$, and $\underline{g}(u)$ if $e = \underline{e}$.

We assume that high effort improves performance. This is formalized by the standard monotone likelihood ratio property:

$$\frac{\bar{f}}{\underline{f}} \quad \text{is strictly increasing in } v, \tag{4}$$

$$\frac{\bar{g}}{\underline{g}} \quad \text{is increasing in } u. \tag{4'}$$

The bank's final profit is realized in period 2. It depends on the choice at the end of period 1, after the signals are revealed, of some action A (see below). The density and cumulative distribution of η conditional on signal u and action A are $h_A(\eta|u)$ and $H_A(\eta|u)$.

For simplicity we focus on two possible actions: S, which consists in "stopping" or "intervening," and C, which stands for "continuing" or "being passive" vis-à-vis the manager. Action S thus represents a reorganization, a partial asset sale, a reduction in the scope of the bank, layoffs and firings or even liquidation. It may be useful to illustrate action S further. One may have in mind U.S.-style "cease and desist powers" according to which the banking regulators can stop a bank from engaging in a practice they consider harmful to safety and soundness; see Garber-Weisbrod 1992, 542. Similarly the U.S. authorities can force a bank to increase its provisions for loan losses, thus reducing its solvency ratio and, indirectly, its investments in risky assets. Other types of "action S" can be observed in countries where regulators have even more discretionary powers. For instance, in Norway the Government Bank Insurance Fund, which was established in 1991 to deal with the widespread banking problems, had substantial powers to force troubled banks to refocus on some core business (activity or geographic area), to reduce the volume of risky assets (shipping activities, foreign business, etc.), to close branches, and more generally to adjust strategy (see Hope 1993 for a detailed account).

The choice between C and S is made on the basis of the realizations of u and v by the party to whom the control rights have been conferred; for, we will assume that these actions are noncontractible.[2] The model focuses on *external interference as a managerial discipline* device. Because the action is noncontractible, the controlling party must be given proper incentives in the form of return streams attached to a claim so as to induce the manager to choose the high effort.

We assume that the manager cares little, actually not at all, about monetary incentives. His salary is equal to his salary in an alternative job and is normalized at zero.[3] In contrast, the manager derives a private benefit $B > 0$ (perks, social status, ego) from running the bank as long as there is no external interference. So, in the absence of renegotiation between the controlling party and the other parties, the manager receives B if the controlling party prefers (and therefore chooses) action C, and 0 if the controlling party prefers (and therefore chooses) action S. When renegotiation is feasible, the manager may lose his private benefit even when action C ends up being chosen if he has to make concessions to prevent action S (see appendix A for more detail). Let us summarize the timing:

---

2. See Dewatripont-Tirole (1993b) for a reinterpretation of this basic model in terms of a complete contract and "double moral hazard."

3. The results obtained here can be generalized under some assumptions to the opposite polar case in which the manager has no private benefit, but cares about monetary rewards; see Dewatripont-Tirole (1993b).

At date 0

1. A control right that is contingent on v is allocated, and the initial balance sheet is determined

At date 1

2. Manager chooses e
3. (u, v) is realized
4. Renegotiation takes place
5. Action $A \in \{S, C\}$ is chosen by controlling party

At date 2

6. η is realized

All but stage 4 of this timing were previously described. Renegotiation may be relevant because the controlling party may not choose the ex post socially efficient action. Indeed ex ante efficient decisions, which take into account the effect on managerial incentives, typically are not ex post optimal, as we will see later. The parties (claimholders, manager) will therefore have an incentive to renegotiate toward an efficient decision. To check robustness, we will analyze both the case where renegotiation is impossible, and the polar case of perfect renegotiation. Conclusions regarding the optimal managerial incentive scheme and implementation are identical, but the nature of the inefficiencies differs. Under perfect renegotiation the governance structure is meant to force the manager to make concessions in case of poor performance. In the absence of renegotiation, the manager makes no concessions; however the controlling party may choose an inefficient action.

Last, we make the following assumption:

A1 *A higher signal makes action C more desirable:*

$$\frac{\partial}{\partial u} (H_S - H_C) > 0.$$

By this assumption we can define a threshold signal $\hat{u}$ such that the bank's expected profit be the same under either action. Let

$$
\Delta(u) = \int_0^\infty \eta\left[h_C(\eta \mid u) - h_S(\eta \mid u)\right] d\eta
$$

$$
= \int_0^\infty \left[H_S(\eta \mid u) - H_C(\eta \mid u)\right] d\eta.
$$

(5)

$\hat{u}$ is thus defined by

$$
\Delta(\hat{u}) = 0.
$$

(6)

We now derive the optimal managerial incentive scheme in the absence of renegotiation.

7.2   No Renegotiation: Excessive Interference and Passivity

In this section we derive the optimal managerial incentive scheme in the absence of renegotiation. Let $x(v, u)$ denote the probability that the controlling party chooses action C when signals are v and u. For the moment we follow the complete contracting approach and assume that one can commit to this function x. In chapter 8 we will show how this function can be implemented through a financial structure when it cannot be contracted upon.

Maximizing total bank value is equivalent to minimizing the expected profit loss due to inefficient decision making, subject to the constraint that the manager be induced to choose the high effort (we will assume all along that it is optimal to induce the manager to choose $\bar{e}$). The need to introduce distortions in the decision can be understood very simply in the special case where effort affects only the first-period performance v. Since the ex post efficient action is C if and only if $u \geq \hat{u}$, the probability of intervention is independent of the manager's effort under ex post efficient decision making; the manager then "exerts no effort" (chooses $\underline{e}$).

The optimal incentive scheme is obtained (in the general case) in the following way: Let $\Delta^+(u) \equiv \max(\Delta(u), 0) \geq 0$ and $\Delta^-(u) \equiv \min(\Delta(u), 0) \leq 0$, where $\Delta(u) = \Delta^+(u) + \Delta^-(u)$, which is the monetary incentive to choose action C, is defined by equation (5). We minimize the expected ex post inefficiency while preserving managerial incentives:

$$\min_{x(\cdot,\cdot)} \int\int \left[(1 - x(v, u))\Delta^+(u) - x(v, u)\Delta^-(u)\right]\bar{f}(v)\bar{g}(u)\,dv\,du \qquad (7)$$

subject to

$$B \int\int x(v, u)\left[\bar{f}(v)\bar{g}(u)) - \underline{f}(v)\underline{g}(u))\right]dv\,du \geq K, \qquad (8)$$

where $x(v, u) = 1$ if action C is chosen and $x(v, u) = 0$ if action S is chosen. The derivative of the Lagrangian of this program with respect to $x(v, u)$ is

$$\Delta(u)\bar{f}(v)\bar{g}(u) + \mu B\left[\bar{f}(v)\bar{g}(u) - \underline{f}(v)\underline{g}(u)\right],$$

where μ is the multiplier of the incentive constraint. We leave it to the reader to check that this optimization together with monotone likelihood defines a threshold $u^*(v)$ that decreases with v. That is, action C is chosen if and only if $u \geq u^*(v)$. Furthermore $u^*(v) < \hat{u}$ if and only if the pair $(v, u^*(v))$ is more likely under the high effort than under the low effort.

Because high signals v and u indicate a high effort, the manager is rewarded by relative passivity when these signals are high. The threshold $u^*(\cdot)$ is depicted in figure 7.1. Let $\hat{v}$ be defined by

$$u^*(\hat{v}) = \hat{u}.$$

That is, the controlling party's decision rule is ex post efficient when the first-period performance is $\hat{v}$.[4]

---

4. We leave it to the reader to check that the downward sloping curve $u = u^*(v)$ and the horizontal line $u = \hat{u}$ intersect.

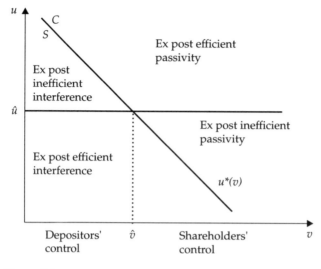

Figure 7.1
The optimal managerial incentive scheme

The optimal incentive scheme threatens the manager with frequent external interference ($u^*(v) > \hat{u}$) in case of *poor performance* ($v < \hat{v}$) and guarantees him a passive attitude ($u^*(v) < \hat{u}$) for *good performance* ($v > \hat{v}$). To implement this rule, we will therefore need to confer control (contingent on v) upon a claimholder with a biased objective compared to that of the community of all claimholders. In other words, a single class of securities (100% equity) cannot implement the optimal managerial incentive scheme.

In appendix A we demonstrate the robustness of this result to renegotiation. As long as the manager's welfare is higher when the controlling party prefers action C to action S, it is optimal to implement a decreasing threshold rule $u^*(\cdot)$ as in figure 7.1. *The idea that poor performance should trigger more interference is the basis for our analysis in the rest of this book.*

**The Investors'
Incentive Scheme**

8.1   A Role for Shareholders and Debtholders

When the performance variable u is not verifiable and/or actions C and S are not contractible, residual rights of control must be conferred on some external party who has an incentive to choose the action appropriately. Since the manager must be punished for poor performance ($v < \hat{v}$) by substantial interference ($u^*(v) > \hat{u}$), control must go to an investor who, in the absence of renegotiation, is particularly prone to interfere. In contrast, when $v > \hat{v}$, control must be allocated to a passive or accommodating investor (since $u^*(v) < \hat{u}$).

The investors' incentives are determined by the effect of actions C and S on the bank's future income. We make the following assumption:

A2 Action S is less risky than action C.   That is, for each u, there exists $\eta_0(u)$ such that

$$H_S(\eta \mid u) < H_C(\eta \mid u) \quad \text{if } 0 < \eta < \eta_0(u)$$

and

$$H_S(\eta \mid u) > H_C(\eta \mid u) \quad \text{if } \eta_0(u) < \eta.$$

Assumption A2 seems natural, since action S is interpreted as a reorganization, partial asset sale, or cancellation of new projects. All

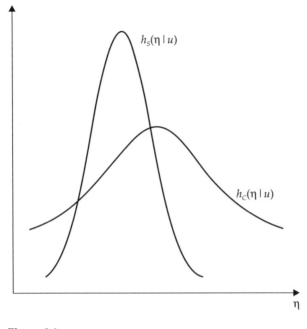

Figure 8.1
Densities

of these actions reduce the bank's risk. Figures 8.1 and 8.2 illustrate this assumption.

How can the ex ante optimal intervention policy be implemented? Let us note, first, that maximizing the bank's expected income would lead to choose action C if and only if

$$\int_0^\infty \eta \, [h_C(\eta \mid u) - h_S(\eta \mid u)] \, d\eta \geq 0,$$

or equivalently, $u \geq \hat{u}$. This ex post efficient rule can be implemented by using a single claim (100% equity).

The ex ante optimal intervention policy, however, requires allocating control to investors who do *not* maximize the bank's expected profit but rather have biased incentives. Because action C is riskier than action S, the holder of a security with a convex return

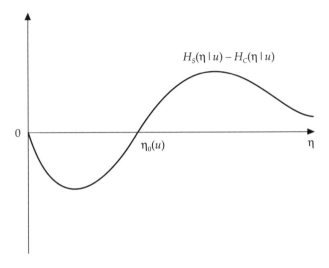

$H_S(\eta \,|\, u) - H_C(\eta \,|\, u)$

0

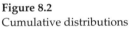

$\eta_0(u)$

η

Figure 8.2
Cumulative distributions

stream will tend to favor action C, while the holder of a security with a concave return stream will have a bias toward action S.

This reasoning suggests splitting control rights between shareholders and debtholders (whose return streams are depicted in figure 8.3). Shareholders, because of their convex return stream, should be given control when the bank's performance is satisfactory $(v \geq \hat{v})$. Debtholders or depositors,[1] who have a concave return stream, would get control in case of bad performance $(v < \hat{v})$.

Let D denote the value of deposits to be reimbursed in period 2. At date 1, v is realized, and the net debt, $D - v$, is to be reimbursed from the uncertain income η. Assuming for the moment that depositors are not insured, their incentive to choose action C over action S is

---

1. Here we do not distinguish between debtholders and depositors. We will do so later by introducing a collective action problem for depositors.

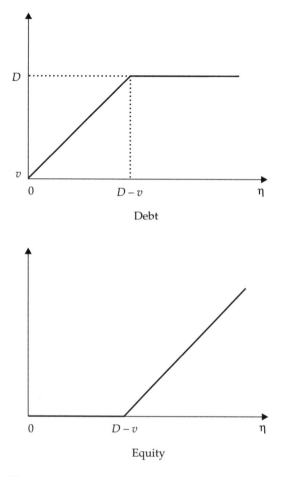

Figure 8.3
Return streams

$$\int_0^{D-v} \eta\,[h_C(\eta\,|\,u) - h_S(\eta\,|\,u)]\,d\eta$$

$$= \int_0^{D-v} [H_S(\eta\,|\,u) - H_C(\eta\,|\,u)]\,d\eta \equiv \Delta_D(D - v, u).$$

Similarly the shareholders'net gain of choosing action C rather than action S is

$$\int_{D-v}^{\infty} \eta\,[h_C(\eta\,|\,u) - h_S(\eta\,|\,u)]\,d\eta$$

$$= \int_{D-v}^{\infty} [H_S(\eta\,|\,u) - H_C(\eta\,|\,u)]\,d\eta \equiv \Delta_E(D - v, u).$$

Figures 8.4 and 8.5 confirm our previous observation that noninsured depositors have a bias in favor of action S, while shareholders tend to favor action C.[2]

Figure 8.4 further shows that the shareholders are more prone to being passive, the higher the net debt $D - v$. To see this, suppose that $\Delta_E = 0$. That is, the area above and under $H_S - H_C$ and to the right of the net debt $D - v$ is equal to zero. An increase in the net debt reduces the negative area and makes Δ_E strictly positive. So the shareholders, who initially were indifferent between the two actions, now strictly prefer action C. The intuition for this is that when the bank is poorly capitalized, shareholders will make money only if the second-period income is very high, which induces them to gamble. Similarly figure 8.5 shows that depositors are more willing to take risks, the higher the net debt $D - v$. Indeed depositors become almost like equityholders when the bank is very undercapitalized.

Assume now that control shifts from shareholders to depositors when performance v falls under the threshold $\hat{v}$. Fix the level of deposits D, and assume that all loans combined yield η, have risk

---

2. These biases refer to the choice of action by a representative claimholder (choose action C if and only if $u \geq \hat{u}$) and ignore the manager's private benefit in case of passivity.

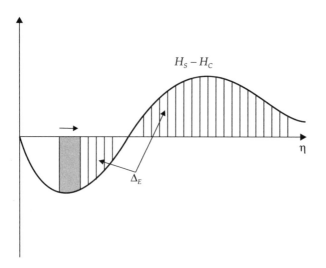

Figure 8.4
Shareholders' incentives

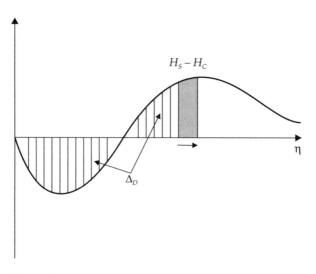

Figure 8.5
Debtholders' incentives

weight equal to 1 as in the Basle accords (while v, which is reinvested in a safe asset, has weight 0). Under historical cost accounting the bank's net worth at the end of period 1 is $\overline{E}_1 = v + \bar{\eta} - D$, where $\bar{\eta}$ is the accounting value of the principal on those loans realized in period 2. The solvency ratio is then $\overline{E}_1/\bar{\eta} = [v + \bar{\eta} - D]/\bar{\eta}$. We can then interpret

$$r^{min} = \frac{\hat{v} + \bar{\eta} - D}{\bar{\eta}}$$

as a minimum solvency ratio required for shareholders to keep control. A lower solvency implies a transfer of control to depositors (or, as we will see, to a regulator). The bank must then have a solvency ratio

$$r = \frac{v + \bar{\eta} - D}{\bar{\eta}} \geq r^{min}$$

to prevent a transfer of control to depositors.

To summarize, shareholders (or more generally any claimholder with a convex return stream) favor risk, while depositors (or more generally any claimholder with a concave return stream) are conservative. Furthermore *the shareholders' bias toward risk is stronger, the lower the bank's solvency. The depositors' bias against risk is also weaker, the lower the bank's solvency.*

Remark ("Bankers' Conservatism")
It is often argued that bankers fear risk. It is useful here to distinguish between shareholders and managers. We have noted (and it is well-known) that shareholders have an incentive to take risk. This may not hold for bank managers. Indeed managers may love risk in some circumstances and hate it at other times. The following example gives an extreme case but illustrates well the complexity of bank managers' preferences toward risk. Suppose that performance v can take one of only five values: $v_0 < v_1 < v_2 < v_3 < v_4$, that u contains no information on effort, and that action C is chosen if and

only if $v = v_2$, v_3, or v_4. Suppose that after effort is chosen but before v is realized, the manager receives a signal $\sigma \in \{\sigma_1, \sigma_2, \sigma_3\}$. If $\sigma = \sigma_i$, the manager chooses between a conservative action that guarantees v_i and a risky action with support $\{v_{i-1}, v_i, v_{i+1}\}$. Clearly the manager prefers the risky action when $\sigma = \sigma_1$, since gambling is the only way of not triggering action S for sure. In contrast, when the bank is healthier but might still have a performance triggering action S (i.e., when $\sigma = \sigma_2$), the manager is better off not taking any risk. Last, when the bank is very healthy ($\sigma = \sigma_3$), the manager is indifferent between the risky and the conservative actions; only in a richer model with some monetary incentives or more periods would this indifference be resolved. The analysis of managerial attitudes toward risk is therefore more complex than that of shareholders'. However, the focus of our argument is on claimholders' interference rather than on managers'choice of risk.

8.2   Exact Implementation

We have seen that control should go to conservative claimholders in case of bad performance ($v < \hat{v}$) and to risk-loving claimholders in case of good performance ($v > \hat{v}$). The bank's financial structure furthermore must be adjusted in order to obtain an exact implementation of the optimal policy $u^*(\cdot)$; for, the decrease in interference with better first-period performance must be continuous and occur not only at $\hat{v}$. We describe three of the several ways of implementing the optimal policy. We will return to the strengths and weaknesses of these methods in chapter 11, where we discuss in detail the adjustments defined by current regulation.

8.2.1   Composite Claims

A continuous decrease in interference with first-period performance can be obtained through composite claims made of $\beta(v)$

units of debt and $1 - \beta(v)$ shares, where $\beta(\cdot)$ is a decreasing function that, for a certain level of debt D,[3] is given by

$$\beta(v)\Delta_D(D - v, u^*(v)) + (1 - \beta(v))\Delta_E(D - v, u^*(v)) = 0.$$

The optimal policy is implemented by giving control to holders of composite claim $(\beta(v), 1 - \beta(v))$ when the performance is v. The better the first-period performance, the more "equitylike" is the controlling claim. This is meant to soften the controlling claimholders as performance improves.[4]

8.2.2   Implementation by Debt and Equity with Net Worth Adjustments

The optimal policy can alternatively be implemented with only the two standard claims, by giving control to shareholders if $v \geq \hat{v}$, and to debtholders if $v < \hat{v}$. An exact implementation of $u^*(\cdot)$ requires a net worth adjustment in each region of control, or equivalently an adjustment of net debt $D - v$ as a function of v:

1. *Shareholder control* $(v \geq \hat{v})$. To implement the optimal policy, *net debt* $D - v$ *must grow with the bank's performance*, for shareholders must be indifferent between the two actions when $u = u^*(v)$:

$$\Delta_E\left(D - v, u^*(v)\right) = 0.$$

The conclusion is then apparent from figure 8.4 which shows that an increase in net debt makes shareholders less prone to intervene.

---

3. For β to be between 0 and 1 for all v, it is necessary and sufficient that for all v, equityholders prefer C while debtholders prefer S, that is, that v "do not vary much." If this is not the case, one must adjust the debt level the way we will in subsection 8.2.2.

4. The notion that equitylike claims are softer is illustrated by the following analogy in the corporate world: Those German and Japanese banks with equity links with their borrowers tend to be softer on them than banks without such equity links (see, e.g., Goodhart 1993a).

The positive relationship between net debt and performance means that *for given levels of deposits and risky loans, the allowed ceiling on dividend distribution must grow faster than first-period performance*. This rule will be called the *multiplicative rule*. Incidentally, we should note that shareholders (as well as the manager) always favor distributing the largest possible dividend.[5] The multiplicative rule implies that a minimum solvency ratio *per se* cannot implement the optimal rule, since it implies that the dividend grows only *proportionnally* with the first-period performance. Instead, under the multiplicative rule, *the minimum solvency ratio must decrease when the bank's income increases*.

Our analysis argues firmly against lowering the minimum solvency ratio when the bank is in trouble. Indeed it is easy to see why this policy has *perverse effects*: If the solvency ratio decreases with the bank's income, a better performance results in more interference. Such a policy gives the manager exactly the wrong incentives.

2. *Debtholder control* $(v < \hat{v})$. The conclusions are the same as for shareholder control. Debtholders are more passive, the higher the level of net debt (see figure 8.5).

3. *Switch between debt and equity control* $(v = \hat{v})$. The sudden switch from equity to debt control has one drawback in this (and any other) model: At the point where control has to be transferred, avoiding discontinuity in the managerial incentive scheme $(u^*(v))$ requires discontinuity in the net debt level $D - v$. Indeed, at $v = \hat{v}$, the choice of action has to be ex post efficient $(u^*(\hat{v}) = \hat{u})$. This is possible only under an all-equity or an all-debt firm. For v tending to $\hat{v}$ *from below*, net debt $D - v$ has thus to tend to infinity (to make

---

5. In a model with more than two periods shareholders might voluntarily limit dividend distribution for fear of losing control in the future. Further, if the manager exerts a new effort after the signals are realized, investors would like to avoid excessive undercapitalization that would discourage the manager by making debtholder control unavoidable in the future (on the discouragement effect, see appendix A).

equity worthless); instead, for v tending to $\hat{v}$ *from above*, net debt $D - v$ has to tend to zero. However, as we will show in the next subsection, allowing shareholders to retain control for low v's, provided they recapitalize the bank, can eliminate such discontinuous behavior.

8.2.3 Implementation through Adjusted Voluntary Recapitalization

Now we will eliminate the discontinuity in the net debt level $D - v$ at verifiable performance $\hat{v}$ and address two other potential objections of the previous implementation method $u^*(v)$. First, in the previous section we assumed that shareholders are always willing to recapitalize the bank in bad times. For example, in the region of debtholder control ($v < \hat{v}$), the lower the v, the lower one should set $D - v$, in order to increase debtholder toughness. This may mean substantial recapitalization by shareholders, who may be reluctant to infuse money when the bank is in trouble. This section takes into account their incentives to recapitalize.

Second, until now we have assumed that each controlling party was able to implement action C or action S, and that its choices only depended on its income stream. In practice, the characteristics of the controlling party, namely its dispersed nature (small debtholders or depositors) or its limited means of action (deposit insurance with a specific mission), may limit its available options. For example, action C, while more accommodating toward management, may still require more knowledge than action S, if S simply means a sale (as a whole or in parts) which can easily be delegated. Our aim here is not to detail imperfections in the external control of banks, which we address in chapters 11 through 13. Instead we will show how exact implementation can be obtained when creditors-depositors, or their representatives, always choose action S when they are in control.

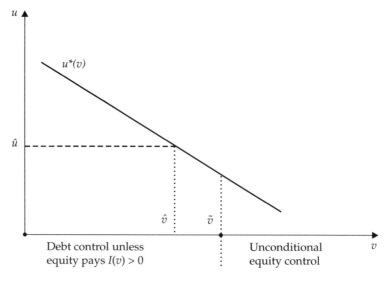

Figure 8.6
Control allocation with voluntary recapitalization

The idea of adjusted voluntary recapitalization is pictured in figures 8.6 and 8.7. Control is allocated noncontingently to shareholders (with capital adequacy ratio such that $\Delta_E(D - v, u^*(v)) = 0$, as in subsection 8.2.2) for all $v \geq \tilde{v}$, where $\tilde{v}$ is higher than $\hat{v}$. For $v < \tilde{v}$ control is allocated to debtholders *unless shareholders are willing to recapitalize the bank* by injecting $I(v)$. $I(v)$ is computed so as to equalize, when $u = u^*(v)$, the value of equity without recapitalization (with S chosen by debtholders) and the (net) value of equity with recapitalization (with C chosen by shareholders).[6] $\tilde{D}$ is the debt level computed in subsection 8.2.2 for $v = \tilde{v}$, such that $\Delta_E(\tilde{D} - \tilde{v}, u^*(\tilde{v})) = 0$. Thus, for v tending to $\tilde{v}$ from below, $I(\tilde{v})$ tends to zero, since

---

6. Specifically, $I(v)$ must satisfy

$$\int_{\tilde{D}-v}^{\infty} (\eta - \tilde{D} + v) h_S(\eta | u^*(v)) d\eta = \int_{\tilde{D}-v-I(v)}^{\infty} (\eta - \tilde{D} + v + I(v)) h_C(\eta | u^*(v)) d\eta - I(v).$$

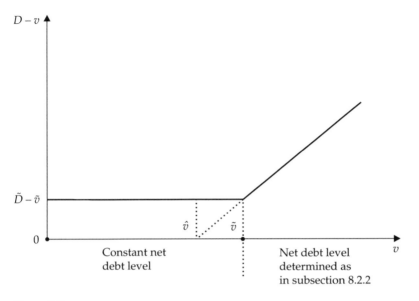

Figure 8.7
Net debt level with voluntary recapitalization

shareholders are indifferent between C and S when $v = \tilde{v}$ and $u = u^*(\tilde{v})$. Moreover, for a given $I(v)$, the incentive to pay $I(v)$ rises with u (which raises the gain to continue).[7] The definition of $I(v)$ will thus induce shareholders to recapitalize if and only if $u \geq u^*(v)$. Of course shareholders will recapitalize to choose action C instead of S. This mechanism leads to exact implementation of $u^*(v)$.

What can we say about $I(v)$? It is positive for $v < \tilde{v}$, and tends to zero for $v \to \tilde{v}$, as mentioned above. However, while continuous, it

---

7. The shareholders' net gain to injecting $I(v)$ can be rewritten

$$- \int_{\tilde{D}-v}^{\infty} [1 - H_S(\eta|u)]d\eta + \int_{\tilde{D}-v-I(v)}^{\infty} [1 - H_C(\eta|u)]d\eta - I(v)$$

or

$$\int_{\tilde{D}-v}^{\infty} [H_S(\eta|u) - H_C(\eta|u))]d\eta - \int_{\tilde{D}-v-I(v)}^{\tilde{D}-v} H_C(\eta|u)d\eta,$$

which grows with u since $(H_S - H_C)$ grows with u and H_C decreases with u.

is not necessarily monotonically decreasing in v: When v decreases, recapitalization must be more costly in order to make shareholders more reluctant to undertake it (they will undertake it only if $u \geq u^*(v)$, where $u^*(v)$ is decreasing). This does not necessarily imply a higher $I(v)$, since each dollar of recapitalization is *more expensive* for shareholders when the bank is less capitalized and thus has a higher probability of being insolvent at the end of period 2.

9

Relative Solvency Ratios, Securitization, and Market Value Accounting

An important observation of agency theory is that managerial incentive schemes should be based on accurate information about managers' performance. The incentive scheme should not depend on random events that are not controlled by the manager but should reflect a "sufficient statistic" of performance.[1] This is a straightforward idea that has significant implications for important topics such as relative solvency ratios, securitization and market value accounting. The policy debate on these topics is often confused, and therefore it is useful to analyze these implications in detail. The common thread of our analysis will be the need to adjust the implementation derived in chapter 8 to insulate the manager from irrelevant random events.

9.1   Relative Solvency Ratios

9.1.1   Controllable and Exogenous Risks

The issue of whether the minimum solvency ratio of a bank should be adjusted to reflect the solvency of other banks has given rise to one of the most important banking policy debates. At one extremity of the policy spectrum, the Basle accords look at each bank in

---

1. See Holmström (1979) and Shavell (1979).

isolation and define minimum solvency requirements that are independent of the solvency of other banks. In contrast, banking authorities sometimes lower the net worth requirements in recessions. A case in point is the strong reduction in capital requirements during the early years of the S&L crisis (see chapter 4). As is usual, this regulatory change can be interpreted either as efficiency enhancing or as stemming from political economy considerations. The political economy approach ascribes the loosening of capital requirements to some intrinsic weakness of the regulatory process, and perhaps to regulatory capture by the banking industry. We will return to this issue in chapter 12. The efficiency approach, on the other hand, considers the regulatory response to the S&L crisis as an attempt to prevent a credit crunch, or else as an ingenious application of "yardstick competition" or "relative performance evaluation." On these two grounds advocates of relative ratios argue for a solvency requirement that covaries positively with the health of the banking sector. In this book we will have little to say about macroeconomic aspects and therefore about the credit crunch,[2] but we will offer some insights on relative performance evaluation.

Let us recall that banks face idiosyncratic (controllable) as well as aggregate (industrywide, exogenous) shocks. Real estate conditions, variations in interest rates, or economic and political evolutions of debtor countries, for example, affect all banks who have had an opportunity to invest in corresponding markets. In the presence of aggregate shocks, a bank manager's incentive structure can be improved upon by comparing the solvency of his or her bank with that of other banks facing similar opportunities for assets and liabilities. In the same way that managers of nonfinancial firms are often rewarded (positively) with their firms' profits and (nega-

---

2. See, for example, Holmström-Tirole (1994). A credit crunch is defined by a shortage of loanable funds by intermediaries (due in turn to insufficient capital in these intermediaries).

tively) with industry profits, the allocation of the residual rights of control over a bank, which affect its managers' incentives, can be tied to the solvency of other banks.

While ideas related to relative performance evaluation are well established in economic theory, they do not seem to have made their way into the banking policy debate. In our view, advocates of a relative ratio have drawn an erroneous conclusion from a correct idea. That a bank manager should indeed be isolated from exogenous (aggregate) shocks does not warrant the use of a relative ratio. In fact our model partially supports the "isolationist" position, implying that the minimum capital ratio of a bank should not depend on the performance of other banks. A minimum capital ratio independent of aggregate shocks means that shareholders can distribute dividends that vary one for one with this shock. This adjustment *isolates* management from any change of outsider behavior due to these shocks. In contrast, indexing minimum capital ratios on these shocks means the manager will face excessive interventionism under positive aggregate shocks and excessive passivity (as in the S&L case) under negative aggregate shocks. To be sure, the isolationist position reaches its limits when shareholders become reluctant to recapitalize. A transfer of control to debtholders may then excessively penalize management. For this reason we suggest "subsidized" recapitalization for big negative shocks.

As an illustration, suppose that the minimum solvency ratio is equal to 8% in the absence of aggregate shock and that an aggregate shock lowers the solvency ratio of all banks by 6%. A bank that in the absence of aggregate shock would have reached a solvency ratio equal to 8.5% now has a ratio of 2.5%. An absolute ratio would then give control to depositors (or their representative), implying more interference than management deserves. It is therefore worth lowering the minimum solvency ratio by 6% to reflect industry conditions and thus leave control with shareholders. Yet, in the absence of recapitalization (note that shareholders have no incentive to re-capitalize as long as the minimum ratio is 2%), shareholders have a strong incentive to take risk (see chapter 8). Absolute and relative ratio rules thus have opposite flaws: In the event of a banking reces-sion a relative ratio rule leads to gambling for resurrection, while an absolute ratio rule encourages excessive conservatism. To comple-ment the relative ratio rule, recapitalization must occur at the 8% level. More generally, *the bank should be required to recapitalize by an amount contingent on the average profitability of banks facing similar op-portunities.* We now make this reasoning more formal.

9.1.2 Relative Performance Evaluation Does Not Imply a Relative Ratio

For simplicity, let us assume that the aggregate shock affects only v, and not u. Suppose that bank i's verifiable first-period performance v_i can be decomposed into an aggregate shock v^A and an idiosyn-cratic shock v_i^I:

$$v_i = v^A + v_i^I. \tag{9}$$

Let $F^A(\cdot)$ denote the cumulative distribution of v^A, and $\bar{F}^I$ and $\underline{F}^I$ denote those of v_i^I when effort is high and low. By definition, man-agerial effort affects the idiosyncratic shock and not the aggregate one. Therefore the manager's utility in an optimal incentive scheme should depend on v_i^I, but not on v^A. But the bank's accounting only reveals the sum of the two, namely the first-period performance v_i. To infer v_i^I, we compute v^A using the first-period performance of similar banks. Let us assume that there are a large number of ex ante identical banks (e.g., they have the same balance sheet structure). Let $av(v_j)$ denote the average performance in the banking industry. And let $v^I = \int v_i^I d\bar{F}^I(v_i^I)$ denote the expectation of the idiosyncratic shock for a high effort. We have

$$v^A = av(v_j) - v^I.$$

The realization of v_i^I can thus be inferred from available data:

$$v_i^I = [v_i - av(v_j)] + v^I. \tag{10}$$

We can now apply the analysis of chapter 7 by simply replacing $u^*(v)$ by $u^*(v_i^I)$![3] This guarantees that the manager is not rewarded (punished) for a positive (negative) aggregate shock.

So far we have concurred with the advocates of relative ratios. Our point of departure from their reasoning relates to implementation. How can one implement the rule defined by $u^*(v_i^I)$? Let us first consider noncontingent control for a given $v = v_i^I$: As in subsection 8.2.2, we would allocate control to shareholders when $v_i^I \geq \hat{v}$ and to debtholders for $v_i^I < \hat{v}$. For the sake of brevity, let us focus on the case where shareholders have control.

We now show that while implementing $u^*(v_i^I)$ requires using *relative ratios* for the *allocation of control*, the *minimum solvency ratio* must remain the same *in absolute terms* in order to avoid perverse incentives. Subsection 8.2.2 showed that a deposit ceiling $D(v)$ should be selected for each first-period performance v, so as to make shareholders indifferent between intervening and being passive when $v_i^I = v$ and $u = u^*(v)$:

$$\Delta_E(D - v, u^*(v)) = 0.$$

The manager is isolated from the aggregate shock v^A if debt reacts to this aggregate shock in the following way:

$$D(v^A) = D + v^A = D + [av(v_j) - v^I], \tag{11}$$

that is, if *the bank's net debt grows one for one with the average income of other banks*. Note that (11) can be implemented by letting the bank

---

3. The new curve $u^*(\cdot)$ is obtained by replacing the densities $\bar{f}$ and $\underline{f}$ by the densities $\bar{f}^I$ and $\underline{f}^I$ corresponding to the cumulative distributions $\bar{F}^I$ and $\underline{F}^I$.

distribute *dividends equal* (up to a constant) *to industry performance* (these dividends may be positive or negative, in which case recapitalization occurs).

Let us consider again the relative solvency ratio debate. As in chapter 8, let $\bar{\eta}$ denote the accounting value of loans maturing at date 2 according to generally accepted accounting principles. Bank i's solvency ratio is then independent of v^A:

$$r_i = \frac{v_i + \bar{\eta} - (D + v^A)}{\bar{\eta}} = \frac{v_i^l + \bar{\eta} - D}{\bar{\eta}}.$$

Yet, in the absence of an adjustment in the bank's net worth, shareholders' incentives in general are not optimal as v^A varies. Their preference ordering between the two actions depends on net debt and therefore on v^A. Ceteris paribus, interference occurs too often when the banking industry is doing well (high v^A), and there is too much gambling in recession times (low v^A). Aggregate shocks thus influence decision making.

Our argument then is that relative performance evaluation should apply, but not in the form of a relative solvency ratio. Indexing the minimum solvency ratio on industry performance preserves an adequate allocation of control rights; it has, however, no effect on the controlling party's behavior. The controlling party, for instance, will often gamble in banking recessions. A *dividend distribution (or a recapitalization) indexed on industry performance* restores proper incentives.

In our discussion we have assumed that the distribution of dividends or recapitalization can be imposed to the bank or its shareholders. While limits on dividends are realistic, forced recapitalization is less so. Shareholders will recapitalize only if they find it profitable to do so. This argument leads us to qualify our conclusions above for *very negative shocks*. Let us thus come back to the implementation scheme described in subsection 8.2.3, where for v very negative, shareholders must choose between action S, implemented by debtholders, and action C, that they can "buy" by injecting $I(v)$ into the bank. This recapitalization is supposed to be more costly for lower v's, in order to discipline management through a higher $u^*(v)$. This implies that *one should reduce $I(v)$ when v is low because of an aggregate shock.*

On the other hand, completely offsetting the aggregate shock, through a recapitalization requirement $I(v_i^I)$ would not be appropriate: A change in v^A changes shareholders' incentive to recapitalize, and it may be optimal to reduce $I(v_i^I)$ when v^A is very negative: The first dollars of recapitalization go with a very high probability to debtholders, since the bank will then quite probably be insolvent in period 2. It may thus be optimal to "subsidize" recapitalization, for example, through pro-cyclical deposit insurance premiums.[4] We should, however, point out that cyclical (proportional) deposit insurance premiums distort the bank's choice of level of deposits (see chapter 13 for a study of the effect of insurance premiums on deposits). An alternative support can be provided by monetary policy.

9.1.3   Addressing Some Potential Concerns

Some readers may wonder about the *applicability* of relative performance evaluation ideas in prudential regulation. Except for the issue that to be comparable, banks must have similar balance and off-balance activities, we see no serious obstacle to the implementation of these ideas. Indeed some of these ideas have filtered into the corporate world where managerial performance seems to be assessed on a relative as well as absolute basis. But, more to the point, comparative assessment has already made its way into the prudential arena. In the United States the Federal Reserve Board and the

---

4. The cycle is that of the banking industry and obviously does not need to coincide with the economic cycle.

Office of the Controller of the Currency screens banks on the basis of peer groups. They use their early warning systems[5] to identify banks at the bottom of a group. They also separate multinational, regional, and community banks, since they engage in different activities and face different diversification opportunities.

A potentially serious concern about the views expressed in this section concerns the *definition of a peer group*. To put the matter simply, why should bank managers be insulated from shocks that they can avoid? For instance, why should banks that wrongly entered a collapsing real estate market not bear the cost of their mistakes?

In fact this issue of bank foresight relates to the implementation of our reasoning, though not to its conceptual foundations. In the framework of the previous subsection, a bank manager who correctly foresees a negative aggregate shock (v^A) on the real estate market and invests instead in, say, a higher-yield safe asset, is rewarded as the government's effort to help the banks is independent of the bank's actual performance. A bank that escapes the real estate crash therefore gets ahead of the others.

In our conceptual framework a peer group should be defined *ex ante* as a group of banks with roughly the same opportunity set for investments and liabilities, and not *ex post* as the group of banks with similar realized balance sheets. Let us return to the real estate example to illustrate this distinction. Suppose that half of the banks foolishly invest in the real estate market, while the more clever half shy away from it. The ex ante approach lumps both subgroups into a single one. Clever banks are rewarded for their wise decision, and foolish ones are punished. In contrast, an ex post definition based on the realized balance sheets leads to a decomposition into two peer groups. For example, a bank that has invested in real estate is not penalized because it is compared only to banks that have made

---

5. See subsection 3.3.1.

the same mistake. Similarly banks that have stayed away from that market are not rewarded.

So, while there is no issue with the foundations, the implementation should ignore the convenient concept of peer group based on realized balance sheets and focus on the practically less attractive concept of peer group based on ex ante opportunity sets. The practical question is then: How large should the ex ante comparison group be, given that banks' opportunity sets may differ? This is obviously a difficult issue, but we should point out that it is a very general one that transcends the problem posed here. The issue surfaces in the most basic prudential rules: Why should all banks be subjected to a uniform 8% capital requirement or to the same risk weights? Such uniformity is firmly justified only if all banks start from similar conditions and face similar investment opportunities.[6]

9.2   Securitization

Securitization has developed in the late 1970s in the United States. At the end of 1992, 55% of mortgages, 3% of automobile loans, 27% of credit card receivables, and 5% of other consumption loans were securitized.[7] Securitization means that the bank sells its assets, either one by one or, more frequently, as a package (pool).[8] Whether the asset sold by the bank becomes a liquid security on an active

---

6. Absent such uniformity, economic theory pleads for the design of *menus* of regulatory rules, in which each individual bank selects a rule in an incentive compatible manner (see section 5.5).

7. *Les Echos*, March 1, 1993, pp. 20–21. Securitization is a more recent phenomenon in most countries. For instance, the securitization of bank loans was introduced by the December 23, 1988, law in France.

8. The mechanics of securitization are described, for example, in the Basle Committee on Banking Supervision (1992, ch. 9), Berger-Udell (1993), Bryan (1988), Gorton-Pennacchi (1993a), Norton-Spellman (1991), and Pennacchi (1988). In a typical securitization operation the bank sells the assets to a special purpose corporation or trust, which then issues marketable securities backed by the pooled assets. There are at least two important characteristics to note here:

market or whether it is simply sold to another economic agent will prove irrelevant for our purpose. We will therefore use "securitization" in both contexts and will focus on the effect of the deletion of the asset in the bank's balance sheet. We will further assume that the bank indeed sells the asset and thereby obtains perfect insurance with respect to the asset's future yields (sale "without recourse"), a sine qua non condition for the asset to be removed from the balance sheet. We will not be interested in "false securitization," in which the originator (the bank) explicitly or implicitly guarantees the buyer against asset risk (sale "with recourse"); the bank then still bears the risk even if it is no longer entitled to the asset's principal, which it traded against cash, and one can hardly view the transaction as one of "securitization."

Securitization is attractive to shareholders and managers of a bank when the Cooke ratio becomes binding. It allows the bank to increase its solvency ratio by transforming into cash a risky asset that requires partial backing by equity. The key issue is then whether securitization provides proper incentives to bank managers. To study this, recall that securitization is a form of insurance. Providing managers with insurance is optimal when the underlying risk is not controlled by the managers, but in general this policy is not optimal when it destroys a measure of managers' performance.

First, securitized assets typically are high-quality assets (mortgages, credit card receivables, etc.). Despite a sharp growth in loan sales in the 1980s, loan sales still represent a small volume (e.g., $35 billion out of $4.4 trillion of loans in 1986; see Bryan 1988). Further most loans are sold with recourse (i.e., not really sold), and those sold without recourse are often loans to high-grade corporations (i.e., very liquid assets in the first place); see Bryan (1988).

Second, credit enhancement at the date of securitization (which often coincides with or follows shortly after the loan's origination) is pervasive. Three parties are concerned with the quality of the new securities: the originator, who may keep some of the risk of the loans (sales with recourse), a rating agency, and a credit enhancer (another institution such as a bank or an insurance company or often the government). The corresponding guarantees or certification substantially enhance the liquidity of the assets.

Assume, for simplicity, that there is a single asset maturing at date 1. In this section only, we will let w denote the first-period income. We decompose the noise on first-period performance into two parts:

$$w = v + \epsilon$$

(Our discussion applies more generally to other periods' incomes.) As earlier, the effort choice stochastically determines the expected income v. [The density of v is $\bar{f}(v)$ if effort is $\bar{e}$ and $f(v)$ if effort is $\underline{e}$.] The first-period income also depends on some exogenous noise ϵ. This noise may be macroeconomic noise (unanticipated changes in interest or exchange rates, or evolution of the economy, industry, or region) or asset specific (death of a borrower's manager, court decision on a product liability suit or on the protection of a patent).

The second noise is independent of effort and should have no effect on the manager's utility. We consider two timings for the resolution of the noise: The noise can be learned before the first-period income (early noise) or simultaneously (late noise). So the two first-period timings are

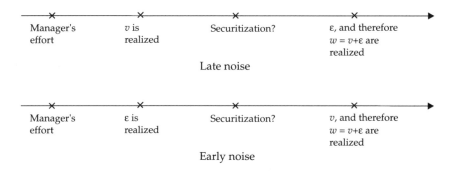

In the case of late noise, the market quickly learns the quality of the bank's loan. This is a reasonable description when the bank's initial acquisition of information on the quality of the loan boils down to a short-term forecast, while long-term evolution is hard to

analyze.[9] An illustration might be mortgage loans (which are heavily securitized in practice), whose long-term evolution follows those of the local economy and of interest rates.[10] The case of early noise is meant to depict situations in which the quality of the loan is (partially) revealed only in the long term, so many exogenous events may occur in the meantime. For example, a bank lends to a firm for a long-term R&D project which (maybe) will pay off ten years from now; the quality of the loan will be (imperfectly) revealed only in ten years when the innovation may occur. In-between exogenous information about the development of rival technologies or on macroeconomic variables affecting the demand for the innovation will accrue.

• The case of *late noise* is the ideal case for securitization. It creates an early measure of managerial performance that is not yet garbled by future noise. Indeed the balance sheet records the asset's market price v in case of securitization, and $w = v + \epsilon$ in the absence of securitization. Securitization thus raises the informational value of income.

• In contrast, the case of *early noise* illustrates what can go wrong with securitization. Here the sale price is equal to the market's assessment v^e of the asset's expected value (whatever this assessment is) plus the realization of ϵ. This has two unfortunate consequences. The first is unavoidable and would exist even in the absence of securitization: The bank's balance sheet is affected by the exogenous noise ϵ. The second is created by securitization. Because the sale

---

9. Introduce subperiods τ of period 1. Suppose that the yield d_τ of the asset follows a first-order Markov process. The yield d_τ is realized at date τ; its process is defined by distribution $H_\tau(d_{\tau+1}|d_\tau)$. The quality of the asset is then measured by the accuracy of the bank's estimate of the first parameter d_0 when the bank commits the principal (e.g., in subperiod 0).

10. Here we should distinguish between these shocks and the risk of borrower default. Default risk is much more dependent on the bank's monitoring activity and is not always revealed in the short run.

price is independent of the quality of the asset, the manager has no incentive to exert effort (at least as far as the first period is concerned.) The asset therefore should not be securitized.[11] A better way of isolating the manager from exogenous shocks such as interest rate shocks is to trade swaps (as long as they do not involve substantial credit risks). Market value accounting may also be useful in this respect, and it is studied next.

9.3   Historical Cost or Market Value Accounting?

Capital requirements confer an important role to accounting methods. It is therefore not surprising that banks and regulators pay much attention to accounting practices. For instance, some proposals for accounting reform simply aim at disguising bank insolvencies, as the accounting reforms for the S&Ls in the early 1980s illustrate (see chapter 4.) Another example is provided by the creation of foreign bank subsidiaries that are endowed with shaky loans (whose accounting value exceeds their real value) when accounts are not consolidated to compute the Cooke ratio. For some observers, another recent example is the proposal (backed by the banking industry) of splitting nonperforming loans into a bad part to be written off and a good part whose payments would, contrary to accepted accounting rules, be reported as income (loan splitting).

Many economists (e.g., Kane 1989; Benston 1991; Mishkin 1992b; White 1991) endorse market value accounting on the correct premise that it produces a more accurate measure of the assets and liabilities of a bank than does historical cost accounting. Another advantage of market value accounting is to reduce the scope for

---

11. Alternatively, the bank could sell the asset but remain residual claimant for its gains and losses. This would reintroduce (up to a constant) the realization of v into the balance sheet, and thus boost managerial incentives. But, as we have already noted, this boils down to not securitizing.

gains trading (see section 10.2). Yet none of the banking reforms introduces market value accounting.[12]

Before assessing the merits of market value accounting, let us recall that its feasibility depends on the nature of the asset. The effect of interest rate changes on some items in the asset or liability sides of the balance sheet are simple to compute. In contrast, it is hard to mark some illiquid loans to market (see section 10.1.). One must then rely on manipulable estimates of market value by the bank or the regulator.[13] Indeed it does not suffice to put up an asset for sale to obtain a reliable estimate of its true value. First, it must be the case that the bank really intends to sell the asset for potential acquirers to have an incentive to obtain information about asset value. But a sale may be inefficient. Second, adverse selection may imply that such illiquid long-term assets are undervalued by the market. This may induce the bank not to invest in such assets and thus to shy away from their liquidity transformation role (O'Hara 1991).[14]

To study the choice between the two accounting rules, suppose that the second-period income is equal to $\eta + \epsilon$, where η is a random variable whose distribution depends on signal u (itself dependent on effort) and ϵ is some noise on second-period income realized in period 1. To make the best case for market value accounting, we assume that the noise ϵ is perfectly measured in period 1. Ignoring for simplicity signal u (which can be easily reintroduced), one can compare the balance sheets under the two accounting rules:

---

12. The 1991 Treasury plan suggests reporting market values, but only in a supplementary balance sheet. The Australian Accounting Research Foundation however offered in 1993 to apply market value accounting on both sides of the balance sheet of a bank (see Hogan 1993.) The exception to historical cost accounting in current regulations concerns the securities "intended for quick turnover," and which are put in a "trading book" valued at market prices.

13. See Berger et al. (1991) on the challenges of market value accounting and on ways to get approximations to true market values.

14. See Lucas-Mc Donald (1987) for a description of the lemons problem in a banking context.

Assets	Liabilities
$v + \epsilon$	D
$\bar{\eta}$	E

$$r = \frac{v + \epsilon + \bar{\eta} - D}{\bar{\eta}}$$

Market value

Assets	Liabilities
v	D
$\bar{\eta}$	E

$$r = \frac{v + \bar{\eta} - D}{\bar{\eta}}$$

Historical cost

The drawback of market value accounting is apparent: The bank's solvency measure, and therefore the allocation of control, is sensitive to the noise. For instance, with a negative shock ϵ, control may unduly be transferred to creditors (or to their representative, the regulator). This indeed reflects the bankers' traditional suspicion toward market value accounting: The Cooke ratio would plummet, and in difficult times perhaps become negative. Of course, the incorrect allocation of control might countervail another effect of the noise. As chapter 8 showed, an increase (decrease) in the bank's net worth makes the controlling party (shareholders, creditors) more conservative (more risk loving). It may thus be the case that an improper transfer of control to creditors be partially offset by risk-taking behavior on their part.

We should not, however, be deceived by the isolation of the bank's balance sheet from the noise ϵ under *historical cost* accounting. While this accounting rule insulates the allocation of the control right from the noise, it does not consider the altered incentives of the controlling party. Indeed a positive (negative) shock makes the controlling party more conservative (risk taking.) Ideally the incentives of the controlling party should not be affected by the noise.

To sum up, historical cost accounting induces too much conservatism (risk taking) when a positive (negative) shock occurs. Market value accounting tends to yield the opposite bias, although the conclusions are more ambiguous. This effect is clearly analogous to that discussed in relation to relative solvency ratios in section 9.1.

Historical cost accounting is similar to the relative ratio rule in that both insulate the allocation of control from exogenous noise but take no account of the fact that this noise changes the bank's solvency and therefore the claimholders' incentives. Market value accounting resembles the absolute ratio rule in that the allocation of control improperly depends on exogenous noise in both cases.

As in our discussion of the relative solvency ratio, we are led to an intermediate position consisting in neutralizing the effect of the exogenous noise. The idea is to follow market value accounting in recognizing the noise in the balance sheet while requiring a recapitalization (in case of negative shock) equal to the corresponding accounting adjustment, possibly with a subsidy to avoid extensive toughness for managers.

We thus favor market value accounting if it goes together with a real, and not only accounting, net worth adjustment.[15] Last, this idea applies only to adjustments of the balance sheet to changes in exogenous variables. The manager should of course not be insulated from the consequences of his or her own performance, good or bad.

---

15. Market value accounting cum a solvency requirement, as in the Basle accords, is in this spirit. See chapter 11 for an analysis of the regulation defined by the Basle accords.

10 Manipulating Performance Measures and Gains Trading

Thus far we have assumed that the first-period performance v cannot be altered by the manager for a given level of effort. In practice, asset purchases and sales or the management of commercial loans affect this measure of performance. The manager who is concerned by possible interference has the incentive to reach a good performance level. He or she may want to sell undervalued assets—that is, assets with a market price in excess of their accounting value—even when it would be profitable for the bank to keep those assets. Similarly the bank may want to demand the payment of a loan even if this hurts the borrower, rather than reschedule reimbursements. Conversely, the bank may keep overvalued assets, even if these assets could be better managed outside the bank; it may also grant new loans to an illiquid borrower in order not to recognize losses, hoping that the external auditor and the regulator will not force it to make corresponding specific reserves and provisions. This practice is called *gains trading*. Before studying it, we analyze the costs and benefits of portfolio management.

10.1 Portfolio Management, Liquidity, and Securitization

Many bank assets (and even more assets of nonfinancial companies) are illiquid. But what is illiquidity? After all, any asset can be sold rapidly provided that its price is sufficiently low. One possible measure of the illiquidity of an asset is the difference between the expected monetary value of the asset when kept by the bank and the expected price in case of sale. An asset is liquid if this "discount" is small. Treasury bonds, for instance, are liquid. A commercial loan usually is not. Besides brokerage costs and taxes, there are at least three factors of illiquidity:

1. *An asset is best managed by its initial owner.* We already noted that banks have private information about their borrowers. The issuing bank therefore may be better equipped to manage the future relationship with the borrower than other financial institutions that would acquire the loan. The corresponding discount of course would not exist if at the date of the sale the issuing bank could cheaply and clearly describe all pieces of information that may shed light on the future relationship. But this information transfer is generally costly and hard to contract on. To be sure, the bank could sell the asset but keep managing it thereafter. Yet this arrangement creates moral hazard. The bank has low incentive to manage the asset properly unless it receives a substantial share of the corresponding profits. In the latter case, however, one can hardly describe the transaction as a sale.

2. *Buyers are concerned about adverse selection.* The bank's private information has other implications. The bank has an incentive to sell those assets that it alone knows to have poor prospects and to keep assets that it believes will do well. Since buyers are aware of this incentive, the trading volume is likely to be suboptimal. In fact, when the potential buyers know that the bank values the sale at the purchase price (there is no other incentive to sell), the bank ends up not selling any asset. This is Akerlof's (1970) famous "lemons problem," which has often been studied in financial economics (e.g., by Myers and Majluf 1984 to explain why share offerings lead to a fall

in the stock price). Let us also note that the issuing bank as well may be concerned by the potential buyers' private information. Such buyers may have inside information about, say, the future of the borrower's industry or even the borrower. The bank may then be reluctant to sell the asset.

3. *Seller faces monopsony power.* The number of potential buyers of an asset is often limited by the cost of acquiring information about the asset. The uninformed buyers, on the other hand, fear the winner's curse, for they infer that their purchasing the asset signals a lack of interest from informed buyers and therefore low prospects. This implies that informed buyers have monopsony power and that the bank, even if it has no private information, cannot sell the asset at an expected price equal to the ex ante value of the asset.[1]

Despite these costs the bank may still want to sell assets. On the one hand, prudential regulation and in particular minimal net worth requirements provide the banks with an incentive to sell risky assets when they do not meet these capital adequacy requirements. This explains a fair share of sales by financial intermediaries. We, however, do not want to take this motivation for asset sale for granted since the design of the regulatory environment is endogenous in our approach. On the other hand, it is often hard to assess the true value of bank assets without creating a market for them. Measuring this value is central to designing proper managerial reward schemes. This is particularly clear when the payment or default on loans occurs past the tenure of the manager who issued those loans. The lack of accounting measurement of the value of such loans prevents performance-based managerial rewards. Even if the profitability of the loans is measured during the tenure of

---

1. See, for example, Harstad (1991).

the manager who issued the loans, it may be useful to obtain intermediate measures of the value of the loans that are not garbled by future noise.[2]

The discussion above focused on asset *sales* to third parties. The decision to simply terminate a commercial relationship with a borrower would not exhibit the information costs described above. In this case the cost would be the loss of future gains from trade with the borrower; the gain would relate to potential savings in nonprofitable loans. Although the conceptual issues differ somewhat from those for sales, there are a number of similarities in terms of portfolio management.

10.2   Gains Trading

A complete analysis of gains trading is beyond the scope of this book. We look at a stylized example based on the idea that some assets are best managed by the bank while some others ought to be sold, in order to illustrate some of the main features of gains trading. In this example, which is further developed in appendix B, the bank makes short-term (maturing in period 1) and long-term (maturing in period 2) loans. The manager learns at the end of period 1 the two characteristics of each long-term loan: its current sale or liquidation value ℓ and its appreciation potential a relative to this liquidation value if the asset is kept within the bank. We allow the bank to be a better or poorer manager of a particular loan than potential buyers. The manager is instructed to divest some (optimal or nonoptimal) fraction of the long-term assets at date 1.

Suppose, first, that there is a single controlling party, who is residual claimant for the bank's profit (equity without debt, i.e., *100%*

---

2. This is the same argument as that according to which the sequence of profits of a firm is not a sufficient statistic for the performance of its manager, which provides informational value for the stock market (Holmström-Tirole 1993).

equity). The manager then sells those assets whose appreciation potential lies below some cutoff value. There is *no gains trading* in that the sunk capital gains or losses on assets do not affect the decision of whether to liquidate them. As we showed in chapter 8, 100% equity banks are however not optimal because then the nature of interference by claimholders is not affected by the current performance of the bank. Instead, we saw that more interference should follow bad current performance. As a result the bank's manager will want to inflate the first-period performance, namely the yield on short-term loans plus the revenue on liquidated long-term assets. *To reach a good performance and thus induce the controlling party to be passive, the manager must depart from the maximization of expected future profits in portfolio management. The manager will want to sell assets with a high market price (the "crown jewels") to the detriment of other, lower-value assets that otherwise should be divested.*

IV

Picking a Regulatory Framework

11   Analysis of the Basle Accords

We now apply our conceptual framework to examine the incentive properties of the international prudential standards. The Basle accords, in line with most regulatory practice, view the government as the representative of small depositors. Yet the government, unlike a large creditor such as a bank, has little discretion. In this chapter we make no attempt at deriving foundations for limited discretion but rather take the regulation as given and analyze its implications. In the next chapter we will discuss the political economy of discretionary regulation.

As we noted in chapter 3, the Basle accords link risk taking and equity level. In the final section of this chapter we will consider the impact of this link by an analysis that endogenizes the amount of risky assets.

11.1   The Basle Voluntary Recapitalization Scheme

The main elements of the Basle accords can be summarized as follows within the context of our model:

1. The bank must hold capital up to at least 8% of its risk-weighted assets.

2. When performance causes capital to fall below this ratio, shareholders can retain control provided that they bring the bank back to at least 8% through recapitalization.

3. If they fail to do so, the public representative (the regulatory agency) will sell or liquidate the bank.

4. The degree of expropriation of equity when sales or liquidation proceeds exceed the value of the deposits of the bank is left unspecified (or "open") in the accords.

5. Idiosyncratic and aggregate shocks are not distinguished in the accords.

In this section we will compare the Basle accords with the benchmark case of optimal voluntary recapitalization developed in subsection 8.2.3.

11.1.1   Risk Weighting

We are interested in the level of equity just before the choice of action C or S, that is, after v has been realized. At that time, v is a *safe* asset, while η is a risky asset with expected value $\bar{\eta}$. The Basle regulation requires that

$$r^{\min} \leq \frac{E}{\bar{\eta}} = \frac{v + \bar{\eta} - D}{\bar{\eta}} = \frac{\bar{\eta} - (D - v)}{\bar{\eta}}.$$

Consequently only "net debt" $D - v$ matters, which, as noted earlier, is optimal. Equity is needed only as a protection for that part of deposits that is at risk because it is unbacked by safe assets.

In practice, risk weighting is more complex; its limitations cannot be addressed in a model with a single risky asset. In section 11.3, however, we will look at changes in the level and composition of η.

11.1.2   Constant Capital Requirement

To keep the Basle regulation as close as possible to subsection 8.2.3, we will assume (1) the absence of macroeconomic shocks, (2) no expropriation of equity even when the bank violates its capital requirement and shareholders refuse to recapitalize, and (3) "sale" or "liquidation" by the depositors' representative amounting to action S. We will relax these assumptions in turn in the following subsections. With these assumptions, we introduce only one difference between the Basle regulation and subsection 8.2.3, and that is the requirement of *constant net debt* $D - v$, which has different consequences for low and high v's.

1. For high v's each additional increase in v can be fully distributed as dividends. Net debt $D - v$ and the shareholders' preferences between actions S and C are unchanged when v grows. Recall that subsection 8.2.3 had instead a *multiplicative rule*, allowing $D - v$ to *grow* with v, in order to reward the manager for a higher v. In this model then shareholders have no incentive to recapitalize beyond the minimum capital ratio. Any extra dollar contributed to the bank goes to the deposit insurance corporation with a probability equal to the probability of bankruptcy. Recapitalization is therefore always costly for shareholders and will always be minimal. (In practice, shareholders may want to go beyond the minimum solvency ratio to appeal to noninsured investors such as subordinate debtholders or partners in swaps.[1])

2. For low v's each additional cut in v has to be *fully* compensated by an equivalent recapitalization if shareholders want to retain control. The lower the v, the higher must be the recapitalization, and the more reluctant will be shareholders to accept it.[2] Managers thus

---

1. Some banks such as J.P. Morgan and Deutsche Bank exceed their solvency requirements and have very good ratings. Sometimes financial intermediaries such as Merrill Lynch create subsidiaries that specialize in swaps and are much better capitalized than the parent company (see, e.g., *The Economist*, February 13, 1993, p. 80).

2. Recapitalization takes place at a time where η is not yet realized and is thus accounted for as its expectation $\bar{\eta}$. Recapitalization is necessary if $(v + \bar{\eta} - D)/\bar{\eta} < r^{min}$, and it must exceed a level I given by $(v + \bar{\eta} - D + I)/\bar{\eta} = r^{min}$, or $I = D - v - \bar{\eta}(1 - r^{min})$. Without expropriation shareholders recapitalize only if they prefer C over S. If they do recapitalize, their payoff is

face a higher probability of action S for lower $v's$, as shown in figure 11.1.

In figure 11.1 the cutoff rule $\tilde{u}(v)$ can never coincide exactly with the optimal scheme $u^*(v)$ depicted in figure 7.1, which depends on the precise parameters facing the bank. Here u^0, which is chosen when shareholders are at the capital ratio r^{min}, is optimal only for one single level of v. The qualitative feature of figure 11.1 we want to stress is that its cutoff schedule $\tilde{u}(v)$ is downward sloping when the bank falls below r^{min} before recapitalization, and horizontal otherwise.

A regulation based on voluntary recapitalization thus yields more interference with poorer performance ($\tilde{u}$ is downward sloping), but above a certain threshold the shareholders' decision is independent of the first-period performance. All incentives are provided by the threat of liquidation and not by that of shareholder interference.

We observed in chapter 8 that the balance sheet cannot be left to evolve naturally with the bank's income, since a higher income makes shareholders more prone to interfere. The manager may then be punished for a good performance and rewarded for a bad one. The idea of dividend distribution for a good performance and of recapitalization for a bad one in order to eliminate this perverse effect

$$\tilde{\Delta}_E = \int_{D-v-I}^{\infty} (v + \eta - D + I)h_C(\eta|u)d\eta - I$$

$$= \int_{\bar{\eta}(1-r^{min})}^{\infty} [1 - H_C(\eta|u)]d\eta - [D - v - \bar{\eta}(1 - r^{min})].$$

Their net gain to recapitalize is thus

$$\tilde{\tilde{\Delta}}_E = \tilde{\Delta}_E - \int_{D-v}^{\infty} [1 - H_S(\eta|u)]d\eta.$$

Since $\partial\tilde{\tilde{\Delta}}_E/\partial v = H_S(D - v|u) > 0$, the lower the v, the higher will be the reluctance to recapitalize, and since $\partial\tilde{\Delta}_E/\partial u = \int_{D-v-I}^{D-v}(-\partial H_C/\partial u)d\eta + \int_{D-v}^{\infty}[\partial(H_S - H_C)/\partial u]d\eta > 0$, the higher the u, the lower will be the reluctance to recapitalize.

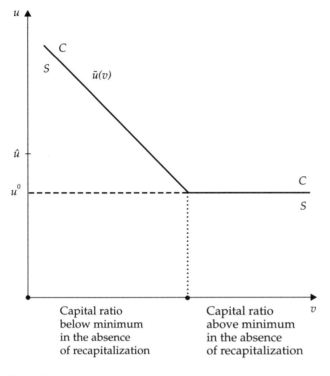

Figure 11.1
Constant net debt requirement ("8% rule")

is very compelling. The Basle accords content themselves with neutralizing the perverse effect by a one-for-one adjustment. They do not go quite as far as implementing the multiplicative rule of subsection 8.2.2, according to which the (positive or negative) dividend would grow more than proportionally with income.

Such a multiplicative rule could, however, create some problems. For example, a multiplicative (i.e., more than proportional) dividend rule may induce shareholders to *manipulate* performance. Shareholders are motivated to secretly recapitalize the bank, even if there is no threat of transfer of control. They would then receive more than what they give. For every $1 that they add to

v, the multiplicative rule implies that their dividend would increase by $\$(1 + \theta)$, where $\theta > 0$. Thus at date 1 the shareholders would gain $\$\theta$. But suppose that net debt increases by $\$\theta$. Then the second-period dividend is reduced by $\$\theta$ in the states of nature in which the bank does not go bankrupt. Overall shareholders gain $\$\theta$ multiplied by the probability of bankruptcy. This argument of course is only relevant if shareholders are able to secretly raise the bank's capital and (when they are numerous) to solve the collective action problem associated with a transfer. Still it is a possible drawback for the multiplicative dividend distribution rule.

Another problem with the multiplicative rule is that it ignores *future managerial incentives*. In our stylized model the manager exerts effort only once, so the multiplicative adjustment has no effect on future incentives. In practice, banking management is a continuous activity that must maintain adequate incentives over time. The multiplicative rule implies that a high income results in a low net worth, and that unless minimum solvency ratios are adjusted downward in the future, creditors are likely to seize control. The manager will then be discouraged in that she may lose her private benefit, even with hard work in the future (on this, see also appendix A). Conversely, a low income results in a well capitalized bank. In this case the manager may be overconfident that creditors will not seize control. In each case the incentives are not quite right. Clearly the strong nonstationarities associated with a pure dividend adjustment do not fit with the relative stationarity of incentive problems. A constant solvency requirement as in the Basle accords is preferable from this point of view.

In the absence of multiplicative adjustment, an alternative way of rewarding the manager for a good performance in the region of shareholder control may be in the form of an authorization to invest in risky assets, provided that the manager can benefit from managing risky assets. We will study this topic in section 11.3.[3]

11.1.3 Macroeconomic Shocks

An important weakness of the Basle accords is that there is no distinction between idiosyncratic shocks (partly controlled by the manager) and macroeconomic shocks. By this we mean that if we decompose the verifiable performance of bank i, v_i, into $v_i^I + v^A$ as in chapter 9, we have an optimal regulation defined by $u^*(v_i^I)$, whereas the Basle accords are defined by $\tilde{u}(v_i^I + v^A)$. From this observation we can draw the following conclusions:

1. In the region where v_i maintains bank capital above its minimum ratio, a change in v_i does not affect outside intervention: This is optimal if v_i varies only because of v^A. On the other hand, a change in v_i^I has no consequence for the manager, which is suboptimal.

2. In the region where $\tilde{u}(v_i)$ decreases with v_i, the manager is punished for a decrease in v^A as well as for a decrease in v_i^I. While punishing the manager for a poor idiosyncratic performance "goes in the right direction," punishing the manager for a fall in v^A is inappropriate. It may therefore be argued that the Basle accords are excessively tough on bank managers in recessions.

11.1.4 Expropriation of Equity Interests

National regulators are free to adjust the degree to which they penalize equityholders for a refusal to recapitalize a bank that has fallen below its minimal capital requirement. If the regulatory lag

---

3. Alternatively, such incentives could be provided by managerial shareholdings (if the manager responded to monetary incentives; see Dewatripont-Tirole 1993b) or by career concerns (if there were incomplete information about managerial talent, and if this talent affected the second-period profit not only through u).

is large relative to the speed at which the situation deteriorates, liquidation proceeds may be insufficient to cover deposits. In that case there is nothing to expropriate. However, in the opposite case, the regulator may choose to fine (e.g., expropriate) equityholders for a refusal to recapitalize. Such a threat actually increases the incentive to recapitalize and thus implies, ceteris paribus, a *softer* behavior toward managers.

Note that such fines also imply, ceteris paribus, a lower cost of deposit insurance for the insurance fund, not only thanks to the revenue from fines but also because of the increased incentive to recapitalize. Regulators, who are typically concerned about limiting the intervention of the insurance fund, thus have two instruments in this respect:[4] the level of capital requirements and the degree of expropriation of equity of failed institutions. This last instrument has the advantage of *solely* affecting the equityholders of poorly performing banks.

11.1.5   Mechanical Intervention by the Regulator

One final way in which the Basle regulation differs from the optimal scheme in subsection 8.2.3 is that the regulator is limited to a mechanical action L (liquidation or sale), while action S may require more discretion (partial reorganization or sale, restructuring) that goes beyond the traditional missions of government agencies. This would alter figure 11.1 for low performance levels: The inefficient action L would be taken in the absence of recapitalization, and the incentive to recapitalize would also be altered, even though lower v's would still imply costlier recapitalization. If managers prefer action C to both S and L, they will still be facing tougher times after poor performance.

---

4. A more complete analysis would of course also consider the impact of an expropriation policy on the optimal deposit insurance premium and on managerial incentives.

We might ask why the regulator would be unable to manage the troubled bank (and choose C or S) and be forced to choose only action L. Offhand, some might attribute this to incompetence.[5] But there could also be political economy considerations. These are factors investigated in chapter 12.

11.1.6 Overall Evaluation

The Basle accords are a second-best policy. They have good incentive properties to the extent that shareholders are more likely to recapitalize, as the income v and the signal u become larger. However, the exact implementation of the optimal policy rule $u^*(\cdot)$ would require adjustments that seem inconsistent with the premise of limited regulatory discretion. Further the shareholders' refusal to recapitalize may lead to too extreme an intervention. Finally, by treating idiosyncratic and macroeconomic shocks alike, the regulation is too tough on bank managers in recessions.

11.2 Recapitalization or Securitization?

Earlier in chapter 9 we mentioned securitization as a way of eluding the solvency requirement. Under the Basle accords (and the other prudential regulations) banks are free to replace recapitalization by a reduction in assets in order to meet the solvency requirement. When do shareholders prefer to sell assets rather than to recapitalize? Consider a bank whose balance sheet at date 1 is

---

5. A standard argument for a mechanistic regulation is that regulatory agencies generally are understaffed and cannot run failing banks even temporarily. The lack of personnel is clearly a problem, but it should not be taken for granted. If regulatory agencies could be entrusted with failing banks and would manage them properly they might well be allocated higher budgets.

Assets	Liabilities
v	D
$\bar{\eta}_1$	E
$\bar{\eta}_2$	

This bank holds two risky long-term assets, a rather liquid η_1 with principal $\bar{\eta}_1$, and an illiquid η_2 with principal $\bar{\eta}_2$. Assume that asset η_1 can be sold at price $\bar{\eta}_1 - \tau$. If the principal $\bar{\eta}_1$ is also the expected value of the asset when it is retained by the bank, τ can be interpreted as a transaction cost. More generally, $\tau \,(\leqq 0)$ is the decrease in accounting value implied by the securitization of the asset. The initial solvency ratio r^i becomes a final ratio r^f with securitization, where

$$r^i = \frac{v + \bar{\eta}_1 + \bar{\eta}_2 - D}{\bar{\eta}_1 + \bar{\eta}_2} \quad \text{and} \quad r^f = \frac{v + \bar{\eta}_1 + \bar{\eta}_2 - D - \tau}{\bar{\eta}_2}.$$

Securitization raises the solvency ratio ($r^f > r^i$) if and only if

$$\frac{\tau}{\bar{\eta}_1} < r^i,$$

or equivalently,

$$\frac{\tau}{\bar{\eta}_1} < r^f.$$

We now can formulate a simple rule: The decrease in accounting value divided by the principal of the asset must not exceed the ex ante or ex post solvency ratio. Unless historical cost undervalues the asset ($\tau < 0$), its securitization does not raise the solvency ratio when the bank's solvency is low or negative.

Securitization is particularly effective in raising the solvency ratio when the bank's solvency is not far from its minimum requirement. But this is precisely what makes recapitalization cheap for shareholders. Let us compare these two ways of meeting the solvency requirements. Shareholders may prefer one or the other instrument depending on the circumstances.

Suppose that a securitizable asset is fairly safe and is unfairly assigned weight 1 in the computation of the Cooke ratio, and that this asset is very liquid in that it can be sold at a price close to its true value (whether or not the latter is the accounting value). Securitization is then but an accounting gimmick; it does not affect the value of equity. It is therefore preferred to recapitalization. Conversely, for a given positive transaction cost, recapitalization dominates securitization when shareholders need only bring in a small amount of capital to meet the solvency requirements.

11.3   Reallocation of the Bank Portfolio between Risky and Safe Assets

Current banking regulation uses the composition of the asset portfolio as an instrument to control banks. The Basle accords assign higher weights to risky assets in the computation of the denominator of the solvency ratio (see chapter 3). Consequently only equity-rich banks can substantially invest in such assets. Similarly the FDIC Improvement Act requires (more explicitly than the Basle accords) that risk taking can take place only in well-capitalized banks. In this section we consider the incentive properties attached to the reinvestment of the first-period income into risky assets.

There are *two natural links between the bank's net worth and its holding of risky assets*. First, *riskier assets in general require a better quality of management* than safe assets. The management of loans to a small enterprise, of securities, or of commercial real estate investments demand more attention than the purchase of Treasury bonds. Now recall that an excessively high performance threshold discourages the manager. To put it differently, an undercapitalized bank is likely to go bankrupt and therefore offers insufficient prospects, thus reducing managerial incentive to exert the high effort. Clearly *the manager of an undercapitalized bank should focus on low moral hazard activities, which tend to coincide with the management of safe assets.*[6]

The second motivation for the link between banking capitalization and portfolio composition is more related to the possibility of partly replacing the net worth adjustment by another instrument. The idea is to *reward the manager for good performance, reflected in the bank's capitalization, by allowing him to manage riskier assets.* It is important here to distinguish between managers and shareholders. As we will see, *shareholders* benefit from an increase in risk because their claim corresponds to a convex return stream. Yet the goal is to reward the *manager,* who is in charge of the bank's affairs rather than to favor one group of claimholders to the detriment of other groups. We must then ask whether the possibility of increasing the risk of the bank's portfolio benefits the manager.

One can think of several reasons why the manager could directly enjoy an increase in risk. First, the manager's human capital is likely to grow faster when there are more complex assets involved. Second, the private benefit of managing the bank may be greater for nonroutine tasks. We will not study these two direct benefits for the manager and will rather focus on the indirect benefit associated with the impact of increasing risk taking on the probability of external interference. Are shareholders more passive when the bank holds a higher proportion of its portfolio in risky assets? We can at most offer a preliminary analysis of this complex question. We must distinguish between two cases, depending on whether the new risky assets purchased, thanks to the bank's high solvency, are correlated with the old ones. In appendix C we present two such simple cases. In the bank "expansion" case, the new assets are sim-

---

6. Rochet et al. (1993) study the screening problem in *entrepreneurial banks.* In their model risky assets ought to be managed by efficient entrepreneurs. Indeed in equilibrium efficient entrepreneurs select risky portfolios. Our focus in this discussion is on moral hazard, but adverse selection issues such as those considered by Rochet et al. are also relevant.

ilar to (actually perfectly correlated with) the existing assets and benefit from managerial experience. But in the bank "diversification" case, the bank invests in new assets that are uncorrelated with the existing assets. In both cases shareholders benefit from an increase in risk. Under weak conditions the increase in risk reduces the probability of shareholder interference and therefore rewards the manager in the bank expansion case. By contrast diversification may trigger more or less shareholder interference.

12   The Political Economy of Public Regulation

The holders of bank debt are often poorly informed, free-riding small depositors. These small depositors need to be *represented*. In this chapter we study the advantages and drawbacks of more discretionary public regulation than the current one.

12.1   Optimal Discretionary Regulation

Suppose that the regulator can choose between actions C and S, as in subsection 8.2.2. To implement the optimal regulation then the regulator must, on behalf of small depositors, choose action S when he or she receives control rights and when the signal on the bank's prospects is below the threshold $u^*(v)$. We saw that the regulator must be allocated control rights when the bank's solvency falls below the minimum solvency ratio. The regulator's interference policy then must be biased toward action S compared to the preferences of the community of claimholders. The bias will be stronger, the lower the bank's solvency.

One way of implementing the optimal regulatory policy is to give the regulator the same incentive as that of noninsured depositors. That is, the regulator should internalize the stake Δ_D defined in chapter 8. Control is transferred to the regulator when the first-period performance is lower than $\hat{v}$.

A simple way of implementing this internalization of depositors'preferences is to institute full deposit insurance. (This motivation for deposit insurance differs from the ones discussed in chapter 5.) It is then appropriate to give control rights to the deposit insurer who has monetary stake Δ_D. Where the bank's solvency is adequate $(v \geq \hat{v})$, the shareholders would instead receive control rights, but the regulator could still exercise control by imposing ceilings on dividend distribution and on risk taking that grow with the bank's solvency.

12.2 Limitations of Discretionary Regulation

Let us stress the point that *discipline in the banking industry requires that the regulator maximize the value of deposits* and *not ex post social welfare*. To maximize ex ante welfare, the regulator cannot maximize ex post welfare. A social welfare maximizing regulator would be too passive; for, if the depositors' incentives to continue Δ_D is positive, the shareholders' incentive also is positive (see figures 8.4 and 8.5). Therefore

$$\Delta_D + \Delta_E + B > 0.$$

Passivity then is socially optimal. A welfare-maximizing regulator never interferes "too much." By contrast, in some states of nature a utilitarian regulator can be passive against the will of depositors (or taxpayers in case of full deposit insurance).

The regulator is even more passive when, instead of putting equal weights on the surpluses of all economic agents, the regulator is captured by the industry and rather puts more weight on the welfare of shareholders and management than on that of depositors. The possibility of capture is very real of course, but it is important to note that the regulator may be too passive even in the absence of capture.

The internalization of depositors' welfare by the government through full deposit insurance is a straightforward matter, but it may be difficult to ensure that regulators focus entirely on the stake Δ_D. Political pressure may induce the regulator to internalize other interests. An incentive scheme based on the financial health of the deposit insurance system then does not guarantee that regulators intervene properly. This leads us to a discussion of the regulators' incentives.

The (monetary) compensation of civil servants and politicians is in general fairly insensitive to their performance (i.e., the financial health of deposit insurance). Civil servants and politicians may instead be driven by public service mindedness, ego gratification, and career concerns. Civil servants may eye promotions to desirable jobs in the public sector or glamorous or lucrative jobs in the private sector. Politicians are of course motivated by the thought of reelection.

In his book on the S&L debacle, Kane (1989) provides an ample description of the incentives that led regulators and politicians (the Congress and the president) not to intervene on time to prevent excessive risk taking by undercapitalized savings banks. By analogy with the banks' gambling for resurrection, Kane describes the government's behavior as "regulatory gambling," the decision to conceal the difficulties facing the deposit insurance system in the hope that very favorable macroeconomic developments would recapitalize the savings and loans, or at least that the buck could be passed to future administrations. Most other authors (e.g., Dab 1991; White 1991) have also stressed the excessive and deliberate passivity of regulatory authorities for several years in the early 1980s (see chapter 4).

The proper policy—which would have hurt managers and shareholders much more than passivity—would have been to recognize the solvency problems of a fraction of the S&Ls and to force them to recapitalize under the threat of reorganizing or selling them. In normal times only a minority of banks are exposed to the threat of regulatory intervention, and therefore lobbying (whether directly on the regulator, or indirectly through the political system) is limited. In the 1980s by contrast, a substantial fraction of S&Ls were concerned, and lobbying was intense. The deposit insurance system itself was undercapitalized, and to the extent that in many S&Ls shareholders would not have recapitalized their bank, a strict intervention policy would have required a recapitalization of the deposit insurance system by taxpayers.

In this respect, a conscientious enforcement of solvency requirements and intervention policy just after the macroeconomic shock of 1981–82 might have been perceived as a confession of inefficient monitoring. It is interesting that the 1989 U.S. reform censures the S&L regulators by transferring their control to the commercial banks' deposit insurance agency, despite the fact that S&L regulators had intervened with energy in the previous two years. Regulators were used as scapegoats (Kane 1989; White 1991).

The regulators' hesitation in the early 1980s to recognize that banks were in trouble may have stemmed from the career concerns, and from *a basic conflict between monitoring and intervention* for the regulators. Our model may shed some light on why intervention would signal imperfect monitoring by the regulator and hurt his or her career. Let us look at a simple example in which the regulator's potential (private or public) employers try to infer the regulator's ability from his or her observed performance on the job.[1]

We enrich the model by introducing a (simpleminded) monitoring activity: The manager now chooses among the possible efforts $\bar{e}$, $\underline{e}$, and $\tilde{e}$. Efforts $\bar{e}$ and $\underline{e}$ have the same cost and the same effects as described earlier. The new effort $\tilde{e}$ generates the same distribution on v as effort $\bar{e}$. However, it yields a worse distribution for u: In the relevant range $\tilde{G}(u^*(v)) > \bar{G}(u^*(v))$. Effort $\bar{e}$ and $\tilde{e}$ thus differ in the

---

1. Related models of coverups are offered by Boot-Thakor (1993), Gale-Vives (1993), and Seabright (1993). See also Mailath-Mester (1993).

long-term management dimension. Effort $\tilde{e}$ furthermore generates at date 1 a high private benefit (e.g., higher than B), so the manager chooses $\tilde{e}$ unless she is prevented by the regulator from doing so.[2] Suppose now that there are two types of regulator: competent and incompetent. The prior probability that the regulator is competent is α. A competent regulator costlessly identifies effort $\tilde{e}$, can reduce the managerial choice set to $\{\underline{e}, \bar{e}\}$, and thus can induce the high effort under the managerial incentive scheme described in chapter 7. In contrast, an incompetent regulator cannot tell the various managerial choices apart and must therefore let the manager choose $\tilde{e}$.

Suppose, first, that the regulator ignores his or her career and implements the optimal policy defined by a threshold rule $u^*(\cdot)$.[3] Let us also assume that the voters (for a politician) or the potential employers (for a civil servant) observe the regulator's decision of whether to intervene but not the information u on which it is based. The posterior probability that the regulator is competent is

$$\beta = \frac{\alpha \bar{G}\left(u^*(v)\right)}{\alpha \bar{G}\left(u^*(v)\right) + (1-\alpha)\tilde{G}\left(u^*(v)\right)}$$

if the regulator intervenes, and

$$\beta' = \frac{\alpha[1 - \bar{G}\left(u^*(v)\right)]}{\alpha[1 - \bar{G}\left(u^*(v)\right)] + (1-\alpha)[1 - \tilde{G}\left(u^*(v)\right)]}$$

if the regulator stays passive. Clearly $\beta' > \beta$. The regulator hence should not intervene if he or she cares about his or her career

---

2. Note that we ignore shareholder monitoring. This assumption is particularly reasonable if effort $\tilde{e}$ corresponds to a risky strategy, or if shareholders cannot solve their collective action problem.

3. $u^*(\cdot)$ is obtained as in chapter 7, except that the objective function accounts for the fact that with probability $(1 - \alpha)$ the manager chooses action $\tilde{e}$. We ignore the social value of the information about the regulator's ability for future decision making. A proper modeling of this value would require a full description of future job allocations.

and therefore prefers to look competent in fulfilling the mission of representing the depositors. This example thus predicts a passive regulatory behavior similar to that observed for the U.S. savings and loans.

The conflict between monitoring and intervention suggests that one may want to *split the regulatory tasks*. The regulator in charge of intervention would be less reluctant to intervene if someone else were in charge of monitoring the bank. Split authority, however, is not a panacea. First, information acquisition costs about the bank are duplicated. Then collusion among regulators must be prevented. Last, multiple regulators face "moral hazard in teams": Each regulator will try to shift the responsibility for a bad outcome onto other regulators. The regulator in charge of monitoring will invoke delays in intervention, while the regulator in charge of intervening will argue that he or she was not informed about the bank's condition or that he or she has inherited a "wastebasket" (this can be illustrated using the previous example and assuming that each regulator is competent or incompetent and may work or shirk).

Last, we note that the conflict between the monitoring and closing tasks is but one instance of a more general issue. Governments generally are concerned not only with banks' solvency but also with monetary and exchange rate targets, with the functioning of the payment system, with the impact on the real sector, or with the competition between banks and nonbanks. Goodhart and Schoenmaker (1993) offer an extensive discussion of the separation of responsibilities between monetary authorities and prudential regulators,[4] and Repullo (1993) provides a first attempt at modeling this separation.

---

4. For a theoretical account of incentives and split of responsibilities in government, in general, see Tirole (1994).

12.3 Drawbacks of Nondiscretionary Regulation

The problems with discretionary regulation have led some economists to recommend a mechanistic form of regulation. Indeed the Basle accords, like most regulations, are based on rules and leave little discretion to regulators by focusing on decisions based on information that are easily specified in the regulatory statutes. It is therefore worth reminding the reader of a couple drawbacks of nondiscretionary regulation (these drawbacks are linked in our model to the choice of A and to the use of soft information u):

1. *Crudeness of intervention policy.* It is difficult to specify in advance the nature of the desirable intervention in the bank. Liquidation of the bank and the firing of its manager can be prescribed, but these are extreme policies. Finer interventions such as putting limits on borrowing, restricting the scope of assets, reducing their correlation and the interest rate risk, or selling assets are much more discretionary. A mechanistic regulation such as the one defined by the Basle accords leaves discretion with shareholders but not with regulators (see section 11.1).

2. *Nonresponsiveness to soft information.* The previous comments also apply to nonverifiable information, which may not be used or else be improperly used.[5]

---

5. We do not need to imply that soft information is not used in a mechanistic regulation. Indeed we have seen in chapter 11 that in a voluntary recapitalization policy decision making is affected by soft information.

13

Private Regulation

Discouraged by the difficulties intrinsic to the public regulation of banks some economists have advocated private remedies.[1] This section analyzes some of the most fashionable proposals.

13.1 Private Deposit Insurance

Banks could buy deposit insurance from a private insurance company on behalf of their depositors (or at least those who wish to be insured). A private insurance company is likely to have better incentives to measure the bank's risk precisely and to charge insurance premiums related to this risk than officers of a public deposit insurance corporation who do not bear the financial consequences of their acts.[2] Of course advocates of private deposit

---

1. The ideas of free competition or a lighthanded regulation in banking have been around for a long time. See the book edited by Capie and Wood (1991) for some case studies and for some recent analyses.

2. No one, to the best of our knowledge, has really explained why the incentives of the managers of private insurance companies cannot be duplicated in the public sector. After all, the managers of the Federal Deposit Insurance Corporation could be rewarded on the basis of its financial health. A possible reason for this discrepancy between the incentives of private and public insurance companies' managers may lie in the difficulty of specifying good incentive contracts in the public sector where a troubled deposit insurance corporation is more likely to be recapitalized. We, however, do not have at this time a fully worked-out argument to offer the reader.

insurance do not fully rule out public regulation. Indeed someone has to check that the insurance company itself is well
capitalized.[3]

It is often argued that this proposal[4] ignores systemic risk. Even
well-capitalized insurance companies may not be solvent in the
event of a severe macroeconomic shock. It is therefore hard to con-
ceive that the government would not perform its role of lender
of last resort in such circumstances. An illustration is supplied
by the case of Norway where the guarantee fund of the banking
sector (based on member banks' assets) was emptied in 1991, at
what point the government had to pour in substantial amounts of
money.[5]

Even in the absence of systemic risk, private deposit insurance
does not seem to be satisfactory. That insurance premiums grow
with the bank's risk is generally considered a good thing, but it
can also have perverse effects. We saw that the bank should behave
more conservatively when its solvency is reduced. However, *an increase in the deposit insurance premium induces the bank's shareholders
to take more risk for a given level of deposits. The change in the premium
aggravates the perverse effect associated with a reduction in solvency* due
to, say, a poor performance.

---

3. See Mishkin (1992a, 377) for an account of some recent bank runs in three American states (Ohio, Maryland, and Rhode Island) where the payment of deposits was
guaranteed by private insurance funds.
4. More common than, but related to, private insurance are industry guaranty associations. For instance, the Swiss bankers' association shares losses in case of losses
due to failure of one of its members. Such arrangements are also common in the insurance industry. For instance, many U.S. insurance contracts are partly covered by
guaranty associations in most states.
  Another analogy for private deposit insurance is the policies sold by private
specialized insurance companies to issuer municipalities. These policies guarantee
interest and principal payments to the holders of municipal bonds (on this, see Merton 1993).
5. Total bank support in Norway was 2% of GDP in 1991 and 1.7% of GDP in 1992
(see 63rd annual report of the Bank for International Settlements 1993, 172).

Let us use our model to assess the impact of a private deposit insurance policy. For the moment we take the level of deposits D to be reimbursed in period 2 and the level of risky assets as given. For instance, the bank's current risky assets are very illiquid, and there is no new opportunity of investment in risky assets. We will later study the effect of the deposit insurance premium on the level of deposits (or net debt). The first-period income net of the deposit insurance premium (γ per unit of deposits) is now $v - \gamma D$. Under a private insurance system, γ decreases with D: The premium amplifies the impact of a bad performance. That is, the net debt, $(1 + \gamma)D - v$, grows faster than v decreases. But we know that a higher net debt induces more passivity from shareholders. Private deposit insurance has wrong incentive properties in that it reinforces the incentive to take risk in hard times. In contrast, by focusing on solvency and by not adjusting insurance premiums, the Basle accords do not have this drawback.

To be fair, advocates of private deposit insurance have in mind that the increase in the premium induces the bank to reduce deposits and assets and thus to recapitalize. We now analyze the validity of this argument.

Suppose that the bank's second-period income is $\eta \Phi(I)$, where I is the increase in deposits beyond D at the end of period 1 ($I > 0$ if deposits increase, $I < 0$ if they decrease), $\Phi(0) = 1$ (the analysis generalizes the previous one), and Φ is increasing and concave (decreasing returns assumption).[6] This example presumes some specialization of the bank to the extent that its returns from different projects are correlated. Let us assume that shareholders have control and choose the level of deposits, or equivalently I. For a given action A (we have previously studied the choice of this action), the shareholders' profit is

---

6. The case of a fixed level of deposits ($I = 0$) we just considered is a special case in which Φ is very concave at $I = 0$.

$$\int_{[(1+\gamma)(D+I)-v]/\Phi(I)}^{\infty} [v - (1+\gamma)(D+I) + \eta\Phi(I)]h_A(\eta \mid u)\, d\eta$$

$$= \Phi(I) \int_{[(1+\gamma)(D+I)-v]/\Phi(I)}^{\infty} [1 - H_A(\eta \mid u)]\, d\eta.$$

The derivative of this profit with respect to the premium γ is equal to

$$-(D+I)\left[1 - H_A\left(\frac{(1+\gamma)(D+I) - v}{\Phi(I)}\middle| u\right)\right].$$

That is, a unit increase in the insurance premium decreases shareholder profit by the amount of deposits $(D + I)$, but only when the bank can reimburse its depositors, namely with probability $(1 - H_A)$. Were this derivative to increase with the level of deposits, a standard revealed preference argument would show that shareholders would decrease deposits when the premium increases. However, an increase in deposits implies that the insurance premium is paid by shareholders with a smaller probability (the probability of bankruptcy increases); hence *an increase in the deposit insurance premium may induce the bank to attract more deposits.* The previous derivative demonstrates two countervailing effects: An increase in I raises $(D + I)$ but lowers $(1 - H_A)$. The effect of γ on the choice of I is therefore ambiguous.[7]

Our discussion of private deposit insurance is likely to be too narrow. First, we have focused on a linear insurance tariff (as is

---

7. Here is an example of an increase in the premium leading to an increase in the level of deposits. Suppose that investment is indivisible: $I = 0$ or D, so that $\Phi(D) \equiv k < 2$. Suppose that η can take one or two values: high (η_H) or low (η_L), with respective probabilities y and $1 - y$, where $y < 1/2$. Suppose, last, that $v - (1+\gamma)D + \eta_L > 0 > v - 2(1+\gamma)D + k\eta_L$ and that $v - (1+\gamma)D + [y\eta_H + (1-y)\eta_L] = y[v - 2(1+\gamma)D + k\eta_H] + \epsilon$, where ϵ is positive and small. The bank goes bankrupt only if $I = D$ and $\eta = \eta_L$. Further γ is such that $I = 0$ slightly dominates $I = D$. Increase γ a bit by $d\gamma$. The profit corresponding to $I = 0$ decreases by $Dd\gamma$, and the profit corresponding to $I = D$ decreases by only $2yDd\gamma < Dd\gamma$. The high deposit level may then become optimal.

usually the case for public deposit insurance). A private insurer might want to offer a nonlinear tariff. Second, and more important, the insurance company is restricted to offer insurance services. It is prevented from intervening in bank management. Yet we know that control rights should be exerted by a conservative claimholder when the bank's solvency is low. In fact, since the insurance company internalizes the welfare of bank debtholders, it could act as a tough claimholder. It would then resemble a large debtholder, whose desirability we will report on later. For the moment we content ourselves with *stressing the crucial role of external interference when the bank's solvency is low.* Private deposit insurance by itself does not create an effective advocate for rigor.

13.2   Independent Rating Agencies

Some public policymakers have proposed to deregulate those banks that accept to post at their branches a rating of their debt by an independent rating agency.[8] The idea behind this reform proposal is that depositors would refuse to deposit money in the bank or else would demand a higher interest rate if the bank's solvency is low.

Relying solely on ratings to create managerial discipline has several drawbacks. First, the absence of deposit insurance is likely to generate bank runs. Even a slight drop in the rating of the bank may give rise to serious liquidity problems. Second, even in the absence of bank runs, depositors may not be able to unite to prevent the dilution of the value of their deposits. (New deposits exert a negative externality on existing long term ones.) Third, there are

---

8. Such a proposal was made in 1993 by the governor of New Zealand's Reserve Bank (see *The Economist*, July 26, 1993, for details). Essentially the proposal hands the regulatory job as much as possible over to the market. The central bank would (1) register banks, (2) enforce a minimum capital requirement and strict disclosure rule, and (3) force banks to display on their windows a credit rating from a recognized rating agency.

the same two issues concerning external interference in the bank as for the case of a private deposit insurance (see section 13.1). On the one hand, there is no mechanism for transferring control to and organizing the representation of depositors when the bank's solvency is low. On the other hand, the increase in the interest rate paid to depositors when the rating is low increases the shareholders' incentive to take more risk. (It is interesting to note that a rating agency can sometimes give two ratings that are both self-fulfilling. A good rating reduces the interest rate to be paid by the bank and may cause the shareholders to behave conservatively; the value of debt is then indeed high. A bad rating increases the interest rate, induces shareholders to choose a risky strategy, and reduces the value of debt.)

13.3 Private External Control in Case of Low Solvency

The previous two subsections stressed the absence of a mechanism for removing control from shareholders when the bank's solvency is low, under either private deposit insurance or credit rating. One popular suggestion is to let the banking industry *self-regulate* through a bank club. The idea is that inside the club, banks exert peer-monitoring and insure each other's deposits. The club has the right to control membership and to exclude members. The obvious benefit of self-regulation is the competence of the monitors. Its drawbacks are equally clear: First, the club must be prevented from erecting barriers to entry. Second, insolvency may propagate among banks of the club, especially in a macroeconomic shock. In such circumstances the government would likely become the lender of last resort. Third, there is the issue of free riding in the monitoring of the club's banks. Fourth, it must be clear to the members and depositors what would happen to insolvent banks that are thrown out of the club.

Given these drawbacks of self-regulation, a number of reform proposals have advocated a serious strengthening of the currently very minor role of uninsured debt. These proposals of course assume that the government can credibly commit not to (implicitly) insure such deposits. Yet formally uninsured deposits (especially in big banks) are almost always reimbursed (these big banks are "too big to fail"). The commitment problem is important, but we will assume for the sake of the following argument that it is solved and that the holders of uninsured debt know they will not be reimbursed in case of bankruptcy.

13.3.1   The Proposals

There are two strands in the literature on uninsured debt. The first is theoretical and focuses on the discipline brought about by short-term debt and bank runs. The second is policy-oriented, less favorable to deposit withdrawal, and more interested in the role of long-term debt.

The first literature (Calomiris et al. 1991; Emmons 1991; Rey-Stiglitz 1992) argues that uninsured short-term debt acts as a managerial disciplining device. If the bank is in trouble, well-informed short-term depositors will withdraw their money and prevent the bank from continuing, which ex ante induces the manager to work hard. The withdrawal of deposits cannot be duplicated through a nondiscretionary regulation, stating that the bank must reduce its deposits if its solvency is low, as long as the information on the bank's solvency is soft. On the other hand, the social cost of bank runs leads other authors (e.g., Diamond and Dybvig 1986) to reject this solution.[9]

---

9. Diamond (1992) uses similar arguments as Calomiris et al., Emmons, and Rey-Stiglitz to identify the benefit of short-term debt in the corporate world (in an adverse selection model rather than in a moral hazard model) but does not apply his argument to the banking industry.

We will focus on the proposal of Benston et al. (1986) and White (1991), among others, that banks be forced to collect a nonnegligible fraction of deposits in uninsured subordinated debt.[10] This subordinated debt is meant to substitute for the regulator, to impose covenants on the bank, and to exert residual rights of control. Benston (1990, 223) and White (1991, 239) both argue that subordinated debt should be added to equity in the computation of solvency ratios. In contrast, as we mentioned earlier, the Basle accords allow subordinated debt to be counted as equity only to a limited extent, and further require it to be long term and not to have control rights.

One possible motivation for uninsured debt to be junior to insured debt is the threat of dilution of insured debt by uninsured debt in the case of equal seniority. Benston et al., as well as regulators, also mention the fact that subordinated debt acts as a "cushion" to protect the deposit insurance fund in case of bankruptcy.

13.3.2 Analysis

The main purpose of introducing large uninsured depositors is to minimize the extent of public regulation. One drawback of subordinated debt is that its holders cannot quite represent senior debtholders and therefore small depositors. The incentives of subordinated debtholders who have a claim d on the bank's profit, in the presence of senior debt equal to D and of equity, are depicted in figure 13.1 by the hatched area.

The holders of subordinated debt do not care about variations of profit under the level of senior debt (because they are then not reimbursed) nor about variations of profit above the total debt (because they are then fully reimbursed). As figure 13.1 shows, subordinated debt is always more interventionist than equity and more passive than senior debt. Allocating control to holders of subordinated debt is fine for an average performance but inappropriate for

---

10. Subordinated debt is senior only to equity in case of bankruptcy.

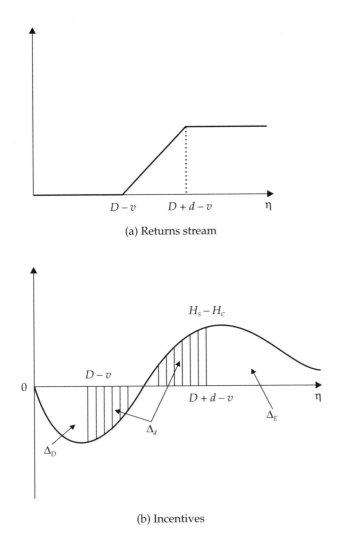

(a) Returns stream

(b) Incentives

Figure 13.1
Subordinated debt

a bad one. In particular, they do not internalize the stake Δ_D of senior debtholders (or the deposit insurance fund). If they were to represent senior debtholders, their decision making would be biased in favor of excessive risk taking. Indeed, when a bank's solvency is very low and equity is almost worthless, subordinated debt is almost equity and is therefore excessively passive. This bias in favor of risk taking would disappear if there were no priority structure between insured and uninsured debt.

Another question with an extensive use of uninsured debt is the availability of such debt in financial markets. Who will be the big debtholders of the theory? Benston et al. (1986) suggest that they might be other banks, and White (1991) refers to institutional investors such as pension funds, insurance companies, or investment funds. The risk of propagation of bankruptcies among financial intermediaries would then be serious, all the more that, contrary to the current situation in which the bank's liabilities in the wholesale market are quite dispersed, monitoring would require uninsured debt to be held by one or two financial intermediaries.[11] On the other hand, the holders of subordinated debt do not have an adequate incentive to monitor if their claims are insured by the government in order to avoid systemic risk.

13.4   Calibrating Capital Requirements: Mixed Public-Private Regulation

So far we have analyzed pure public and private regulations. Now we consider using the private sector to help the public sector calibrate its regulatory requirements and to act as a check against supervisory collusion with the industry or cover-ups. Mixing public and private controls is not a new idea. Indeed the 1991 U.S. Treasury proposal discusses the possibility of a mixed public-private *in-*

---

11. Uninsured debt must also be sizable in order to reduce the risk of collusion of its holder(s) with shareholders.

surance system. The idea is to calibrate the pricing of public deposit insurance through a small amount of private insurance. Namely private insurers would bid for the right to cover a fraction (5% or 10%) of depositor losses. The public insurer would cover the rest and set its premium rate equal to that charged by the private insurer. Such a scheme has several drawbacks, as we have described earlier: The private deposit insurers would themselves need to comply with capital requirements. They should not collude with the bank, whose gain from an aggressive bid (low premium) far exceeds the loss incurred by the low bidder. Last, the scheme must prevent the bank from gambling in hard times (see section 13.1) and must trigger external interference when necessary. Clearly the scheme preserves the need for regulation. On the other hand, the introduction of the private sector in the regulatory process offers a convenient benchmark that can be used to either guide or control the regulators' behavior.

The same principles extend beyond the specific issue of pricing deposit insurance. Indeed private sector calibration could be used to help with the design of capital requirements, the primary focus of this book. Let us come back to the idea of using a big debtholder as a discipline device (see section 13.3). We can transpose the discussion on the public-private deposit insurance scheme. Since large debtholders are scarce, one might demand that a bank borrow a small fraction (5% or 10%) of its insured deposits as uninsured liabilities with the *same priority* as insured deposits in order to align incentives of uninsured creditors and the public deposit insurance fund. The uninsured deposits would exert the same function of pricing risk as the private insurers considered in the U.S. Treasury proposal. The riskiness of insured deposits could be measured by the interest rate charged by uninsured creditors.[12]

---

12. The measurement of this risk is slightly more complex than in the case of deposit insurance, especially if the maturity structure of the uninsured debt is not constrained to match that of insured deposits.

This big debtholder (or twin, the large deposit insurer) can then be used as a second representative of depositors. Like the regulator, the big debtholder could be allowed to impose debt covenants, including capital requirements and to intervene when these covenants are violated. In case of conflict the more stringent covenant or interference could apply. Equivalently, the bank could choose its level of capitalization and commit to other covenants, knowing that the resulting pricing of the uninsured debt would also be reflected in that of the insured debt.[13] As long as the big debtholder maximizes the expected profit of his or her uninsured claim (absent limited liability), regulation becomes superfluous: The small depositors are represented. We therefore argue that the idea of private sector calibration could in theory be used to calibrate prudential regulation and not only deposit insurance premiums. It offers a clue to addressing the nagging question that will be posed by any agency-theoretic approach: "Why 8%?"

While we find the idea of using private sector benchmarking appealing, we ought to once again emphasize its limits. First, the large debtholder holds only a small fraction of total debt and therefore has suboptimal incentives in his or her monitoring, interference, and covenant writing functions. Worse, he or she may have an incentive to collude with management and shareholders against the public deposit insurance fund by charging low interest rates in exchange of a nice deal on another operation. Second, the government is still in need of checking the capitalization of this large debtholder; an undercapitalized debtholder might bid aggressively

---

13. Of course the premium charged on public deposit insurance should not be equal to the difference between the bank's uninsured and insured rates. The bank would then have no incentive to keep insured deposit costs down or could be tempted to enter "sweet deals" with its customers by bundling high deposit rates with lucrative products or low bank services. Rather the insured deposit rate taken to compute public deposit insurance premium should be some industry average in order to make the bank internalize the cost of its insured deposits.

for the bank's uninsured debt in a general attempt to gamble for resurrection. More generally, in the absence of such regulation, one might envision low-interest-rate equilibria in hard times, in which undercapitalized intermediaries price uninsured debt to each other low in order to "go for broke."

Given these drawbacks, we might still consider the general idea of using a private benchmark on some scale in order to observe the privately determined solvency ratios, and then adjusting the capital requirement of the traditionally regulated banking sector accordingly. But further thought needs to be given to the implications of this scheme.

V   Conclusion

14 Lessons for Banking Regulation

Our premise for this book is that banking regulation should encourage efficient banking while protecting depositors and guaranteeing the stability of the industry and the payment mechanism. Like for any managerial firm, efficiency is obtained partly through the threat of external interference. Namely a good performance should leave control with relatively passive shareholders, while a bad performance should lead to control by more interventionist debtholders. The threshold for the transfer of control from shareholders to debtholders can be interpreted as a minimum solvency requirement.

According to this view an efficient governance of banks requires (I) accurate measures of its solvency and of the nature of its activities (in particular its portfolio risk), and (II) an increase in interference when performance deteriorates, and, in particular, a credible mechanism for the transfer of control to an interventionist party when the bank's solvency is low. The first requirement leads to some standard recommendations:

1. Bank solvency could be measured more precisely than is currently done by requiring banks to report assets at their market values when this is feasible (liquid assets). Of course market value accounting is not feasible for a number of assets held by banks (e.g.,

commercial loans to small firms). Yet a partial introduction of market value accounting would give a more precise picture of the balance sheet and would reduce the amount of gains trading.

2. A bank's global risk should be better assessed by measuring not only credit risk as in the current Cooke ratio but also interest rate and other market risks. In the same spirit, credit risk should be measured at the portfolio level, and not only at the level of individual assets.

3. Ratings by private rating agencies could play a more substantial role, since they incorporate (soft) information that cannot make its way into nondiscretionary regulatory measures of solvency. Banks could be required to be rated (the current system involves voluntary rating where the bank may or may not disclose its rating). The benefit of using a private rating agency (or a private deposit insurance company) is to generate information from sources other than the bank or the regulator.

To be sure, the *exclusive* use of ratings or private deposit insurance has two serious drawbacks. First, by aggravating the bank's condition, a bad rating reinforces the perverse effect of a greater incentive for risk taking in a situation of low solvency. Second, the use of ratings or private deposit insurance is consistent with requirement (I), but it does nothing to meet requirement (II). It leaves open the issue of who will control the bank in tough times. In this respect our analysis yields the following conclusions:

4. Most holders of bank debt have only a faint idea of the bank's real solvency. This holds especially for small depositors but also, to a lesser extent, for nonfinancial firms with little expertise in banking and for other banks with lines of credit in hundreds of other banks. Exposing these debtholders to risk is likely to generate more bank runs than careful monitoring. This volatility is a somewhat ill-targeted managerial disciplining device. A broad deposit insurance, explicit or implicit as is nowadays the case, seems to be a preferable

alternative. This of course does not foreclose a requirement for the bank to have a large uninsured debtholder:

5. Some proposals argue that large, long-term debtholders should receive control when the bank's solvency is low. Their incentive to monitor the bank would be provided by the lack of insurance on the corresponding debt. Several forms of such debt can be considered:

- *Unsubordinated debt.* The large debtholders would be representative of other depositors and, in the absence of collusion with shareholders and management, would have the proper incentives to intervene. On the other hand, the large debtholders, to the extent that they share losses with other depositors, have suboptimal incentives to monitor the bank. Alternatively, the large debtholders would have the proper incentive to monitor if they gave full deposit insurance to the other depositors and therefore internalized their welfare. This would be similar to giving control rights to a private deposit insurance corporation, and it raises the issue of the large debtholder's solvency.
- *Subordinated debt.* The Basle accords allow regulated banks to issue subordinated debt provided that its holders receive no control rights. However, we saw that the large debtholders should be allowed to intervene in tough times. On the other hand, allocating control to holders of subordinated debt has a substantial drawback: When the bank is poorly capitalized, subordinated debt de facto becomes equity (since actual equity is almost worthless). Holders of subordinated debt then have no incentive to impose discipline. Therefore subordinated debt does not eliminate the need for a mechanism of intervention in bad times.

Regardless of the priority of their claims, we may wonder about the identity of the large debtholders. If they are financial intermediaries, we may question both the availability of such risky investments and the credibility of their lack of insurance. Concerning the credibility issue, let us note that an implicit insurance motivated by the fear of propagation in the financial system completely destroys the large debtholders' incentives to monitor and interfere.

6. In view of the drawbacks of the reform proposals discussed above, banking regulation is typically conducted within the public sector. There are two approaches to public regulation:

• *Discretionary regulation.* The regulatory agency has discretionary power and is allocated control when the bank's solvency falls under some threshold. It is instructed to minimize the disbursement incurred in indemnifying fully insured depositors. This mission thus consists in representing the depositors and requires the agency to be more conservative and interventionist than the maximization of ex post social welfare would call for. Internalizing the welfare of depositors only is the optimal mission once the ex ante goal of banking efficiency is taken into account. However, one may have doubts about the commitment of regulatory agencies not to be lax ex post. If it proves difficult to guarantee the independence of the regulatory agency from political pressure and interest groups, there may be a need for less discretionary regulation.

• *Nondiscretionary regulation.* The more common approach consists in giving a precise mission or rule to be implemented by the regulatory agency when it receives control (e.g., sell or liquidate the bank), while allowing shareholders to repurchase control through a recapitalization. This approach is in the spirit of the Basle accords. While it sets up only a rough substitute for the optimal banking governance structure, it has some nice features; in particular, the less solvent the bank, the more costly it is for shareholders to keep control and the higher is the probability that the management will face interference.

While the Basle accords define a fairly reasonable nondiscretionary mechanism for representing depositors in bad times, the credibility and the opportunity of this mechanism in an unfavorable macroeconomic shock have been disputed. In this respect our analysis has led to the following observations:

7. Because managers (by definition) do not control macroeconomic shocks, their welfare, and therefore their compensation and the interference they face from outsiders, should be insensitive to such shocks. Since interference by shareholders depends on the bank's capitalization, the macroeconomic shock should be perfectly offset by an equal distribution of dividends if the bank's performance exceeds the minimum solvency ratio. Conversely, if the macroeconomic shock puts the bank's solvency below the minimum ratio, managers are unduly punished if control shifts to debtholders, or (in the context of voluntary recapitalization as in the Basle accords) if shareholders refuse to recapitalize and leave control with the regulator. A mere adjustment in the minimum solvency ratio to the average solvency of banks is, however, too lax a policy, since shareholders are more prone to take risk when the bank is poorly capitalized. This reasoning thus calls for a recapitalization requirement softened by some contribution of the regulatory agency in bad times, for example, through monetary policy or pro-cyclical deposit insurance premiums.

8. Market value accounting allows the balance sheet of the bank to fully reflect macroeconomic shocks. It may generate quite a lot of volatility in solvency ratios. To insulate bank managers from shocks that are beyond their control, an automatic net worth adjustment is called for to offset any change in shareholders' incentives. Such a policy is preferable to historical cost accounting which induces softer (tougher) behavior by shareholders in the case of an adverse (favorable) macroeconomic shock.

Let us conclude by offering a few general thoughts and by identifying some areas for future research. As we have seen, regulating banks is a very complex matter. This fact could be used to build a case for light-handed regulation. However, lenders to private corporations (or bank headquarters vis-à-vis their divisions) do not have a much easier time than bank regulators. They also struggle to formulate proper risk weights, performance measures, capital requirements, and more generally covenants. To this extent our book contributes to the design of the private regulation of banks and other financial or nonfinancial entities.

We have argued that the government supplies a very valuable service by representing depositors. The government is by no means the only potential provider of this service. Indeed, it would seem natural to allow private yardsticks in order to obtain a better assessment of the performance of regulators. As we noted, such private yardsticks would not eliminate the need for (light-handedly) regulating those banks that choose to have private regulators; depositors would still need to be clearly warned of the risk they face, informed about the bank's governance structure, and be given a clear assessment of the solvency of the bank's deposit insurers, if any. There is one issue that must be given careful consideration, though. The government has a comparative advantage as an "insurer of last resort"; thanks to its taxing ability, it (but not the financial sector) can guarantee claims against systemic risk. Yet competition between private and public regulators requires a level playing field. This raises the issue of a fair access of the private regulators to this coverage against large economy wide risks, and the concomitant issue of government taking control over its stake in the privately regulated sector. This complex issue is worth some serious thinking.

Last, we have mainly built a conceptual framework for studying prudential regulation and left many questions for future research. Some are purely microeconomic issues. For example, our treatment of the Basle accords has remained fairly general. Our framework could be used to assess more specific issues such as the differential treatment of borrower classes or the concentration of large risks. It might also suggest some alternatives to the current single-dimensional measure of solvency. We here have in mind the measurement of liquidity and the foundations for early warning systems. It could even serve to assess the regulation of conglomerates and of other intermediaries, such as insurance companies and pension funds. Last, it could be used to evaluate alternative regulatory institutions, such as mixed public and private regulatory structures.

The most unexplored topics for research relate to the macroeconomics of banking. A coherent general equilibrium framework is required in order to study optimal risk sharing among shareholders, uninsured debtholders (holding junior or senior debt), and the deposit insurance fund. This question is crucial for a proper assessment of more radical reform proposals such as those limiting deposit insurance to "narrow banks" (i.e., banks that can invest only in very liquid assets). We leave this integration of incentives and risk sharing in a macroeconomic context to future research.

Appendixes

A

Perfect Renegotiation and Managerial Rent Extraction

Section 7.2 showed that in the absence of renegotiation a poor performance should trigger more interference. Let us now consider the polar case of perfect renegotiation. The assumption of perfect renegotiation, that is, of the choice of an action that maximizes the sum of the surpluses, in general requires transferable utility: For instance, the manager must be able to concede part of her private benefit if the controlling party and the other investors prefer S— and therefore the total stake $\Delta(u)$ of claimholders is negative—and if action C is ex post efficient (if $\Delta(u) + B > 0$).

The assumption that is crucial for our results to carry over to the perfect renegotiation case is that *the manager's utility after renegotiation be increasing in the utility she would obtain in the absence of renegotiation (the status quo).*[1] We illustrate this assumption with an example, but it should be clear that the idea applies to more general models.

---

1. A case in point is supplied by the concessions extracted from banks by the Government Bank Insurance Fund in Norway. It has imposed a reduction in operating costs on managers. It has also forced banks to write down ordinary share capital, which penalizes not only shareholders but also managers to the extent the latter are given stocks and stock options in their banks. In the model presented here bank managers do not respond to monetary incentives and therefore do not receive stocks or stock options. But the model can be extended to allow responsiveness to monetary incentives and to predict that managers hold stocks or options; see Dewatripont-Tirole (1993b).

A.1   Example

The manager loses her private benefits in either of two cases: (1) if action S is chosen and (2) if, under the *credible* threat of action S, she reduces her perks as part of a reorganization package imposed by the controlling party. We assume that the manager is *indispensable* to implement action C but she can be costlessly replaced when implementing action S. Indeed the manager is fired when S is implemented.

One could, in principle, let the managerial contract specify whether she keeps her job as a function of the verifiable performance v. However, the controlling claimholder cannot credibly commit to fire her and deprive her of B if he prefers action C (because it is then optimal for the controlling party to keep the manager). In contrast, a controlling claimholder who prefers S can threaten the manager and force her to make concessions.

Renegotiation occurs in two cases: when the controlling claimholder prefers ex post inefficient action C and when he prefers ex post inefficient action S. Let us assume that renegotiation is voluntary and that the manager obtains the same utility before and after renegotiation. Regardless of the final decision the manager's utility is B (respectively, 0) if the controlling claimholder prefers C (respectively, S) in the absence of renegotiation. More generally, our results hold if the threat of action S induces the manager to concede more of B than when the controlling claimholder prefers C. In this example, we assume that the private benefit B is fully transferable; that is, the investors' gain is equal to the manager's loss in private benefit. One has in mind that the manager is compelled to propose a plan reducing cost by B in order to keep her job, and fully internalizes this cost reduction. This assumption will simplify notation because it implies that the final allocation maximizes the sum of the surpluses in society, but it is not crucial.

Table A.1
Pre- and postrenegotiation actions and payoffs

	Ex post efficient action	Choice of A in the absence of renegotiation	Ex post choice (after renegotiation)	Who gets B?
1	C	C	C	Initial manager
2	C	S	C	Investors
3	S	C	S	Initial manager
4	S	S	S	Investors

Table A.1 summarizes the assumptions concerning the impact of renegotiation on utilities.

• In case 1 the manager does not face interference, keeps running the bank, and receives her private benefit. This is *business as usual*.

• In case 4 the controlling party's preferred action (interfere) is also ex post efficient. As in case 1, no renegotiation occurs. In this *hostile reorganization* the manager loses her private benefit in the midst of asset sales, reorganization, firing, and so on.

• In case 2 the threat of interference by a tough controlling party forces the manager to concede her private benefit to keep her job. There is a *continuity in the banking strategy* but with a tighter management (cost control, reduction of perks, etc.).

• In case 3 the controlling party is excessively passive. The manager need not forgo her private benefit and is compensated in the renegotiation process. This may be termed a *friendly reorganization*.

Ex post efficient renegotiation implies that expected total surplus (manager's plus investors') is entirely determined by the optimal choice of effort, $e = \bar{e}$. The optimal financial structure is designed so as to minimize expected managerial rent (MR) while inducing a high effort. As in section 7.2 the manager's individual rationality constraint is satisfied if her reservation utility is equal to zero, and we can focus on the incentive constraint. The optimal incentive scheme solves

$$\min_{x(\cdot,\cdot)} MR = B \iint \bar{f}(v)\bar{g}(u)x(v,u)\,dv\,du$$

subject to

$$MR \geq B \iint \underline{f}(v)\underline{g}(u)x(v,u)\,dv\,du + K,$$

where $x(v,u) = 1$ if action C is chosen, and $= 0$ otherwise.

As in the case of no renegotiation the manager must be rewarded (by the absence of interference) when v and u are high. The optimal incentive scheme is represented as in figure 7.1 by a downward sloping curve $u^*(v)$. The controlling party must prefer action C when $u \geq u^*(v)$, and action S when $u < u^*(v)$.

A.2   Special Case: Effort with Only Short-Term Effects

In this case u is independent of e. The optimal policy $x(\cdot)$ should therefore not depend on u. The minimization of expected managerial rents boils down to

$$\min_{x(\cdot)} MR = B \int \bar{f}(v)x(v)dv$$

subject to

$$MR \geq B \int \underline{f}(v)x(v)dv + K.$$

Because $\bar{f}/\underline{f}$ is increasing in v, there exists a threshold $\hat{v}$ such that at the optimal policy

$$x(v) = \begin{cases} 1 & \text{if } v \geq \hat{v}, \\ 0 & \text{if } v < \hat{v}. \end{cases}$$

Indeed the higher the v, the more likely it is that the manager has chosen effort $\bar{e}$. Action S is chosen if and only if the threshold performance $\hat{v}$ is not reached.

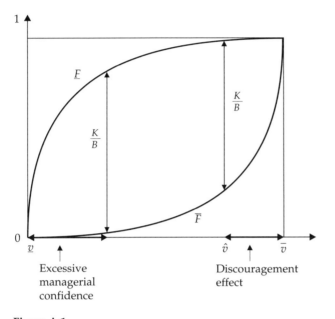

Figure A.1
The discouragement effect

The threshold has a simple expression in this special case because the incentive constraint, which depends only on $\hat{v}$, must be binding:

$$B\left[\underline{F}(\hat{v}) - \bar{F}(\hat{v})\right] = K. \tag{12}$$

From figure A.1 it is clear that (12) has multiple solutions. The threshold $\hat{v}$ is of course the highest solution because this value minimizes the expected rent among the solutions to (12). For any higher threshold than $\hat{v}$, the manager prefers the low effort (see figure A.1); we call this the *discouragement effect*. Rewards must be "reachable" in order for the manager to have proper incentives. This explains that the investors may want to *voluntarily* recapitalize (i.e., increase v) at the initial stage if the initial capitalization is so low that the manager loses her incentives. Conversely, a low threshold also destroys incentives because the manager is quite certain to reach this threshold performance regardless of her effort (see figure A.1).

B

Manipulation of the Performance Measure: An Example

This appendix develops the stylized example of gains trading mentioned in section 10.2. The bank holds two kinds of assets. Short-term assets mature at date 1 and yield v_0. Long-term assets can either be sold or liquidated at date 1 or else be kept and managed by the bank until their maturity date, date 2. All long-term assets are ex ante identical and therefore have the same accounting value. Their yields however differ and are learned by the manager at date 1. A long-term asset yields l if it is liquidated at date 1, and $l + [u_0 + a]$ in expectation if it is kept by the bank until date 2. The value added by the bank, $u_0 + a$, has two components: a shock u_0 that is common to all long-term assets and that reflects the managerial effort as well as the savings in transaction costs associated with their liquidation, and an asset-specific component a. The value added can be positive or negative. The bank's experience with the asset may make it a better manager. But a sale to a new owner or a liquidation may be desirable if new expertise is needed, if a key employee of the bank has quit, or if the relationship with the borrower has deteriorated.

The manager's effort (stochastically) determines the overall quality v_0 of the short-term portfolio and the investment u_0 in the bank's ability to manage long-term assets (more generally, the effort could also affect the liquidation values). In contrast, the asset's idiosyncratic components l and a do not depend on effort. There is a joint distribution over the random variables l and a. The bank holds a large number of long-term assets, a continuum to be precise. The distribution of the realized (l, a) pairs is then identical to the prior distribution.

The manager liquidates a fraction $k \in [0, 1]$ of the long-term assets at date 1. For simplicity we assume that the cash raised in period 1 (v_0 plus the proceeds from liquidations) is reinvested in safe assets at the market rate of interest (equal to 0 in our model). The choice of k will be commented upon later, but our main result holds regardless of its optimality. Our key assumption will be that the manager is responsible for portfolio management, that is, for choosing which assets to liquidate. Before doing so, the manager learns, besides u_0 and v_0, the individual liquidation value l and idiosyncratic value added a of all long-term assets. Let $y(l, a) = 1$ if assets with characteristics (l, a) are kept, and $y(l, a) = 0$ if they are liquidated. The mathematical expectations below will refer to the prior distribution on (l, a). In this highly stylized example, the action C is interpreted as the choice by the controlling party to keep the remaining fraction $(1 - k)$ of risky assets in the bank, and action S consists in selling the entirety of this remaining fraction; that is, investors do not liquidate assets one by one. We can now relate this modeling with our basic framework:

First-period income

$$v = v_0 + E[(1 - y)l].$$

Second-period income

$$\eta = \begin{cases} E[y(l + u_0 + a)] + \epsilon & \text{if } A = C, \\ E[yl] & \text{if } A = S, \end{cases}$$

where ϵ is the portfolio risk when the bank keeps managing it.[1]

---

1. This risk serves no purpose here. It is introduced only to conform to assumption A2 of chapter 8, which conditions the implementation through standard securities. The liquidation value of remaining assets $E[yl]$ is here deterministic. More generally, it could be risky as long as it is less risky than the profit obtained under continuation.

Once the manager has chosen which assets to liquidate, investors observe the first-period performance v, the profit $\pi_S = v_0 + E[yl]$ in case of full liquidation and the expected profit $\pi_C = \pi_S + u$ in case of continuation, where $u = E[y(u_0 + a)]$. The variable v (which is cash) is verifiable, whereas the other two variables are only observable at date 1 (they might result from some informal sampling in the pool of long-term assets). Last, we assume that the manager can always reduce the second-period profit; this assumption is a simple way of guaranteeing that a higher u does not lower the manager's utility. We otherwise will keep assuming that the manager receives his private benefit when action C is chosen.

Because the manager's private benefit cannot decrease with u for given v and π_S, the managerial incentive scheme is necessarily a threshold rule: C is chosen if and only if $u \geq u^*(v, \pi_S)$. The manager manages the bank's portfolio so as to maximize u for given v and π_S. We can thus write

$$\max_{\{y(\cdot,\cdot)\}} E[y(u_0 + a)] \qquad \text{(value added of the remaining assets)}$$

subject to

$$E[y] = k \qquad \text{(trading volume)},$$
$$v_0 + E[(1 - y)l] = v \qquad \text{(first-period performance)}.$$

Let θ and μ denote the multipliers of the two constraints. The first-order condition with respect to $y(l, a)$ is

$$y = \begin{cases} 1 & \text{if } u_0 + a > \mu l - \theta, \\ 0 & \text{if } u_0 + a < \mu l - \theta. \end{cases}$$

The trading rule can thus be summarized by a positively sloped straight line in the space (l, a). For a given level of l, the asset is kept if and only if $a \geq \mu l - (\theta + u_0)$. Moreover we can show that $\mu \geq 0.$[2] The sign of θ depends on the trading volume imposed on

---

2. Suppose that $\mu < 0$, and let the manager replace the decision rule defined by $a \geq \mu l - \theta - u_0$ by a new rule $a \geq \tilde{\mu}l - \tilde{\theta} - u_0$, where $\mu \leq \tilde{\mu} \leq 0$ and $\tilde{\theta}$ is chosen so

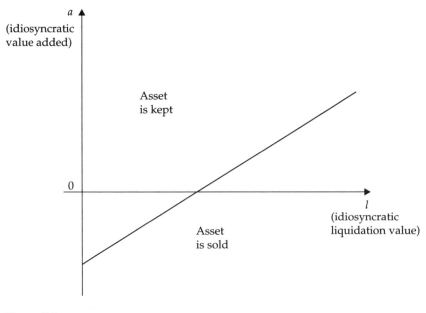

Figure B.1
Gains trading

the manager. For a low trading volume, the first constraint becomes $E[y] \geq k$, and then $\theta \geq 0$. For a high trading volume, the constraint can be written $E[y] \leq k$, and $\theta \leq 0$. The trading rule is depicted in figure B.1.

A controlling party who is residual claimant for the bank's profit (equity without debt, or 100% equity) would compare π_S and π_C to choose between the two actions. It would therefore choose C if and only if $u \geq 0$, regardless of v and π_S. The manager then maximizes the value added $E[ya]$ and therefore chooses $y = 1$ if and only if a exceeds some threshold. There is no gains trading. In particular, in the absence of a constraint on the trading volume, the manager

---

as to keep trading volume equal to k. It is easy to see on a diagram that the value added for the newly kept assets exceeds that of the newly liquidated ones (which are in equal numbers).

keeps those assets with positive value added ($u_0 + a \geq 0$) and liquidates the others. Although the use of a single security prevents gains trading, it should be recalled that the constant decision rule $u^*(v, \pi_S) = \hat{u} = 0$ associated with the single security is not optimal: The manager must be rewarded for a good first-period performance and be punished for a poor one. We can thus conclude that powerful incentive schemes breed gains trading.

The previous paragraph identified low-powered incentives as one way of limiting gains trading. An alternative is to constrain the trading volume. There is of course no gains trading when $k = 1$. But such a policy forces the bank to keep all assets including those it should sell. This implies a trade-off between a flexible portfolio management and gains trading. Giving the manager discretion over the trading volume both enhances the profit opportunities for the bank and triggers more manipulation of the performance.

Portfolio Reallocation between Risky and Safe Assets

This appendix studies the question raised in section 11.3 concerning the impact of a reinvestment of the first-period income into risky assets on the probability of shareholder interference. To keep things simple, we assume that there is no new moral hazard in the management of new assets. An amount $\bar{v}$ (the principal) taken from the first-period income is reinvested in risky assets. The complement $v - \bar{v}$ is reinvested in safe assets (so we had previously assumed that $\bar{v} = 0$). The new risky assets yield random second-period income v. The expectation of v is at least equal to $\bar{v}$. The total profit is then

$$\pi = \eta + v + v - \bar{v}.$$

The bank's balance sheet at the end of date 1 is

Assets	Liabilities
$v - \bar{v}$	D
$\bar{\eta}$	
$\bar{v}$	E

C.1 Perfect Correlation with Previous Investments

Assume first that the bank invests in the same types of risky assets as initially. The yields v and η are then perfectly correlated. We assume that in this expansion the new assets inherit the experience or quality, here measured by u, of previous assets. Assuming that the purchase price is the same for all risky assets, there exists $\lambda > 0$ such that

$$v = \lambda \eta \quad \text{and} \quad \bar{v} = \lambda \bar{\eta}.$$

Do shareholders benefit from the possibility of investing in new risky assets? For a given action A, their expected profit is

$$\int_{(D+\lambda\bar{\eta}-v)/(1+\lambda)}^{\infty} [(1+\lambda)\eta + v - \lambda\bar{\eta} - D] h_A(\eta|u) \, d\eta$$

$$= \int_{(D+\lambda\bar{\eta}-v)/(1+\lambda)}^{\infty} (1+\lambda)[1 - H_A(\eta|u)] \, d\eta.$$

The left-hand side of this equality shows that the derivative of profit with respect to λ is equal to

$$\int_{(D+\lambda\bar{\eta}-v)/(1+\lambda)}^{\infty} (\eta - \bar{\eta}) h_A(\eta|u) d\eta > 0.$$

Shareholders therefore select as high a λ as is permitted by prudential regulation. Further they do not discriminate between old and new risky assets in their choice of action. As before, the manager receives her private benefit if and only if

$$\int_{(D+\lambda\bar{\eta}-v)/(1+\lambda)}^{\infty} (1+\lambda) [H_S(\eta|u) - H_C(\eta|u)] \, d\eta \geq 0.$$

Consider a signal u such that shareholders are indifferent between the two actions, and increase λ slightly. *The probability of bankruptcy, or equivalently $(D + \lambda\bar{\eta} - v)/(1 + \lambda)$, grows with the increase in risk if and only if the bank's solvency ratio is positive ($r \geq 0$) prior to the increase in risk*, that is, if and only if $v + \bar{\eta} - D \geq 0$. Assuming that this condition holds, figure 8.4 shows that the increase in risk makes shareholders more passive. The manager is rewarded for a good performance when the latter permits an increase in risky assets.

C.2 Unrelated Old and New Investments

We now consider the polar case of a diversification in which v and η are independent. In such case it may make sense to assume that the manager is indispensable only to run old risky assets (she has not yet managed the new risky assets). She keeps her private benefit if and only if shareholders choose action C concerning the old risky assets.

A standard result in statistics[1] shows that a claimholder with a convex return stream benefits from adding the new independent risk since $Ev \geq \bar{v}$. Therefore, regardless of their choice of action (S or C) for the old risky assets, the shareholders will want to add on the new risk. But we know that a good performance should bring a reward to the manager rather than to the shareholders. So let us study the impact of the existence of the new independent risk on the interference decision for the old risky assets.

An added independent risk can make shareholders more conservative or more risk taking. To show this, let $\epsilon \equiv v - \bar{v}$. The shareholders' incentive to choose C is

$$\mathring{\Delta}_E = E_\epsilon[\int_{D-v-\epsilon}^{\infty} (v + \eta + \epsilon - D)h_C(\eta \mid u)d\eta$$

$$- \int_{D-v-\epsilon}^{\infty} (v + \eta + \epsilon - D)h_S(\eta \mid u)d\eta]$$

$$= E_\epsilon U(\epsilon),$$

where $U(\epsilon) \equiv \int_{D-v-\epsilon}^{\infty} [H_S(\eta \mid u) - H_C(\eta \mid u)]\,d\eta$. Since $U(\cdot)$ is neither concave nor convex (its second derivative is $h_C(D - v - \epsilon \mid u) - h_S(D - v - \epsilon \mid u)$), the comparison of $\mathring{\Delta}_E$ with the stake $\Delta_E = U(0)$ in case of safe reinvestment depends on the precise distribution of ϵ. We cannot, in general, conclude that the increased risk taking allowed by the Basle accords in case of good performance has good incentive properties.

---

1. See Rothschild-Stiglitz (1970, 1971) for a presentation and analysis of some of its implications.

References

Aghion, P., and P. Bolton. 1992. An incomplete contract approach to financial contracting. *Review of Economic Studies* 59:473–94.

Akerlof, G. 1970. The market for lemons, qualitative uncertainty and the market mechanism. *Quarterly Journal of Economics* 84:488–500.

Akerlof, G., and P. Romer. 1994. Looting: The economic underworld of bankruptcy for profit. *Brookings Papers on Economic Activity*. 2:1–73.

Allen, L., S. Peristiani, and A. Saunders. 1989. Bank size, collateral, and net purchase behavior in the federal funds market: Empirical evidence. *Journal of Business* 62:501–16.

Amihud, Y., and H. Mendelson. 1986. Asset pricing and the bid-ask spread. *Journal of Financial Economics* 17:223–49.

Bank for International Settlements. 1990. *Report of the Committee on Interbank Netting Schemes of the Central Banks of the Group of Ten Countries* (Lamfalussy Report). Basle.

Bank for International Settlements. 1993. *63rd Annual Report*. Basle.

Barth, F., P. Bartholomew, and C. Labich. 1989. Moral hazard and the thrift crisis: An analysis of 1988 resolutions. Presented at the 25th Annual Conference on Bank Structure and Competition, Federal Reserve Bank of Chicago.

Barth, F., D. Brumbaugh, and R. Litan. 1991. Bank failures are sinking the FDIC. *Challenge* 34:4–15.

Barbour, D., J. Norton, and G. Penn. 1991. Capital adequacy concerns: Basle supervisors committee, US and UK. In *Asset Securitization*, J. Norton and P. Spellman, eds. Oxford: Blackwell, ch. 11.

Basle Committee on Banking Supervision. 1992. *Report on International Developments in Banking Supervision*. Report 8. Basle: Bank for International Settlements.

Basle Committee on Banking Supervision. 1993a. *The Supervisory Treatment of Market Risks.* Consultative Proposal. Basle: Bank for International Settlements.

Basle Committee on Banking Supervision. 1993b. *Measurement of Banks' Exposure to Interest Rate Risk.* Consultative Proposal. Basle: Bank for International Settlements.

Basle Committee on Banking Supervision. 1993c. *The Supervisory Recognition of Netting for Capital Adequacy Purposes.* Consultative Proposal. Basle: Bank for International Settlements.

Benston, G. 1990. *The Separation of Commercial and Investment Banking.* New York: Mcmillan.

Benston, G., R. Eisenbeis, P. Horvitz, E. Kane, and G. Kaufman. 1986. *Perspectives on Safe and Sound Banking, Past, Present and Future.* Cambridge: MIT Press.

Berger, A., K. King, and J. O'Brien. 1991. The limitations of market value accounting and a more realistic alternative. *Journal of Banking and Finance* 15:753–83.

Berger, A., and G. Udell. 1993. Securitization, risk, and the liquidity problem in banking. In *Structural Change in Banking*, M. Klausner and L. White, eds. Homewood, IL: Business One Irwin.

Bernanke, B. S. 1990. Clearing and settlement during the crash. *Review of Financial Studies* 3:133–51.

Berkovitch, E., and S. Greenbaum. 1990. The loan commitment as an optimal financing contract. *Journal of Financial and Quantitative Analysis* 26:83–95.

Besanko, D., and A. Thakor. 1993. Relationship banking, deposit insurance and bank portfolio choice. In *Capital Markets and Financial Intermediation*, C. Mayer and X. Vives, eds. Cambridge: Cambridge University Press, 292–318.

Bester, H. 1985. Screening vs. rationing in credit markets with imperfect information. *American Economic Review* 75:850–55.

Bester, H. 1987. The role of collateral in credit markets with imperfect information. *European Economic Review* 31:887–99.

Bhala, R. 1989. *Perspectives on Risk-Based Capital: A Guide to the New Risk-Based Capital Adequacy Rules.* Rolling Meadows, IL: Bank Administration Institute.

Bhattacharya, S. 1982. Aspects of monetary and banking theory under moral hazard. *Journal of Finance* 37:371–84.

Bhattacharya, S., and A. Thakor. 1993. Contemporary Banking Theory. *Journal of Financial Intermediation*, forthcoming.

Bodie, Z., J. Light, R. Mørck, and R. Taggart. 1987. Funding and asset allocation in corporate pension plans: An empirical investigation. In *Issues in Pension Economics*, Z. Bodie, J. Shoven and D. Wise, eds. Chicago: University of Chicago Press, ch. 2.

Boot, A., and A. Thakor. 1991. Off-balance sheet liabilities, deposit insurance and capital regulation. *Journal of Banking and Finance* 15:825–46.

Boot, A., and A. Thakor. 1993. Self-interested regulation. *American Economic Review* 83:206–12.

Boot, A., S. Greenbaum, and A. Thakor. 1993. Reputation and discretion in financial contracting. *American Economic Review* 83:206–12.

Boot, A., A. Thakor, and G. Udell. 1987. Competition, risk neutrality and loan commitments. *Journal of Banking and Finance* 11:449–71.

Boot, A., A. Thakor, and G. Udell. 1991. Credible commitments, contract enforcement problems and banks: Intermediation as credibility assurance. *Journal of Banking and Finance* 15:605–22.

Borio, C., and R. Filosa. 1994. *The Changing Borders of Banking: Trends and Implications*. Basle: Bank for International Settlements.

Bovenzi, J., and M. Muldoon. 1990. Failure-resolution methods and policy considerations. *FDIC Banking Review* 3(Fall):1–11.

Boyd, J., and S. Graham. 1988. The profitability and risk effects of allowing bank holding companies to merge with other financial firms: A simulation review. *Quarterly Review, Federal Reserve Bank of Minneapolis*: 3–20.

Boyd, J., and M. Gertler. 1993. US commercial banking: Trends, cycles, and policy. *NBER Macroeconomic Annual*.

Brealey, R., and S. Myers. 1988. *Principles of Corporate Finance*. 3d ed., New York: McGraw-Hill.

Brock, P., ed. 1992. *If Texas Were Chile: A Primer on Banking Reform*. ICS Press.

Broecker, T. 1990. Credit-worthiness tests and interbank competition. *Econometrica* 58:429–52.

Bryan, L. 1988. *Breaking up the Bank: Rethinking an Industry under Siege*. Homewood, IL: Dow Jones-Invin.

Bryant, J. 1980. A model of reserves, bank runs, and deposit insurance. *Journal of Banking and Finance* 43:749–61.

Bulow, J., and M. Scholes. 1983. Who owns the assets in a defined-benefit pension plan. In *Financial Aspects of the United States Pension System*, Z. Bodie and J. Shoven, eds. Chicago: Chicago University Press, ch. 1.

Burgard, J. C. 1988. *La Banque en France*. Paris: Dalloz.

Calomiris, C., and G. Gorton. 1991. The origins of banking panics. In *Financial Markets and Financial Crises*, G. Hubbard, ed. Chicago: University of Chicago Press.

Calomiris, C., C. Kahn, and S. Krasa. 1991. Optimal contingent bank liquidation under moral hazard. Mimeo. Northwestern University and University of Illinois.

Campbell, T., and W. Kracaw. 1980. Information production, market signalling, and the theory of financial intermediation. *Journal of Finance* 35:863–82.

Capie, F., and G. Wood. 1991. *Unregulated Banking, Chaos or Order?* New York: Macmillan.

Carey, M., S. Prowse, J. Rea, and G. Udell. 1993. Recent developments in the market for privately placed debt. *Federal Reserve Bulletin* (February):77–92.

Carosio, G. 1990. Problems of harmonization of the regulation of financial intermediation in the European Community. *European Economic Review* 34:578–86.

CEA (Comité Européen des Assurances). 1993. *Financial Conglomerates*. Special issue, July.

Chan, Y., S. Greenbaum, and A. Thakor. 1992. Is fairly priced deposit insurance possible? *Journal of Finance* 47:227–46.

Chari, V. V., and R. Jagannathan. 1988. Banking panics, information and rational expectations equilibrium. *Journal of Finance* 43:749–61.

Chiappori, P. A., C. Mayer, D. Neven, and X. Vives. 1991. The microeconomics of monetary union. In *Monitoring European Integration: The Making of Monetary Union*. CEPR Annual Report.

Chiappori, P. A., D. Perez-Castrillo, and T. Verdier. 1993. Spatial competition in the banking system, localization, cross-subsidies and the regulation of interest rates. Mimeo. Delta, Paris.

Cole, R., J. McKenzie, and L. White. 1993. The causes and costs of thrift institution failures: A structure-behavior-outcomes approach. Mimeo. Board of Governors of the Federal Reserve System, Federal Housing Finance Board, and New York University.

Committee on Banking Regulations and Supervisory Practices. 1988. International convergence of capital measurement and capital standards. Mimeo. Bank for International Settlements, Basle.

Cone, K. 1983. Regulation of depository institutions. Ph.D. dissertation. Stanford University.

Corrigan, G. 1991. The risk of a financial crisis. In *The Risk of Economic Crisis*, M. Feldstein, ed. Chicago: University of Chicago Press, pp. 44–53.

Craig Pirrong, S. 1993. The economics of risk-based capital requirements. In *Modernizing US Securities Regulation*, K. Lehn-R. Kamphuis, ed. Homewood, IL: Business One Irwin, pp. 419–26.

Dab, S. 1991. *La Débâcle des caisses d'epargne américaines: Une crise financière sans précédent.* Brussels: Editions de l'Université Libre de Bruxelles.

Daltung, S. 1994. *Risk, Efficiency and Regulation of Banks.* Ph.D. dissertation. Stockholm University. Institute for International Economic Studies Monograph Series 25.

Davies, S., and D. McManus. 1991. The effects of closure policies on bank risk-taking. *Journal of Banking and Finance* 15:917–38.

Davis, E. P. 1993. The structure, regulation and performance of pension funds in nine industrial countries. World Bank, Policy Research Working Paper 1229. December.

Dewatripont, M., and E. Maskin. 1990. Credit and efficiency in centralized and decentralized economies. Harvard Institute for Economic Research Working Paper 1512.

Dewatripont, M., and J. Tirole. 1993a. Efficient governance structure: Implications for banking regulation. In *Capital Markets and Financial Intermediation*, C. Mayer and X. Vives, eds. Cambridge: Cambridge University Press, pp. 12–35.

Dewatripont, M., and J. Tirole. 1993b. A theory of debt and equity: Diversity of securities and manager-shareholder congruence. *Quarterly Journal of Economics*, forthcoming.

Diamond, D. 1984. Financial intermediation and delegated monitoring. *Review of Economic Studies* 59:393–414.

Diamond, D. 1991. Monitoring and reputation: The choice between bank loan and directly placed debt. *Journal of Political Economy* 99:689–721.

Diamond, D. 1993. Bank loan maturity and priority when borrowers can refinance. In *Capital Markets and Financial Intermediation*, C. Mayer and X. Vives, eds. Cambridge: Cambridge University Press, pp. 12–35.

Diamond, D., and P. Dybvig. 1983. Bank runs, deposit insurance and liquidity. *Journal of Political Economy* 91:401–19.

Diamond, D., and P. Dybvig. 1986. Banking theory, deposit insurance and bank regulation. *Journal of Business* 59:53–68.

Diaz-Gimenez, J., E. Prescott, T. Fitzgerald, and F. Alvarez. 1992. Banking in computable general equilibrium economies. *Journal of Economic Dynamics and Control* 16:533–59.

Dimson, E., and P. Marsh. 1994. The debate on international capital requirements. Mimeo. London Business School.

Economic Review. 1983. Commercial bank surveillance. Special Issue. November. Federal Reserve Bank of Atlanta.

Emerick, D., and W. White. 1992. The case for private placements: How sophisticated investors add value to corporate debt issuers. *Journal of Applied Corporate Finance* (Fall):83–91.

Emmons, W. 1991. Deposit insurance and last-resort lending as delegated monitoring: A theory of banking "safety nets." Mimeo. Northwestern Department of Finance.

Fama, E. 1985. What's different about banks? *Journal of Monetary Economics* 15:29–39.

Farrell, J., and N. Gallini. 1987. Second sourcing as a commitment: Monopoly incentives to attract competition. *Quarterly Journal of Economics* 101:488–500.

Franks, J., and C. Mayer. 1989. *Risk, Regulation and Investor Protection: The Case of Investment Management.* Oxford: Clarendon Press.

Freixas, X., and J. C. Rochet. 1994. *Microeconomics of Banking.* Cambridge: MIT Press, forthcoming.

Friedman, M., and A. Schwartz. 1963. *A Monetary History of the United States, 1870–1960.* Princeton: Princeton University Press.

Fudenberg, D., and J. Tirole. 1992. A theory of income and dividend smoothing. *Journal of Political Economy*, forthcoming.

Gale, D., and M. Hellwig. 1985. Incentive-compatible debt contracts: The one-period problem. *Review of Economic Studies* 52:647–63.

Gale, D., and X. Vives. 1993. Separation of authority in financial regulation. Mimeo. Boston University and Universitat Autonoma, Barcelona.

Garber, P., and S. Weisbrod. 1992. *The Economics of Banking, Liquidity, and Money.* Lexington, MA: D.C. Heath.

Gennotte, G. 1990. Deposit insurance and bank competition. Mimeo. University of California at Berkeley.

Gennotte, G., and D. Pyle. 1991. Capital controls and bank risk. *Journal of Banking and Finance* 15:805–24.

Gerschenkron, A. 1962. *Economic Backwardness in Historical Perspective*. Cambridge: Harvard University Press.

Giammarino, R., T. Lewis, and D. Sappington. 1993. An incentive approach to banking regulation. *Journal of Finance* 48:1523–42.

Goldsmith, R. W. 1969. *Financial Structure and Development*. New Haven: Yale University Press.

Goodhart, C. 1987. Why do banks need a central bank? *Oxford Economic Papers* 39:75–89.

Goodhart, C. 1993a. Banks and the control of corporations. Mimeo. London School of Economics.

Goodhart, C. 1993b. Price stability and financial fragility. Mimeo. London School of Economics.

Goodhart, C., and D. Schoenmaker. 1993. Institutional Separation between Supervisory and Monetary Agencies. Mimeo. London School of Economics. FMG Special Paper 52.

Gorton, G. 1985a. Clearinghouses and the origin of central banking in the United States. *Journal of Economic History* 45:277–83.

Gorton, G., and G. Pennacchi. 1990. Financial intermediaries and liquidity creation. *Journal of Finance* 45:49–71.

Gorton, G., and G. Pennacchi. 1993a. Banks and loan sales: Marketing nonmarketable assets. Mimeo. University of Pennsylvania and University of Illinois.

Gorton, G., and G. Pennacchi. 1993b. Money market funds and finance companies: Are they the banks of the future? In *Structural Change in Banking*, M. Klausner and L. White, eds. Homewood, IL: Business One Irwin.

Gual, J., and D. Neven. 1992. Deregulation of the European banking industry. (1980–1991). CEPR Working Paper 703.

Gurley, J., and E. Shaw. 1960. *Money in a Theory of Finance*. Washington: Brookings Institution.

Hall, M. 1993. *Banking Regulation and Supervision: A Comparative Study of the UK, USA and Japan*. Edward Elgar Publishing.

Harstad, R. 1991. Auctions with endogenous bidder participation. Mimeo. Virginia Commonwealth University.

Hart, O., and J. Moore. 1989. Default and renegotiation: A dynamic model of debt. Working paper 89-069. Harvard Business School.

Hart, O., and J. Moore. 1990a. Property rights and the nature of the firm. *Journal of Political Economy* 98:1119–58.

Hart, O., and J. Moore. 1990b. A theory of corporate financial structure based on the seniority of claims. Working paper 560. MIT.

Hart, O., and J. Moore. 1991. A theory of debt based on the inelienability of human capital. *Quarterly Journal of Economics*, November.

Heaton, J., and D. Lucas. 1992. The effects of incomplete insurance markets and trading costs in a consumption-based asset-pricing model. *Journal of Economic Dynamics and Control* 16:601–20.

Hellwig, M. 1991. Banking, financial intermediation and corporate finance. In *European Financial Integration*, A. Giovannini and C. Mayer, eds. Cambridge: Cambridge University Press.

Hellwig, M. 1993. Liquidity provision, banking, and the allocation of interest rate risk. *European Economic Review*, forthcoming.

Hirschman, A. 1970. *Exit, Voice, and Loyalty*. Cambridge: Harvard University Press.

Hogan, W. 1993. Market value accounting in the finance sector. Mimeo. University of Sidney.

Holmström, B. 1979. Moral hazard and observability. *Bell Journal of Economics* 10:74–91.

Holmström, B., and J. Tirole. 1993. Market liquidity and performance monitoring. *Journal of Political Economy* 101:678–709.

Holmström, B., and J. Tirole. 1994. Financial intermediation, loanable funds and the real sector. Mimeo. Yale University and Institut d'Économie Industrielle, Toulouse.

Hope, E. 1993. The banking crisis in Norway: Problems and prospects. Mimeo. Foundation for Research in Economics and Business Administration, Bergen.

Hoshi, T., A. Kashyap, and D. Scharfstein. 1991. An examination of post-deregulation corporate financing in Japan. Mimeo. University of California, San Diego, University of Chicago, and MIT.

Jacklin, C. 1987. Demand deposits, trading restrictions, and risk sharing. In *Contractual Arrangements for Intertemporal Trade*, E. Prescott and N. Wallace, eds. Minneapolis: University of Minnesota Press.

Jacklin, C., and S. Bhattacharya. 1988. Distinguishing panics and information-based bank runs: Welfare and policy implications. *Journal of Political Economy* 96:568–92.

Jensen, M., and W. R. Meckling. 1976. Theory of the firm, managerial behavior, agency costs and ownership structure. *Journal of Financial Economics* 3:305–60.

Kahan, M., and B. Tuckman. 1993. Private vs. public lending: Evidence from covenants. Mimeo. New York University.

Kane, E. 1989. *The S&L Insurance Mess, How Did It Happen?* Washington: Urban Institute Press.

Kareken, J. 1983. Deposit insurance reform; or, deregulation is the cart, not the horse. *Federal Reserve Bank of Minneapolis Quarterly Review* 7:1–9.

Keeton, W. 1979. *Equilibrium Credit Rationing*. New York: Garland Press.

King, R., and R. Levine. 1993. Finance, entrepreneurship, and growth. *Journal of Monetary Economics* 32:513–42.

Koehn, M., and A. Santomero. 1980. Regulation of bank capital and portfolio risk. *Journal of Finance* 15:1235–44.

Kroszner, R., and R. Rajan. 1993. Is the Glass-Steagall Act justified? A study of the U.S. experience with universal banking before 1933. *American Economic Review*, forthcoming.

Leland, H., and D. Pyle. 1977. Information asymmetries, financial structure and financial intermediaries. *Journal of Finance* 32:371–87.

Litan, R. 1994. Financial regulation. In *American Economic Policy in the 1980s*, M. Feldstein, ed. Chicago: University of Chicago Press, ch. 8.

Lucas, D., and R. McDonald. 1987. Bank portfolio choice with private information about loan quality. *Journal of Banking and Finance* 11:473–97.

Mailath, G., and L. Mester. 1993. A positive analysis of bank closures. *Journal of Financial Intermediation*, forthcoming.

Matutes, C., and J. Padilla. 1991. Shared ATM networks and banking competition. Mimeo. IAE, Barcelona and CEMFI, Madrid.

Matutes, C., and X. Vives. 1992. Competition for deposits, risk of failure, and regulation in banking. Mimeo. Universitat Autonoma de Barcelona.

Mayer, C. 1988. New issues in corporate finance. *European Economic Review* 32:1167–88.

Mayer, C. 1990. Financial systems, corporate finance, and economic development. In *Asymmetric Information, Corporate Finance, and Investment*, G. Hubbard, ed. Chicago: University of Chicago Press.

Mayer, C. 1993. The regulation of financial services: Lessons from the United Kingdom. In *European Banking in the 1990s*, J. Dermine, ed. 2d ed. Oxford: Blackwell, pp. 17–37.

McKinnon, R. I. 1973. *Money and Capital in Economic Development.* Washington: Brookings Institution.

Merton, R. 1977. An analytical derivation of the cost of deposit insurance and loan guarantees: An application of modern option pricing theory. *Journal of Banking and Finance* 1:3–11.

Merton, R. 1978. On the costs of deposit insurance when there are surveillance costs. *Journal of Business* 51:439–52.

Merton, R. 1993. Operation and regulation in financial intermediation: A functional perspective. Mimeo. Harvard Business School.

Merton, R., and Z. Bodie. 1992. On the management of financial guarantees. *Financial Management* (Winter):108–109.

Miles, D. 1993. Optimal regulation of deposit taking intermediaries. Mimeo. Birkbeck College and Bank of England.

Miller, M. 1976. Debt and taxes. *Journal of Finance* 32:261–76.

Mishkin, F. 1992a. *The Economics of Money, Banking and Financial Markets.* 3d ed. New York: HarperCollins.

Mishkin, F. 1992b. An evaluation of the Treasury plan for banking reform. *Journal of Economic Perspectives* 6:133–53.

Modigliani, F., and M. Miller. 1958. The cost of capital, corporate finance, and the theory of investment. *American Economic Review* 48:261–97.

Myers, S. and N. Majluf. 1984. Corporate financing and investment decisions when firms have information that investors do not have. *Journal of Financial Economics* 13:187–221.

Narayanan, K. 1991. Bank influence and industrial concentration: A comparative study of post-war West Germany and Japan. Mimeo. MIT.

Newman, A. 1992. The capital market, inequality and the employment relation. Mimeo. Northwestern University.

O' Hara, M. 1991. Real bills revisited, market value accounting and loan maturity. Mimeo. Cornell University.

O' Hara, M., and W. Shaw. 1990. Deposit insurance and wealth effects: The value of being "too big to fail." *Journal of Finance* 45:1587–1600.

Padilla, J., and M. Pagano. 1993. Sharing default information as a borrower discipline device. Mimeo. CEMFI, Madrid and Università Bocconi, Milan.

Pagano, M. 1993. Financial markets and growth: An overview. *European Economic Review* 37:613–22.

Parkinson, P., A. Gilbert, E. Gollob, L. Hargraves, R. Mead, J. Stehm, and M. A. Taylor. 1992. Clearance and settlement in US securities markets. Federal Reserve Board Staff Study 163. March.

Pearce, J. 1991. *The Future of Banking*. New Haven: Yale University Press.

Postlewaite, A., and X. Vives. 1987. Bank runs as an equilibrium phenomenon. *Journal of Political Economy* 95:485–91.

Rajan, R. 1992. Insiders and outsiders: The choice between relationship and arms length debt. *Journal of Finance* 47:1367–1400.

Rajan, R. 1992. A theory of the costs and benefits of universal banking. CRSP Working Paper 346. University of Chicago.

Ramakrishnan, R., and A. Thakor. 1984. Information reliability and a theory of financial intermediation. *Review of Economic Studies* 51:415–32.

Repullo, R. 1993. Who should decide on bank closures? An incomplete contract model. Mimeo. CEMFI, Madrid.

Rey, P., and J. Stiglitz. 1992. Short-term contracts as a monitoring device. Mimeo. INSEE, Paris, and Stanford University.

Riordan, M. 1993. Competition and bank performance: A theoretical perspective. In *Capital Markets and Financial Intermediation*, C. Mayer and X. Vives, eds. Cambridge: Cambridge University Press, pp. 328–43.

Rochet, J. C. 1991. Capital requirements and the behavior of commercial banks. Mimeo. Institut d'Économie Industrielle, Toulouse.

Rochet, J. C., B. Bensaid, and H. Pages. 1993. Toward a theory of optimal banking regulation. Mimeo. Institut d'Économie Industrielle, Toulouse, and Banque de France, Paris.

Rochet, J. C., and J. Tirole. 1994. The industrial organization of the payment system. Mimeo. Institut d'Économie Industrielle, Toulouse.

Ronen, J., A. Saunders, and A. Sondhi. eds. 1990. *Off-Balance Sheet Activities*. Westport, CT: Quorum Books.

Rothschild, M., and J. Stiglitz. 1970. Increasing risk. I: A definition. *Journal of Economic Theory* 2:225–43.

Rothschild, M., and J. Stiglitz. 1971. Increasing risk. II: Its economic consequences. *Journal of Economic Theory* 3:66–84.

Rubinovitz, R. 1990. Moral hazard in the thrift industry. Discussion Paper EAG 90-1. U.S. Department of Justice.

Rudolph, B. 1993. Capital requirements of German banks and the European Community proposals on banking supervision. In *European Banking in the 1990s*, J. Dermine, ed. 2d ed. Oxford: Blackwell, pp. 373–85.

Sahlman, W. 1990. The structure and governance of venture-capital organizations. *Journal of Financial Economics* 27:473–521.

Schaefer, S. 1990. The regulation of banks and securities firms. *European Economic Review* 34:587–97.

Seabright, P. 1993. Cover-ups. Mimeo. Cambridge University.

Sharpe, S. 1990. Asymmetric information, bank lending, and implicit contracts: A stylized model of customer relationships. *Journal of Finance* 55:1069–87.

Shavell, S. 1979. Risk sharing and incentives in the principal and agent relationship. *Bell Journal of Economics* 10:55–73.

Shaw, E. S. 1973. *Financial Deepening in Economic Development*. Oxford: Oxford University Press.

Sheard, P. 1989. The main bank system and corporate monitoring and control in Japan. *Journal of Economic Behavior and Organization* 11:399–422.

Shepard, A. 1988. Licencing to enhance demand for new technologies. *Rand Journal of Economics* 18:360–68.

Smith, C., and J. Warner. 1979. On financial contracting: An analysis of bond covenants. *Journal of Financial Services*, 7:117–61.

Steigum, E. 1992. Financial deregulation, credit boom and the banking crisis: The case of Norway. Discussion paper 15/92. Norwegian School of Economics and Business Administration.

Stiglitz, J., and A. Weiss. 1981. Credit rationing with imperfect information. *American Economic Review* 71:393–410.

Sussman, O., and J. Zeira. 1993. Banking and development. Mimeo. Hebrew University of Jerusalem.

Taggart, R., and S. Greenbaum. 1978. Bank capital and public regulation. *Journal of Money, Credit and Banking* 10:158.

Tirole, J. 1994. The internal organization of government. *Oxford Economic Papers* 46:1–29.

Tobin, J. 1985. Financial innovation and deregulation in perspective. *Bank of Japan Monetary and Economic Studies* 3 (2).

Townsend, R. 1979. Optimal contracts and competitive markets with costly state verification. *Journal of Economic Theory* 21:417–25.

U.S. General Accounting Office. 1987. *Bank Powers: Insulating Banks from the Potential Risks of Expanded Activities*, Washington: GPO.

U.S. Treasury. 1991. *Modernizing the Financial System: Recommendations for Safer, More Competitive Banks*, Washington: GPO.

Vayanos, D., and J. L. Vila. 1992. Equilibrium interest rate and liquidity premium under proportional transaction costs. Mimeo. MIT.

von Thadden, E. L. 1990. Bank finance and long-term investment. Mimeo. Universität Basel.

von Thadden, E. L. 1994a. Optimal liquidity provision and dynamic incentive compatibility. Mimeo. Universität Basel.

von Thadden, E. L. 1994b. The term-structure of investment and the banks' insurance function. Mimeo. Universität Basel.

Wall, L. 1989. A plan for reducing future deposit insurance losses: Puttable subordinated debt. *Federal Reserve Bank of Atlanta Economic Review*. July–August.

Warshawsky, M. 1988. Pension plans: Funding, assets and regulatory environment. *Federal Reserve Bulletin*. November.

White, L. 1984. Competitive payments systems and the unit of account. *American Economic Review* 74:699–712.

White, L. 1991. *The S&L Debacle, Public Policy for Bank and Thrift Regulation*. Oxford: Oxford University Press.

Winton, A. 1991. Competition among financial intermediaries when diversification matters. Mimeo. Northwestern University.

Yanelle, M. O. 1988. On the theory of intermediation. Ph.D. dissertation. Universität Bonn.

Yanelle, M. O. 1989. The strategic analysis of intermediation. *European Economic Review* 33:294–304.

Zimmerman, C. 1977. An approach to writing loan agreement covenants. In *Classics in Commercial Bank Lending*, pp. 213–28.

Index